T0251984

3ds Max Modeling for Games

Volume II

Praise for *3ds Max Modeling for Games,* Volume 1, Second Edition

"This book is a must-have resource for anyone wanting to learn how to make game art in 3ds Max. It has great support on the forums which is a testament to the author's enthusiasm for the subject. My students would be lost without it. If you want to understand how to really make 3d art for games then this is the book you need."

—**David Wilson,** programme leader, BA (Hons) Computer Games Modelling and Animation, University of Derby, UK

"This is a great book covering most aspects of modeling for games including the basics of 3D, Ambient Occlusion, Normal Maps, Character, Vehicle, Scene Creation and much, much more. It covers everything you need to get you started for your career in games."

—**Andy Manns,** lead artist, THQ

"An extremely comprehensive book covering all the basic theory and techniques with 3ds Max, currently used within the best game development studios in the industry."

—**Alex Perkins,** art director, Sony Computer Entertainment Europe

"For a beginner, getting to grip with 3ds Max is a daunting prospect, but this book picks on the relevant features and aims to get you producing usable 3D game art quickly and efficiently. It gives you a great understanding of what goes into make good 3D video-game art and will give you the vocabulary needed to talk with confidence about in-game models."

—**Don Whiteford,** creative director THQ Digital UK Ltd.

"This book is one of the most comprehensive, straight-forward, and easy to follow guides for modeling precise and efficient 3D game assets and environments. Andrew Gahan has heard everything every educator has said about what a textbook needs to do to meet the broad stroke of students' needs and abilities in learning how to master 3D modeling with 3ds Max. With simple understanding and imagination, this text can be used to transform modeling for games into modeling for animation or modeling for simulation."

—**Tim Harrington,** national assistant dean, Game and Simulation Programming, DeVry University

3ds Max Modeling for Games

Insider's Guide to Stylized Modeling

Volume II

Andrew Gahan

Routledge
Taylor & Francis Group

LONDON AND NEW YORK

First published 2012

This edition published 2015 by Focal Press

Published 2017 by Routledge
2 Park Square, Milton Park, Abingdon, Oxon OX14 4RN
711 Third Avenue, New York, NY 10017, USA

First issued in hardback 2017

Routledge is an imprint of the Taylor & Francis Group, an informa business

© 2012, Taylor & Francis.

All rights reserved. No part of this book may be reprinted or reproduced or utilised in any form or by any electronic, mechanical, or other means, now known or hereafter invented, including photocopying and recording, or in any information storage or retrieval system, without permission in writing from the publishers.

Notices
Practitioners and researchers must always rely on their own experience and knowledge in evaluating and using any information, methods, compounds, or experiments described herein. In using such information or methods they should be mindful of their own safety and the safety of others, including parties for whom they have a professional responsibility.

Product or corporate names may be trademarks or registered trademarks, and are used only for identification and explanation without intent to infringe.

Library of Congress Cataloging-in-Publication Data
 Applicationsubmitted

British Library Cataloguing-in-Publication Data
A catalogue record for this book is available from the British Library.

ISBN 13: 978-1-138-40074-0 (hbk)
ISBN 13: 978-0-240-81606-7 (pbk)

Typeset by: diacriTech, Chennai, India

Contents

Contents

Acknowledgments

Thanks to:

Laura and Lauren at Focal Press

Extra special thanks to:

Ant O'Donnell for Vegetation

Seth Nash for Robot

Allan Wales for Robert

Andy Manns for the Scene

Adrian Burrows for the Trashcan

Finally, thank you, for picking up the book.

Introduction

Hello and welcome to *3ds Max Modeling for Games*. We must be kindred spirits, as for the last 20 years I've been reading through books just like this and learning new software just like you are now. I've also spent a lot of time understanding the best way to teach what I've learned to others, so hopefully you'll be able to learn a lot of new things quickly and enjoy this journey.

You'll find that this book isn't just a set of tutorials, it is also an invitation to a great community and the opportunity to make some friends and build your confidence and professional connections along the way.

I'd like to start off by explaining how to use this book in conjunction with the website to help you to get the very best out of this experience in the fastest possible time.

Website and Forum

As previously mentioned, along with the tutorials in this book you also have access to an amazing community and website, which can be found at www.3d-for-games.com.

FIG 1 The 3D for games website.

FIG 2 A view of the forum front page.

Probably the most useful part of the website is the forum. Here you can post questions about the tutorials in this book and the other books that I've written (or any other 3D, art, games, or even film-related questions for that matter).

It's also a place where you can ask for help and advice on your personal or professional work, and there are some great tips on getting into the industry. Quite a few of the forum members have already achieved their dreams of landing their first job in the games industry and are quickly becoming well respected and talented professionals.

Also on the forum, there is a great resource for reference materials and website links to almost all the 2D, 3D software and reference sites that you'll need.

You'll also find free competitions to enter, a showcase gallery to show off your work, as well as a work-in-progress section to postprogress section along with lots of other 3D and game art-related discussion threads.

The forum can be found at www.3d-for-games.com/forum sign in today and have a look at what's going on.

Also, unlike almost every other book, I'll be available to help you on every step of your journey, along with the rest of the community, so don't be shy, log on, and say hello and we can start working with you immediately.

Also, on the forum, there are a number of live projects that you can get involved in. At the time of writing, there is a short film project called Mila (www.milafilm.com) and a games project with The Pixel Bullies – a small independent games developer. These are great ways of learning new skills, improving to a professional level, and meeting some great contacts – not to mention getting to work on published games and films.

Level

This book is mostly aimed at intermediate 3ds Max and Photoshop users. By intermediate, I mean you will have already used 3ds Max to create a few assets and are familiar with basic modeling, unwrapping, and texturing techniques.

If you find that you are struggling with the tutorials and if you feel that you're not familiar enough with all the tools and techniques, don't worry. I've written another book that is published by Focal Press titled **3ds Max Modeling for Games – An Insider's Guide to Game Character, Vehicle, and Environment Modeling**. There is also a 2nd edition available, which has a lot of new and different content. Both books are ideal for getting you to an intermediate/ advanced level of modeling.

The 2nd edition has a new introduction and new tutorials on LOD's, normal maps, creating trees and foliage, and a completely new scene. It was written to complement the 1st edition rather than to replace it.

FIG 3

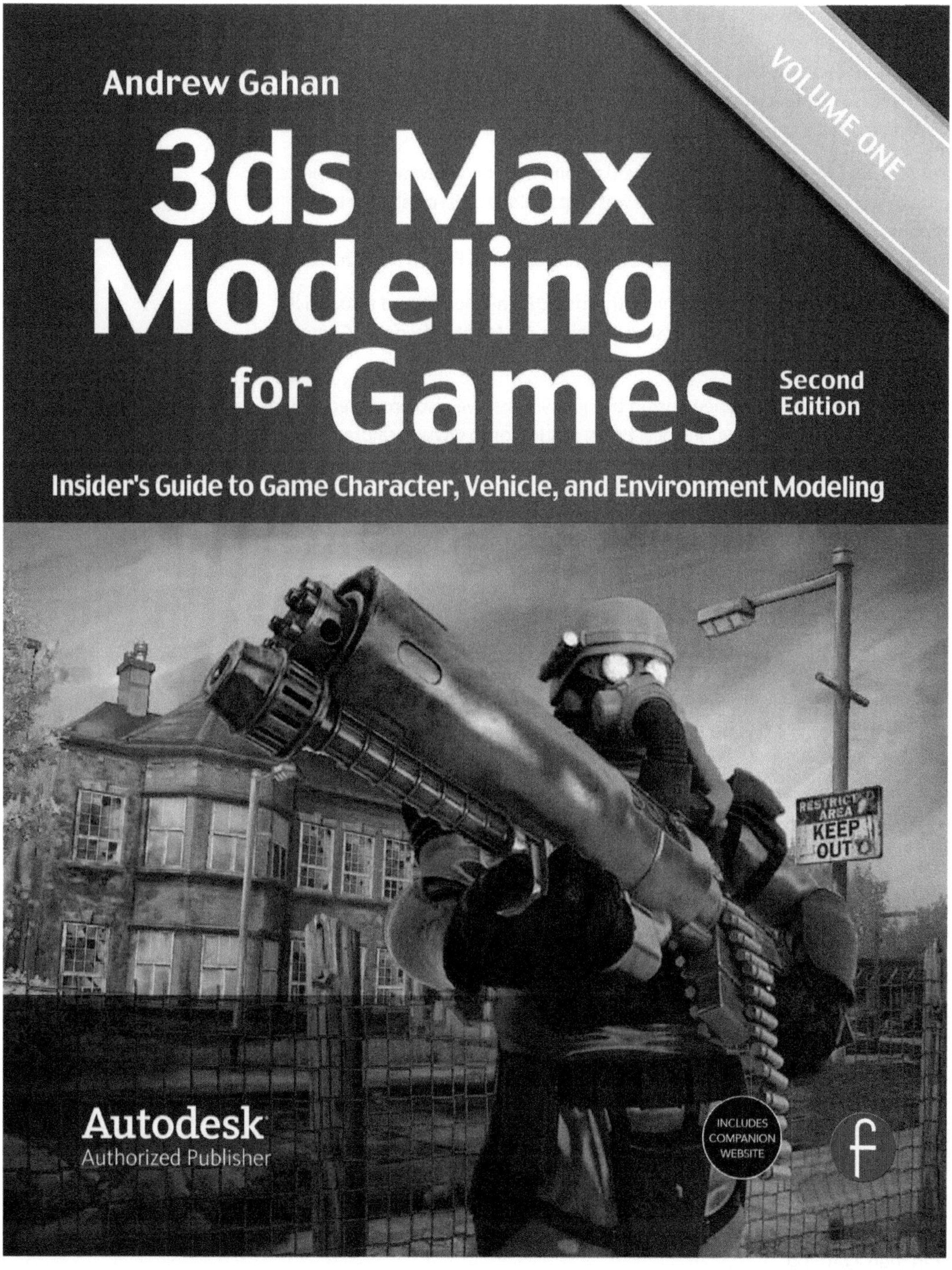

Andrew Gahan

3ds Max
Modeling
for Games

VOLUME ONE

Second
Edition

Insider's Guide to Game Character, Vehicle, and Environment Modeling

RESTRICT
AREA
KEEP
OUT

Autodesk
Authorized Publisher

INCLUDES
COMPANION
WEBSITE

FIG 4

I wrote these books specifically for anyone starting out in 3D modeling or new to game asset creation in 3ds Max. In these books, you'll be taken through the fundamentals of 3ds Max and Adobe Photoshop with some beginner tutorials, and I've also included some intermediate and advanced tutorials to challenge you as your skills improve as you work through the books.

3ds Max Modeling for Games has received a number of great reviews in the press and on websites such as Amazon and was so popular that it has already been reprinted, along with a 2nd edition that is available with lots of new content. *3ds Max Modeling for Games* has also been translated into French and Czech.

So, if you're struggling a little bit with this book, by all means read through it, but work through the first five or six tutorials in *3ds Max Modeling for Games*, and you'll soon be up to speed.

If you prefer to get up to speed using training videos, I've also produced a great Max in Minutes series through Focal Press, just log onto www.focalpress.com/eresources.aspx and search for Max in Minutes. These videos are designed to teach you each of the processes or techniques quickly without any waffle. They are roughly 15 to 20 minutes long and available for a few $ each.

Content

OK, let's get on with the content of the book.

For all of the tutorials, I have chosen the theme **Robert and Robot**. Before we get started, let me tell you a little about this concept…

Back Story

Here's the basic back story that sets the scene and the characters for the book…

Robert lives with his mother, sister, brother, and eccentric inventor father in a suburban town. One night, his father mysteriously disappears, leaving his mother struggling to pay the bills and look after the family by herself. Robert is a young dreamer obsessed with the tales of grand adventure and excitement he sees on TV and in books and comics.

Finding out his mum will soon lose the house, he goes out into their run-down backyard, which is scattered with his dad's failed and broken inventions, to see what he can find to sell. Looking into the starry sky, he wishes on a shooting star that he could escape and find his father wherever he is.

Believing that his dreams will never come true he kicks a piece of scrap in anger, which spirals off into the junk-filled yard. Robert hears a clunk, a buzz, and then a rattling.

He climbs through the discarded junk approaching the dull blue glowing light. He sees a small metal figure rattle to a stop and utter the words ro-bot-fuel…

xvi

FIG 5

feed ro-bot … Robert sees a thin wire dangling loosely from his hand and knows what he must do.

Quickly he scoops the robot up and drags him into the house, without thinking, Robert jams the wire into the socket and BANG! There is an almighty flash and both Robert and robot suddenly find themselves in a strange new place…

The Tutorials

All of the assets that you will complete in the tutorials will all be part of this theme.

This scene will include the main character Robert, who is an 8-year-old boy, his side kick robot, their house and garden, which features an old tree house and a workshop and lots of Robert's fathers' old inventions.

Starting Out

We'll start off with a brief chapter on planning a project. I realize that you probably want to get straight into modeling, but if we spend a little time on thinking about what you want to build, planning it out and breaking it down, it will save you a lot of time in the long run. Also, it will hopefully set you off with some great fundamentals of project planning. This should help you to estimate your work in the future and help you not to take on too much work on later projects.

Next, we'll continue with building a basic box model, just in case there are any readers completely new to 3ds Max. After the box tutorial, the skill curve will increase quite steeply, so don't forget, if we're moving a bit too quickly, pick up a copy of **3ds Max Modeling for Games** and then once you're ready come back here to continue your journey.

Finally, we'll get into the core of the modeling for the project. You'll be generating good-looking assets quickly and efficiently and learning the basics of rendering to give you the skills to create a great portfolio of your own work.

I'll also leave a few gaps in the scene for you to fill in yourself. I've prepared some cool concepts that you can use for inspiration for modeling projects, or to just build and populate your scene.

OK, let's get started…

CHAPTER 1

Introduction to 3ds Max and Basic Modeling Terms

The first part of this chapter is designed to get complete beginners up to speed with an overview of the 3D Studio Max user interface, tools, and some functions. The version we'll be covering is Max 2011; if you happen to have an earlier version a lot of this information will still be accurate.

A trial version of the latest release can be downloaded from the Autodesk website. Just go to www.autodesk.com and look in the Products tab.

First of all let's have a brief look at the layout of the **user interface** (UI). Figure 1a.1 is a screen grab of how 3ds Max looks when it's launched. Let's have a look at each of the main areas of the interface.

1. In the top-left corner, we have a button which is the 3ds Max logo. Click on this to bring up the **Application menu**; this provides the file-management commands such as opening or loading a scene and the saving options.
2. To the right of this is the quick access toolbar – it contains icons for saving, new scene, open file, and the undo and redo commands.

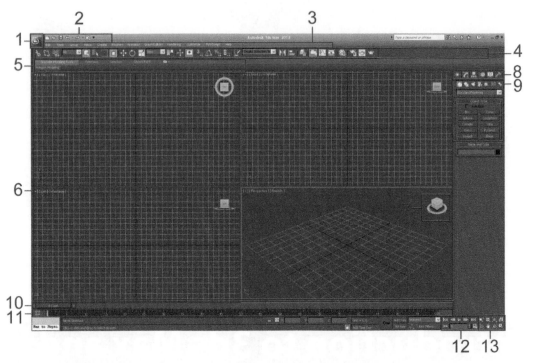

FIG 1a.1 Layout of the user interface.

3. Just below these we have the **menu bar.** This gives you access to all the tools and their settings in max along with the create options for creating 3D shapes. It also contains all the preferences and software settings under **Customize > Preferences.**

4. Below the menu bar is the **main toolbar** – this contains a lot of the basic tools we will need. Highlighted in the screenshot of the toolbar below are the select, move, rotate, and scale buttons. These are the tools we need to manipulate objects and meshes within Max.

   Other options on this bar include the snap settings for snapping components using different methods. The selection options are also available here, including the selection filter, which is a useful dropbox that allows you to restrict selections to certain object types. This is very useful when dealing with complex scenes with many types of objects.

   On the right side of the toolbar, as shown in the image, are the buttons to bring up the material editor and the rendering options.

FIG 1a.2

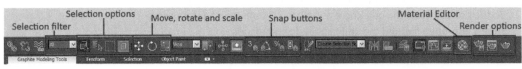

5. Beneath the main toolbar are the Graphite Modeling Tools. This section gathers all the standard edit tools related to poly modeling in one place. It really helps to speed up the modeling process.

6. The four windows highlighted by number 6 are the four default viewports. From the top left, these are the top view, front view, left view, and the perspective view. It is possible to arrange the viewports whichever way you want. To maximize or minimize the active viewport, the shortcut is ALT + W. The currently active viewport will always be highlighted by a yellow border.

    You can also left click and drag into the intersection between viewports to resize them. Right click in the intersection again and select reset layout to restore the default four panel view.

7. Highlighted here is the viewcube. This is a very handy tool for quickly changing the orientation of a camera or changing the viewport with one click. You can do this by clicking on either a direction on the compass around the viewcube or clicking on the cube itself.

    When the cube is displayed in a 3D viewport you can select any corner, side, or face to position the camera. To change to a standard view, click on the center of a face.

    When in a standard view four arrows will appear around the viewcube allowing you to cycle through all the standard viewports, for example front, back, and top. To go back to a 3D view, click on a side or a corner.

    You can also hold the LMB (left mouse button) and drag to rotate the viewcube and viewport.

    Below is an image of the viewcube. The viewcube on the left is from the perspective viewport and the right one is from the front viewport.

FIG 1a.3

8. This is the command panel and comprises six panels that give you access to most of the modeling features of 3ds Max. To display a different panel, you click its tab at the top of the command panel.

The most important panels for beginners are the create panel and the modify panel.

> **Create panel:** This panel gives you access to the primitive shapes that are good starting points for creating models. Also featured within this tab are shapes, lights, and cameras. There are seven categories. All of these can be created by selecting what you want in the menu with the LMB and then clicking the LMB in the viewport. Then, the item will appear.
>
> **Modify panel:** The modify panel is where you can change the creation parameters of an object and also where you can apply modifiers to objects to reshape them. The modify panel's contents will contain different parameters depending on what category or type of object is selected. We will be dealing with all these various parameters as we encounter them throughout the book.

9. These are the **object categories** within the **create panel.** This is the panel which contains the basic primitive objects. The drop-down box below the icons allow you to access more advanced shapes and items. By default, it is on standard primitives.

10. This is the **time slider.** This displays the current frame the time slider is on and how many frames are in the total range. To move the slider, you can either select it and hold the LMB and drag it along back and forth or you could use the playback controls to the right (12).

11. The **track bar** sits below the time slider and is a time line displaying frames in increments. It is mainly used for adjusting keys – moving, copying, or deleting them.

12. These are the **animation playback** controls and they do as they say. You can use them to jump to the start and end frame on the time slider or move one frame at a time.

13. To the right of the animation playback controls are the **viewport navigation controls.** Some of the options here may be different and change depending on the type of viewport that's active. For example whether it is a standard one or you are looking through a camera or light.

To use the controls, select the option you want from the navigation controls with the LMB and then use the LMB in the viewport to carry this action out. If you hold the LMB on the navigation buttons with a triangle in the bottom right-hand corner of the icon, you will get more advanced options for that function.

One example is the rotate tool. You have three options:

> **Arc rotate:** This will rotate the camera within the viewport using the view as the center of rotation.
>
> **Arc rotate sub object:** This will use the component selected, i.e., a vertex as the center of rotation.
>
> **Arc rotate selected:** This will use the selected object as the center of rotation. I tend to leave it on arc rotated selected because this makes sure you are always focused on what you have selected.

Viewport Navigation

To navigate the viewport in Max holding the MMB and moving the mouse will pan the camera. Using the MMB to scroll will zoom in and out.

ALT + W will maximize or minimize the active viewport.

There are also hot key options to switch between views.

Press P to change it to a perspective view, F for a front view, B for a bottom view, and T for a top view.

The Quad Menu

I'm going to briefly mention the Quad menu now as it can help to speed up your work rate when you get used to it.

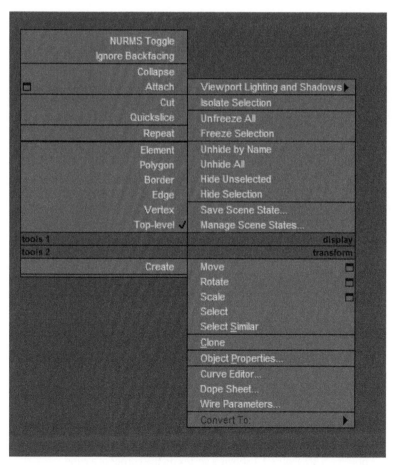

FIG 1a.4 The Quad menu.

The Quad menu will give you access to most commands needed by clicking the RMB in a viewport. If there is no object selected, it will display generic commands seen in the right two quadrants of the image above. The two left quadrants will appear when an objected is selected, and as it is context sensitive, the contents will vary depending on what's selected.

The Quad menu can be heavily customized, and it is worth looking into this further as you develop a workflow and get more experienced with 3ds Max. Max's help section can provide further information on this if you are interested.

Setting Up 3ds Max

To begin with, we'll start with some basic settings for 3ds Max. Go to Customize > Preferences > Files > Enable Auto Backup, and set the number of Auto Backup files to 9, and set Backup Interval (minutes) to 10, then click OK.

Next we'll set up the units we'll be modeling in; these vary from studio to studio, but in this book, one unit equals 1 cm. Go to Customize > Units setup … and, select Metric, and then click OK.

Don't forget that the in-depth help section is always at hand on the main menu or by pressing F1 or just log onto the free help forum at www. 3d-for-games.com/forum and we'll answer your questions as soon as you've registered and logged in.

Game Art Terminology

I'd like to introduce you to the key terms used in the games industry relating to the creation of 3D assets. I am not going to go into great technical detail, as there are plenty of resources online which will explain these terms in greater depth. 3ds Max has a wealth of information in the help section, so don't be afraid to use the F1 key to search for anything that you'd like to know more about. As you progress through this book, you will encounter all the elements listed below, clearly explained in context, and you'll learn how to implement them.

Geometry

3D geometry is made up of vertices, edges, triangles, and polygons. These are the elements that define the surface of a 3D model. We can manipulate each of these in 3ds Max.

> **Vertex** (singular of vertices): A vertex is a single point. It contains information of its position in 3D space using the X, Y, and Z coordinates system found in 3ds Max. Vertices form the basic structure of geometric objects in 3D. Figure 1.1 shows a vertex on the corner of a cube.
> **Edge:** An edge is a line that connects two vertices. The edge is highlighted in red in Fig. 1.2.

FIG 1.1   FIG 1.2

Triangle (face): A triangle is created when three vertices all have edges connecting them. In relation to a 3D model, a triangle is the surface between these three vertices/edges. It is this surface that defines the form of a model. Triangles could also be called faces as these usually have three sides. Figure 1.3 shows a triangle selected on the face of a cube.

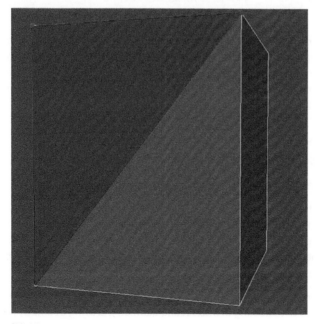

FIG 1.3

Polygon: A polygon is typically the surface between four vertices/edges. This could also be referred to as a quad. Polygons are also referred to as faces as they can have three or more sides. Polygons with more than four sides are referred to as n-gons. A quad consists of two triangles; you can see this in Fig. 1.4. On the left, I have selected a polygon on the side of the box which has two triangles counted in the selection. In the right of the image I have selected an n-gon. Note it's still counted as one poly but three triangles or tri's.

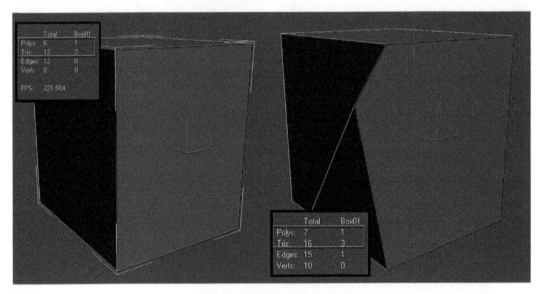

FIG 1.4

When creating 3D models for games, 99% of the time they should be made up of tri's or quads. You can create a model with a mixture of triangles or quads or n-gons, but in the end in game engines and 3ds Max, all polygons are broken down into triangular faces. It's good practice to measure your model's complexity in triangles as this is more accurate.

Stitched Geometry and Floating or Intersecting Geometry

These terms refer to two techniques of constructing a model.

The first, "stitched geometry" or "stitched in geometry" is when every vertex in the model is connected to another creating a water-tight solid mesh. The example on the right of Fig. 1.5 is a cylinder sitting on top of a cube, which is stitched to the cube at a vertex level. All of the faces that are not visible between these meshes have been deleted.

The example on the left of Fig. 1.5, where the cylinder sits on top of the cube, is referred to as floating or intersecting geometry. Leaving geometry floating

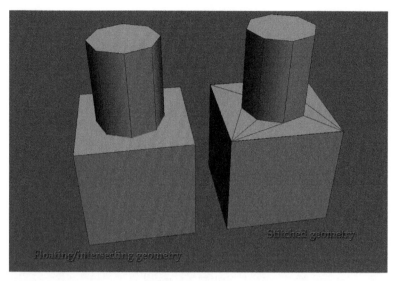

FIG 1.5

will mean that you use less triangles overall, but there is some overdraw in the face of the cube at the point where the cylinder sits over it. This surface area will be calculated in rendering but it is never visible. The stitched in example has no unrendered surface area as it has been deleted during the stitching process.

The decision on which method is best can be determined by a game engine or a project's needs. However, as a general rule, small objects are ok to be placed on meshes as they cause little overdraw. Some examples are handles on doors, switches, posters, or fire alarms.

Large objects such as buildings connected to each other are best using the stitched method as the saving in overdraw is worth the extra triangles when the overdraw consists of a large surface area on screen.

LODs

LOD is the acronym for level of detail. LODs are used in almost every game today. A LOD is a version of an asset which is lower in polygon count than the original. Sometimes LODs have smaller texture maps or simpler shaders too.

For an artist creating LODs you should aim to reduce the polygon detail to around 50% per LOD, more if possible without destroying the outline of the asset.

Figure 1.6 shows a model of an old fire extinguisher with two LODs and the polygon counts of each reduction.

FIG 1.6 An old fire extinguisher.

Textures

The term "textures" or "texture maps" in game art refers to 2D images that are projected onto or wrapped around a 3D mesh. We'll cover this more in the tutorials later on in the book.

These texture pages can be cropped from photographs or hand painted or created using a combination of both. The purpose of texture maps is to define an object's surface, color, or texture, and to visually describe any extra details that are not modeled in polygons.

Here is a brief description of the most common texture types.

> **Diffuse map:** A diffuse map is the main texture applied to most 3D models. This texture should define a surface's main color and detail. A good diffuse map should not have any directional lighting in it. The only lighting that should be present in this texture should be from an ambient light source as if it's being lit evenly from all directions. This means that recesses in the texture will appear darker and raised elements would be lighter. No shadows or highlights should be present in the texture.

FIG 1.7 An example of a diffuse map.

Bump map: A bump map is a grayscale image that affects the shading over a surface. A game engine or 3D program will interpret dark values as being recessed areas and lighter values as being raised areas. Bump maps are used less commonly now due to other more advanced techniques like normal mapping.

FIG 1.8 An example of a bump map.

Specular map: A specular map can be a grayscale or color image. Specular maps define a surface's shininess and highlight color. If you use a grayscale specular map, the lighter the value in the texture the shinier that area will be. Darker values will be less shiny with pure black resulting in a matte surface. A grayscale spec map will give you a white highlight. The example below is of a door. The metallic and glass surfaces are almost white, whereas the wood and dirt are much darker. You can see from the glass panels in the render the benefits of using a specular map.

FIG 1.9 An example of a specular map.

Normal map: Normal maps have become a standard in most current games. A normal map is an RGB texture used to give an object the appearance of having a lot more detail than it really has. Each color channel contains information that represents the direction of a face's surface normal in 3D space using the X, Y, and Z coordinates. This means normal maps work with dynamic lights and will light as if it were geometry. Normal maps can be generated from high-resolution models or can be created from grayscale images.

FIG 1.10 An example of a normal map.

12

Alpha map: An alpha map is a grayscale or black-and-white texture which controls the transparency on a surface. Black pixels appear transparent (or see-through) and white pixels appear opaque (or solid color). Common uses for alpha maps in games are leaves and foliage, wire mesh fencing, glass, cloth, decals, and particles. The example here is a small plant.

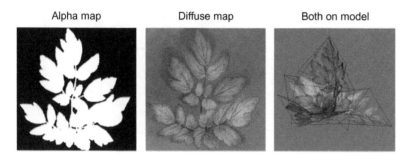

Alpha map   Diffuse map   Both on model

FIG 1.11 An example of an alpha map.

Shader: A shader or material in 3D is what we input all these textures into and then it's applied to a model. A basic explanation for a shader is that it is a set of instructions for the GPU (general processing unit) or a mini program for the software telling it how to render a surface. Shaders can have a lot of parameters that we can adjust further to increase the effects of the assigned texture maps. We'll be using 3ds Max's material editors later in the book.

Types of Texture Layouts

The space where we will layout our texture, the **edit UVWs** window, has three axes just as the viewport does. These axes are referred to as UVW rather than XYZ. The U and V axes correspond to the X and Y axes, respectively. The W axis corresponds to the Z axis and is generally used for procedural maps. For now we'll be referring to the U and V axes.

Tiling Texture

A tiling texture is one that is seamless and can be repeated across a surface. It needs to be seamless for at least one or both of the U and V axes to work. The following image shows the different directions a tiling texture can tile in.

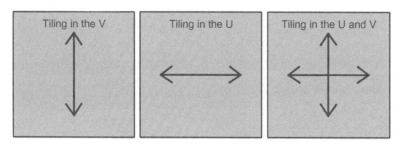

FIG 1.12

Tiling textures are commonly used in games to cover large surfaces or surfaces that do not require any unique details such as the ground, brick walls, or landscape. Here are some examples.

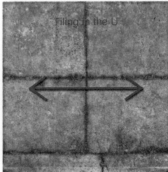

FIG 1.13

Unique Texture

A unique texture is one that contains no tiling elements but many uniquely unwrapped UV shells laid out into the UV space. This type of map is commonly used for objects that require specific details or characters. Figure 1.14 is an example of a unique texture layout.

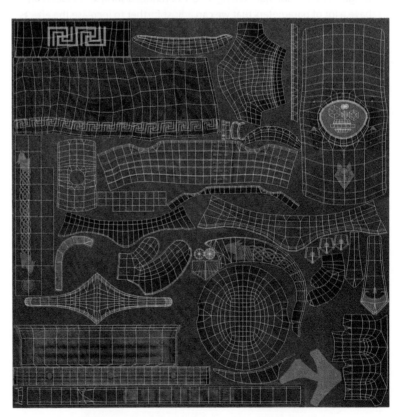

FIG 1.14 An example of a unique texture layout.

A Unique Texture with Tiling Elements

This type of texture layout utilizes both tiling elements, which need to tile in at least one axis, and uniquely unwrapped elements all laid out in the texture sheet. The following example has three strips running along the bottom of the texture sheet tiling in the U axis. The top half of the texture is made up of several uniquely unwrapped elements.

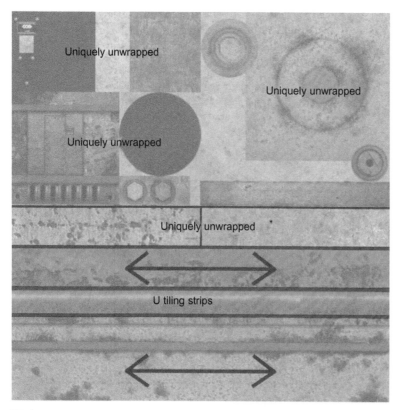

FIG 1.15

Think about how you will create your own texture pages in the future using these techniques.

What's New in 3ds Max 2012

For those of you who have just downloaded 3ds Max 2012 from the Autodesk website to go through the tutorials, I thought I'd cover a few new additions to the software that will be useful for your modeling. Sure, there are lots more stuff that I've not covered, so remember to use the F1 for help and browse at will. These are the most relevant tools and techniques that I think you'll use.

Atfirst glance when you open up 3ds Max 2012, you might not notice the difference in terms of the layout and the viewports and button configuration, but many issues have been addressed since versions 2010 and 2011.

So let's get started with the new stuff.

Nitrous Accelerated Graphic Core

Basically, this allows the user to be able to use render quality display in the real-time viewport. This includes unlimited lights, soft shadows ambient occlusion, tone mapping, and high-quality transparency. These will all help with your decision making in your work.

You also have the Quicksilver hardware renderer, which speeds up the rendering of your scene and also allows you to set the render type as Realistic, Ink, Color Ink, Acrylic, Tech, Graphite, Color Pencil, and Pastel.

The Stylistic Rendering

This can be found in the left-hand corner of any of the viewports. This new feature allows you to create a variety of nonphotorealistic effects that simulate artistic styles with the new ability to render styled images in the viewport with the Quicksilver renderer.

Right click in any viewports' left-hand corner to see the drop-down menu.

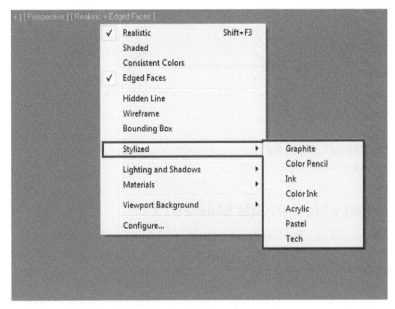

FIG 1.16

The styles included are shown as follows:

FIG 1.17

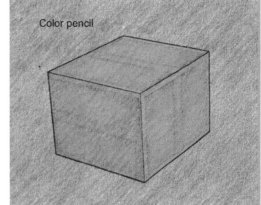

FIG 1.18

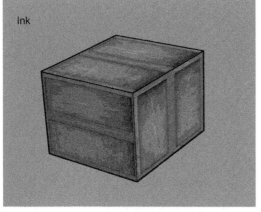

FIG 1.19

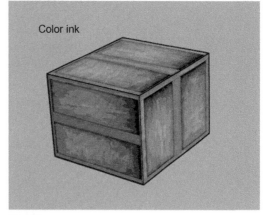

FIG 1.20

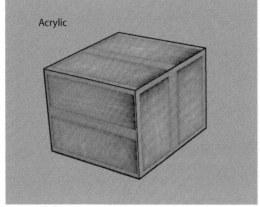

FIG 1.21

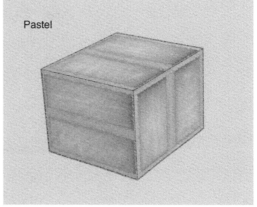

FIG 1.22

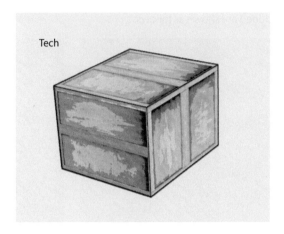

Tech

FIG 1.23

All extremely useful and easy to use.

Updated UV Editor

Long-awaited improvements are the Unwrap UVW Modifier enhancements. It still has the same layout as the UVW Unwrap but with added buttons, to help speed up your unwrapping.

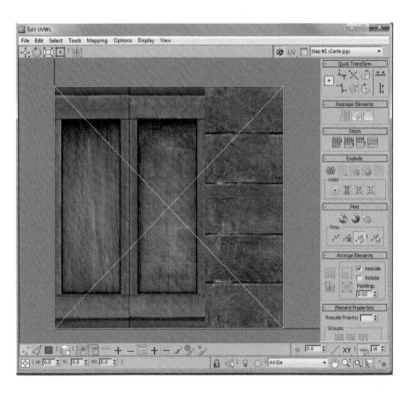

FIG 1.24

18

Autodesk has introduced the commonly used tools Stitch and Weld, but have also added several new tools to make your life a lot easier.

The new icons are simple to understand and more useful to the user.

Quick Transform

This new feature quickly allows you to rotate tilt and move up, down, and side to side, instead of having to use the drop-down menu as in the previous versions.

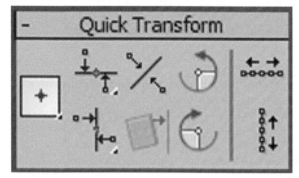

FIG 1.25

Reshape Elements

This allows you to straighten out your mapping by taking curved clusters and straightening them out.

FIG 1.26

Explode

Use the tools in the first row of this rollout for breaking up texture coordinates into separate clusters. The Flatten tools work on selected texture polygons, or if no polygons are selected, just polygons .

FIG 1.27

Weld

Turn on Target Weld, and then drag one vertex to another vertex, or one edge to another edge to weld them.

Peel

Peel will let you take a selection of your model, for instance a leg on a horse, or a characters head. You unwrap it, and then use the "pins" to control the cluster of vertices to get the neat mapping. This is a really useful tool.

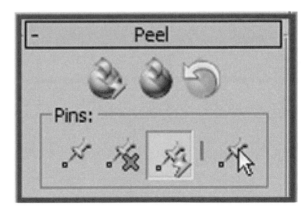

FIG 1.28

Arrange Elements

Use these tools to arrange elements automatically in various ways. Packing is useful for adjusting the layout so that clusters don't overlap. Also use Pack UVs to get accurate scale on mapping.

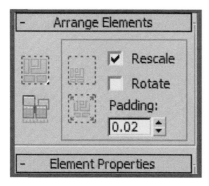

FIG 1.29

New Graphite Modeling Tools

Sculpting and Painting Enhancements

Paint Deform provides tools for deforming mesh geometry interactively and intuitively by dragging the mouse over an object surface. The primary tools are Shift, for moving vertices with falloff in the direction you drag the mouse, and Push/Pull, for moving vertices inward and outward. Additional tools include Smudge, Flatten, Noise, etc.

FIG 1.30

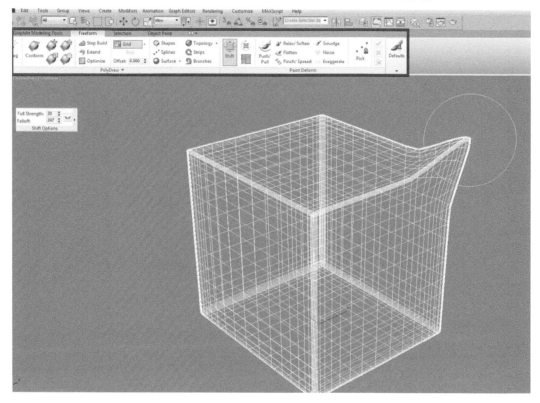

Here is the interface close up, along with the Paint and Deform panels close up.

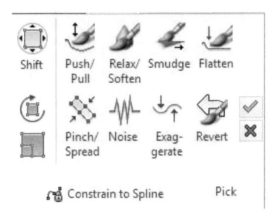

FIG 1.31

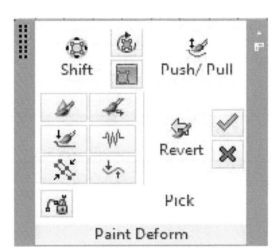

FIG 1.32

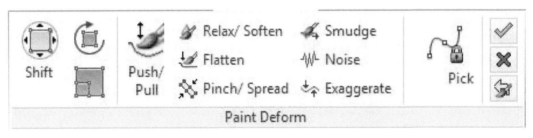

FIG 1.33

Conform Brushes

PolyDraw provides tools for sketching out and editing a mesh on the main grid, projected onto the surface of another object, or onto the selected object itself, depending on the setting. PolyDraw also provides Conform tools for molding one object to the shape of another.

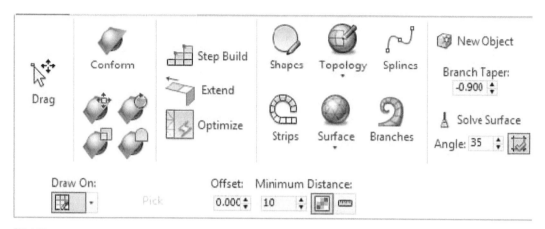

FIG 1.34

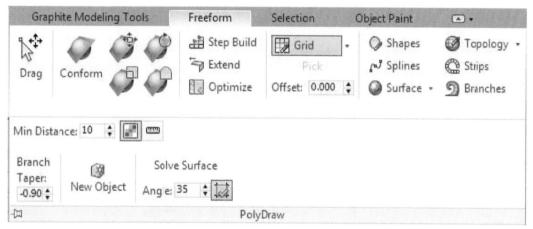

FIG 1.35

The Conform brushes let you mold a conform object into the shape of a target object while moving the conform object's vertices toward the target. You can base the conform direction on the normals of the conforming vertices, or on a line between the target surface and the view plane. Possible modeling applications include painting-raised road markings on a road or a hedge on a hillside.

The Conform brushes are extremely useful tools for creating more organic terrain or creatures; there are some tutorials that would expand on these tools. These are well worth investigating.

ProOptimizer Improvements
You can now optimize models faster, more efficiently, with much better results, using the enhanced ProOptimizer. This includes normal and

UV interpolation, along with the ability to keep your high-resolution normals on your low-resolution model.

The main things to look at are…

- Improved optimization results
- Faster optimization
- UV Interpolation
- Normal Interpolation
- Reduced memory requirements
- Lock Vertex/Point Position option

The New Material Editor

If you've ever used Maya or the Unreal engine, you'll feel pretty comfortable with the new additions to the editor as they feel very similar.

FIG 1.36

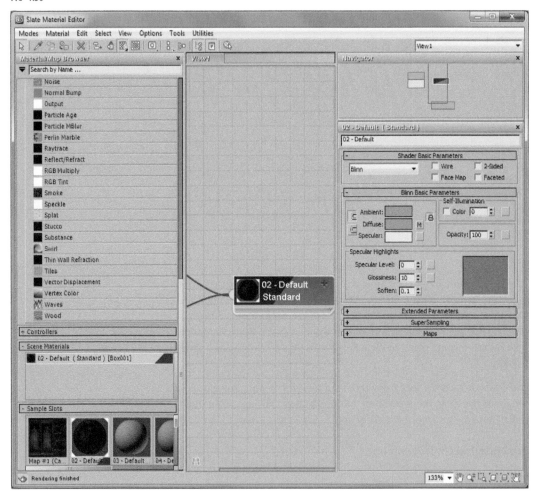

As in previous versions of 3ds Max, pressing (M) will bring up the Material Editor. At first glance it looks totally different, but after a few minutes you can find your way around. The editor now gives you more control over your texture before assigning it to your mesh, letting you link up your normal maps and spec maps with much more control.

This concludes our brief introduction to the most common terms used when creating art for video games as well as some of the key features in 3ds Max 2012. There are many more things to learn, which we will be dealing with later in the book. It's now time to start making some objects, so let's move on to Chapter 2 – good luck!

Planning Your Project Including Making a Plan

Introduction

If you've just picked up this book and are ready to get straight into the modeling, I'd recommend that you read the introduction first. It's short, but explains how the book and website work together, contains useful links, and it also sets the scene and background story for our characters. Have you read it? Great! Let's get started.

What We Are Building and Why

At the start of any project, we first need to decide what it is we're going to create. This may seem like a bit of a simple or insignificant thing to say, but it's not. Far too many people set out on creative projects without knowing what they're going to do and what they want the end result to be. This can waste an awful lot of time and be quite de-motivating.

3ds Max Modeling for Games
© 2012 Taylor & Francis. All rights reserved.

To start off, make a few notes on what it is you're going to do and what the end result will be. In the case of our Robert and Robot tutorials, we will be creating a number of assets to build up a scene. The end result will be a render. The style will be similar to something that Pixar may create in terms of texture style, the film "Up" could be a good reference point for color and texture, though our assets will be lower detail. We will be aiming the complexity at the higher end of game assets but not quite as detailed as the motion picture assets.

Reference Materials Including Mood Boards

The next step is to start to gather reference materials and to create some mood boards. The reference material can be sketches, images found on the Internet, photos, snapshots from films, or anything else that you like the look, tone, texture, or form of.

To create a mood board, just collect all the images in a folder on your PC or print them out and either stick them to a large foam/cardboard board or arrange them digitally in Photoshop. Next, put the boards somewhere prominent next to your PC or set them as your screensaver or desktop background. Alternatively, if you have a dual screen setup, you can have your reference materials on your second screen – most professionals do this.

Brief

If this isn't a personal piece of work, and you're doing it for a college project or professional contract, you should have a brief. If you don't have a brief, always ask for one, and try to ask as many questions as possible, so that you can pull one together yourself.

If you're working to a brief, it's extremely important to ask as many questions as you can before you start, rather than during the project. If you complete this part of the process well, it can save you a lot of time. There are a number of reasons for asking all of the questions up front – here are a few of the more important ones…

- You'll be able to scope to project and ensure that you have enough time and resources to deliver it on time. Always ensure you know the deadline.
- You'll be able to commit to dates (or not), knowing whether you should actually start the work at all. Remember to include reviews, work-in-progress deliveries, and a final delivery.
- You will be able to determine the polygon count, texture resolution specifications, and what types of textures are required (Bump, Specular, Normal maps, etc). Never start a job without knowing these things.
- Ae different versions of the model required? Levels of detail, for example (also known as LODs). These can take at least as long to create again if

four or five LODs are required. This can also be a very costly mistake if you overlook them.

- Does anything need to be *animated ,rigged*, or have *particles* included? Maybe you can only deliver the modeling part of this build.

Most importantly, if you are doing work for someone else and charging for it, agree on a price up front. This can be a fixed price, or if you are working on an hourly rate, estimate a final price, so that you don't put the customer in a difficult position when you submit an invoice five times more than they are expecting.

Even if this is a personal project without a brief, it's a good idea to go through a similar Q&A process as the following one to ensure you are clear with what you are doing. A lot of professionals make this mistake, so try not to get into the habit.

Below is an example of a simple brief…

Now, for the uninitiated, this may look like a pretty good brief. It tells us what we need to build, the poly count and also the price we'll be paid for the work.

This is in fact a very poor brief as there is lots of information missing.

When presented with a brief like this we should first ask a lot of questions. Here are some of the initial ones that I would recommend in this situation and why…

Which Noddy are you referring to?
We could at this point assume that our client means Noddy from the children's books. But it could also mean Noddy from the animated series. Are there any differences between the two? There could also be any number of other Noddy characters. Let's assume the brief refers to the Noddy on the animated series, this leads us on to our next question…

When you say similar, what do you mean? A rough likeness, an exact copy or something else?
This should tell us whether we need to design a car to build or whether we need to obtain reference of the actual car required. In this instance,

---

Title – Cartoon Car

We would like you to create a cartoon car similar to Noddy's for us to use in an animation. We would like the car to be textured and have no more than 15,000 polys.

We don't mind how long you spend on this project as it will be a fixed price of $1000.

Your contact for this project will be Andy Gahan – Info@3d-for-games.com

---

I would ask the client to provide me with reference material or a concept of the car they want built. Always ask for orthographic drawings so you can see the top, side, front, back, and maybe even underneath the vehicle.

If the client doesn't have a sketch, or orthographics, you can always offer to produce them at an extra cost. Make sure this is added to the brief with the costs defined, clearly keeping them separate from the modeling task. You'd keep this priced separately so that your bid won't appear more expensive than another one, and it helps everyone's understanding of what's involved when it's all broken down. Once you have the orthographics or reference material, you should know exactly what you're building, so on to the next question…

When you say 15,000 polys (short for polygons), do you mean four-sided polys or could you possibly mean triangles?

It's quite common to get a brief stating poly count when it actually refers to the triangle count. It may seem a small point, but is well worth checking as your model will be well off the stated detail if you fail to check. No one will mind if you ask questions like this, and could save both you and the client lots of unnecessary conflict.

When would you ideally like delivery of the final asset?

Although the client has specified that this is a fixed price job, so they don't mind how long you spend on it, they could want it in three days time, and it could be a two-week build for you to complete. If this is the case, then you'll have to politely contact the client and say that it's not possible for you to complete the asset in that timescale, but you could complete it in 10 days if all feedback is prompt and there are no major changes in the brief. This covers two important issues. First, you are letting the client know that you need feedback to be prompt on your submissions. You may ask that the client provides feedback within 24 hours for all submissions. If they are late, it will make you late, and you wouldn't want to be penalized for something that isn't your fault.

Also you are stating that you'll only be able to complete on time if the brief doesn't change. Briefs have a habit of changing, and goalposts move quite often on jobs like this, so you want to make sure that if there are major changes, they will be needed to be added as extra tasks, which you will estimate an additional cost for should they come up. Agreeing a day rate for your time is a good way to solve this.

What are the delivery and sign-off steps and schedule?

A good delivery plan could be completed poly model, completed textured model, then final model. If you agree to review at each point, this could save a lot of rework at the end. You could also break the $1000 fee up into three parts, to ensure that you get paid for each signed-off step if you can't get the final delivery signed off. It would be useful to set specific delivery dates for each step too, so that the client can have someone available to review. As a client, there's nothing worse than taking delivery of a load of outsourced work that you weren't expecting, especially if you're really busy.

What format will you want the final model in?
Max, Maya, Zbrush? It's important to get this right, especially the version of software to use.

What is the budget for the texture maps?
How many texture maps of what size are required? Do we need normal maps, specular, anything else?

What scale would you like me to work to?
Again, not a major issue but one you'll need to know, 1 unit = 1 cm maybe?

Payment terms?
Full payment on sign-off within 30 days is common. If this isn't on your estimate, you may have difficulty getting some people to pay on time. Even with terms like this, it can be difficult.

Anyway, I think you get the idea, ask lots of questions of your client, or define exactly what you are planning to do for yourself.

Concept Art

OK, so if we're doing a personal project and we don't have a client brief, we're going to need some concept art. This can be photographic reference, sketches, or orthographic illustrations. As we have the concept art for our project already, we can move on. If you don't have clear and detailed concepts for your project, don't start modeling. It's a lot easier to make changes in 2D and on sketches, than it is halfway through your 3D build. A lot of artists fail to do this – don't fall into the same trap. It's a worthwhile investment of time to make all your decisions up front, and believe me, it really does pay off.

Making a Plan and Estimating Your Work

Now we know exactly what we want to build and we have our concept art and specifications, before we jump in with the modeling we should really make a plan. Now I realize that you probably don't plan out your work much at this point, but you should definitely get into the habit.

The most important reason for this is so that you have a good idea of what you're getting yourself into. All too often I see artists starting out on a project and running into trouble because they took on too much work, or they didn't set deadlines to help them focus on specific goals or milestones leading them to completion.

Now this doesn't have to be a mega Hansoft or Microsoft Project Plan, it can be a simple list of tasks with estimates against them in a notepad.

First of all, you need to break down the project into components. In our case, we will break down our scene into separate assets (Robot, Character, House, Workshop, Tree House, Garden assets, etc.)

For each asset, we now need to break the work down into smaller tasks, adding rough estimates for each one…

House

Modeling	8 days
Detailing	2 days
Unwrapping	1 day
Textures	4 days

So for the house asset we have a rough estimate of 15 days. Continue to do this for all of the other assets in your scene. Don't forget to include all of the details like the trash can, the fence, any plants, or shrubs, absolutely everything.

Once you have the full list of estimates, add up all the totals and it will give you an idea of the scale of the project you are about to embark on. Now, if you're just building a single asset, you shouldn't really have any problems, but if you are building a scene it's essential that you go through this process.

The final part of this is to honestly work out how much time each day you can spend on this work.

Let's say that we have eight main assets that take around 15 days each to complete, and 10 smaller models that will take 3 days each to complete. This will give us a rough total of 150 days (eight main assets totaling 130 days added to 10 smaller ones totaling 30 days).

If we are estimating a day means 8 hours, the grand total is 1200 hours. As you can see this has become a major undertaking. Especially if you consider that you may only be working on this for 3 or 4 hours a day. If this is the case, it's going to take you 300 days without a break to complete this – almost a year!

Now, the good thing about this plan is that you are clear about the amount of work it's going to take to finish the scene without modeling anything. So if you decide that you don't want to invest almost a year on this, then you can redesign and de-scope to something a bit more manageable.

You might decide that you can't see all the assets in the scene at once depending on where the camera is, so you may only need to build half of them to get the first completed render done. You can always do a few other projects and come back to this one if you want to at a later date.

You may decide to reuse assets too, so instead of building three different trees, you may decide to just scale and re-color one tree to fill the scene.

Taking this method, you'll be able to complete more work, and not have so many unfinished projects in your portfolio. This will enable you to bulk up your portfolio with quality work, and none of your effort will be wasted.

Finally, once you have your estimates, add a column next to each one of the date you expect to have each model or component completed by. You can also set up reminders to keep you focused – five days left to complete the house as a meeting request in Microsoft Outlook, or Lotus Notes maybe.

This will keep you motivated, and it will also show you whether you are on track or not. If you're on track or even ahead of schedule, you may want to ease off a little, but if you are behind schedule, it's a good pointer that you either need to work harder or de-scope the work once more.

If you get good at estimating your work and keeping a record of how long assets took you to make, you'll be a lot better at pricing your work as a freelancer, or you'll deliver a lot more time for your lead artist or art director.

Now we have the basics of working out what you're going to build and also a simple plan, let's get on with building the first asset for the scene.

CHAPTER 3

Adapting a Concept

o start off with, Twe will try to keep the brief as 'real' as possible – by changing it right from the beginning. The concept we have been given is for one of the inventions of Robert's father. It is a gadget that uses a prism to split the different spectra of colors in light to make the plant's leaves contain all the colors of the rainbow.

This was originally designed as one of the inventions for an interior scene; but as our scene will be outdoors, we will adapt this concept and scale it up so that we see it nice and big in our final render.

We will keep the gadget the same, but we'll swap out the potted plant for a palm tree so that it is more visible in our scene.

We could do a sketch for this, but in this case, I'm confident that I know what I want to do; so, we'll just get started with the modeling.

We will build the models separately, first the palm tree; and then the gadget, using a variety of techniques.

Before any modeling can begin, we need to gather a selection of palm tree references. This is standard practice for any professional artist when starting any new modeling task. Once we have a good selection, we will pick the best two or three pictures to use as our points of reference. The criteria we're looking for in our key images are form, color, and texture. Don't forget the palm fronds will need texture reference too!

Don't fall into the trap of modeling what you think the tree looks like – a lot of artists do this and generally produce poor-looking models. Always get references and always look at them.

For this chapter, we will customize our modifier set. The modifier set is a group of buttons that you can customize to display your favorite modifiers and make them easily accessible. Modifier-set usage and setup differs from artist to artist, depending on their role or experience; but specialized sets can and should be used by modelers, animators, texture artists, and even designers. These are the tools you will keep coming back to; so any modifiers you use a lot should go here – it will save you a lot of time in the long run.

To begin with, bring up the Configure Modifier Sets dialogue box by clicking the button.

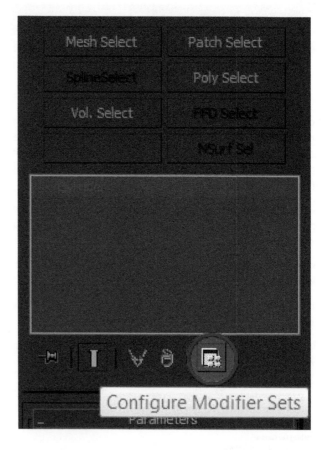

FIG 3.1

36

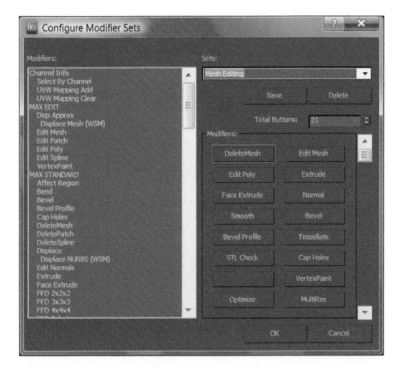

FIG 3.2

Here, we can customize our modifier set from a list of modifiers (on the left) and assign them to the buttons on the right. We'll start off with a default set and then customize it.

Open the Sets rollout and choose Mesh Editing (see Fig. 3.2). This will provide a set with 21 buttons.

Next, we customize the set. First, in the **Total Buttons** rollout, change the number from 21 to 10. Notice the name has now disappeared under the **Sets** header to reflect the fact that the set has been customized. Next, we need to swap out the modifiers we don't want for the ones we want.

Left click, hold, and drag on the **DeleteMesh** button and (while holding) move over to the **Modifiers** window and release. The button will now appear blank. Repeat this procedure for all the buttons except **Edit Poly** and **Edit Mesh** .

Once this has been done, scroll the modifier menu and drag into the empty slots the following functions; **FFD 2x2x2, Bend, Twist, UVW Map, Unwrap UVW, CrossSection, Surface**, and **Edit Spline** .

The layout can be rearranged however you like (see Fig. 3.4). Under the **Sets** header, type in the name for the new set 'Chapter 3.' Additional buttons can be added (they will appear blank until a function is dragged onto it) at any time, but be aware that the name will disappear once a customization has taken place. If you change them, remember to save them.

Once the button layout is finalized, click **Save** and **OK** to close the dialogue box.

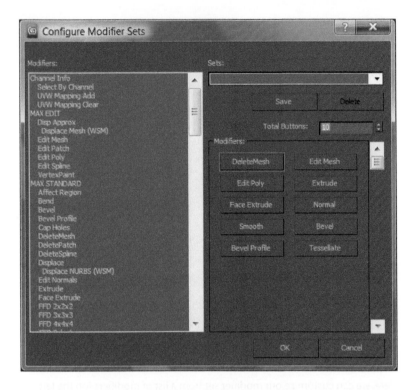

FIG 3.3

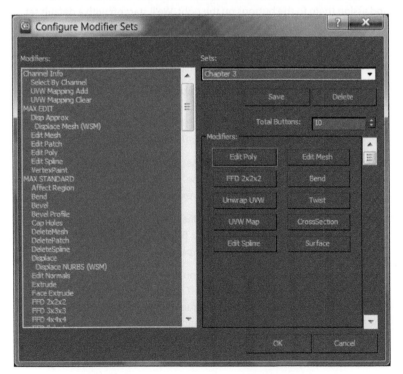

FIG 3.4

Now create two reference or block-out objects as rough estimates of scale and color for the two objects. The machine reference object should be approximately 250 cm and the palm should be approximately 700 cm. Create three basic materials and colors, as shown in Fig. 3.5. After completion, name the objects as Machine ref, Palm ref, and Fronds ref; and hide them.

FIG 3.5

The first model we create will be the palm tree. First we will make the trunk. Before we build the model, we will create the texture map in Photoshop.

As the model will be based around a cylinder, the UV mapping will be cylindrical. Knowing this beforehand affects how we look at texture creation and a little forethought and planning will yield better results.

Mirroring the aspect of the target, the texture will be taller than it is wide. So, with this in mind, create a texture with the dimensions of 1024 pixels tall and 128 pixels wide.

Always create textures at double the size (or resolution) you ultimately need, as Photoshop filters work more efficiently at a high resolution. After the texture is complete, reduce the size by 50% (Image > Size). This is typical industry practice. Another trick is to save the original large texture as a source image that you can apply to your models for portfolio renders. They need to be small and efficient for in game, but can be bigger (and therefore, look better) for your portfolio renders.

The palm texture will be made up of three different segments (as shown in Fig. 3.7). These will be the main body (1), the top (2) and the falloff/roots (3). If you can get all the elements from one reference image, then great; but if not, find up to three images (one for each area).

Layer each part on top of the base (1) and fade them off to make a smooth blend using the layer-mask function. A simple vertical gradient mask should give the desired falloff effect.

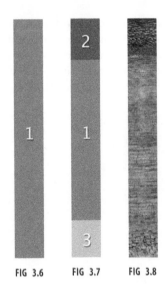

FIG 3.6   FIG 3.7   FIG 3.8

Once this is done, flatten the image. Next, using **Filter > Other > Offset** command, offset the texture in the horizontal plane by 64 pixels. The texture has now wrapped round, revealing any breaks in tiling down the central spine of the texture. Repair this effect using the Heal and Clone tools. With this completed, you can offset the texture again and you should have something resembling Fig. 3.8 .

With the texture ready, we can move back to Max and begin construction of the trunk model. Start by creating a cylindrical primitive object roughly the same scale as the reference object. The starting dimensions should be: radius 75 cm, height 700 cm, and segments 10. The trunk will have varying segment widths, so the radius denotes the absolute maximum. Once this is created, add an Edit Mesh modifier and select the central vertex on the top set of polygons. Pull this up a little to match Fig. 3.9.

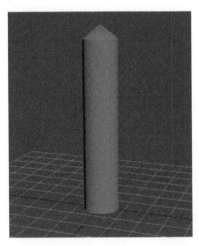

FIG 3.9

Finally, go into polygon mode (4 on the keyboard), select all of the polygons (CTRL + A) and set the Material ID to 1.

The model is now prepared for UV mapping. Add a **UVW Map** modifier to the stack and select cylindrical as the mapping type. Click the **Fit** button and the gizmo should match the dimensions of the model (Fig. 3.10). If the gizmo is horizontal, just rotate it so that it points upward, then use the fit function.

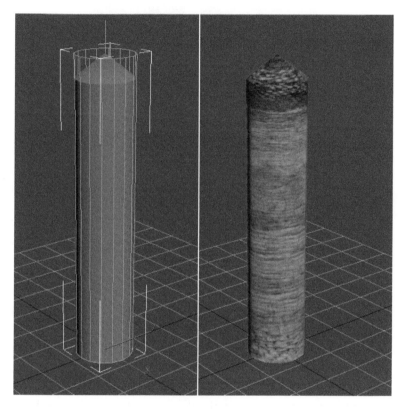

FIG 3.10

The default coordinates are fine for this model, so they don't need to be changed. Create a **Multi-Sub Object** material and change the number of IDs to two. Slot 1 will be for the tree trunk material and Slot 2 will be for the leaves. Name them Trunk and Palm, respectively. Next, just load the texture map for the trunk in the diffuse texture slot and click the Assign Material to Selection button.

Next, checking back against your reference photos and using your reference object an average, add an **Edit Mesh** modifier and adjust the segment scale of the model to make the form more organic, like a real tree trunk. This can be further embellished by rotating the segments too. When you think the model is starting to match the reference, add some subtle modifiers such as **Twist** and **Bend**. Experiment with the values until you are happy with the results. Name the model Trunk.

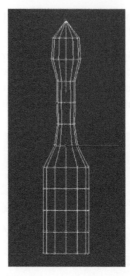

FIG 3.11a   FIG 3.11b

With the trunk complete, we can now move onto the palm leaves. Create a plane with the following dimensions; 375 cm height, 150 cm width, Length Segments 6 and Width Segments 4. This is the basis for the palm leaf object.

Go into Photoshop and create a palm leaf texture from one your reference images (or find some additional images for this). Once you have chosen a key image, create an alpha map and save it. Name the frond texture **Palm_Frond** and the alpha texture **Palm_Frond_Alpha** .

Put these two textures in the second ID slot of the Multi-Sub Object material. They should occupy the diffuse and opacity slots, respectively. Call the material "Palm" if you haven't named it already. Apply the material to the plane, add an **Edit Mesh** to the stack, select all the polygons and change the material ID to 2. The palm leaf texture should appear on the leaf model.

Next, add a Bend modifier to the stack. Select X as the bend axis and set the angle to 90°. The result should match Fig. 3.12. The frond object can now be used to populate the trunk.

FIG 3.12

Move the frond object to the top section of the palm trunk. Again, referring to your reference object, duplicate the frond around the circumference of the top of the trunk, varying the scale and rotation to stop the population looking mechanical. When a density similar to the reference is achieved, group the objects and the trunk together. Name the group **Palm tree** .

Additional form changes such as twists and bends can be applied to the group if need be.

FIG 3.13

With the palm complete, we can now move onto the gadget or invention.

First, we need to make the main hub. This can be done with a simple **Lathe** operation. To begin with, using the spline tools, create a cross section of the main hub. Once this is finished, choose **Lathe** from the drop-down modifier menu and set the segments to 16. The before and after versions of this process can be seen in Fig. 3.14a.

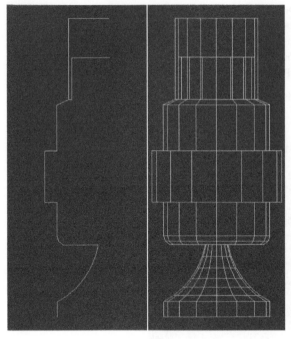

FIG 3.14a

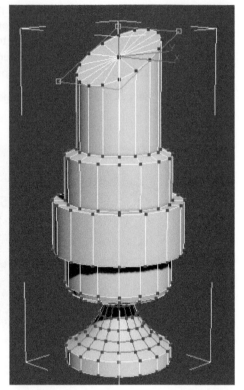

FIG 3.14b

Add an **Edit Mesh** modifier and set up the smoothing groups for the model. An auto smooth set to the default angle of 45° will be fine.

To create the tilt on the central cylinder (what will become the glass section later), select the top vertices and add an **FFD 2x2xv2** modifier. An orange gizmo will appear around the selected vertices.

Go into the **Sub Object** mode **Points** and from the top view, select the bottom points. To prevent de-selection, lock the selection using the **Selection Lock Toggle** button.

Returning to a perspective view, pull the selected points down, as shown in Fig. 3.14b .

The main body of the model is complete and now needs to be split up into its separate components and texture-mapped. Select polygon groups by type (horizontal, cylindrical, etc.). Be sure to also separate by target material type (metal, glass, and liquid).

Using this logic, I separated the model into seven unique parts (Fig. 3.15).

Now, the model has been split up for mapping purposes, we can re-attach by material type, which will reduce the number of materials down to

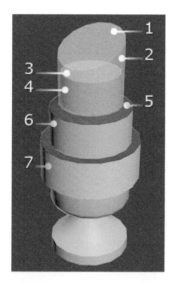

FIG 3.15

three – Metal, Glass, and Liquid. As long as the model isn't welded, there will still be separate parts/elements, making it easy to quickly select and texture-map it.

Once this has been done, map each object. Using the metal base as an example, add an **Edit Mesh** .

 Choose**Element** as a sub-selection and ctrl click each element that will use vertically aligned mapping. Again, as the model is cylindrical, we use cylindrical mapping. If the gizmo appears rotated, alter until you are happy with the alignment and use the **Fit** command.

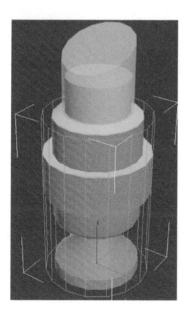

FIG 3.16a

Next, add an **Unwrap UVW** modifier and select the button labeled **Open the UV editor**. Once open, turn off the checker pattern. You can now see the UVs you have just applied laid out in wireframe.

Using the tools provided in the upper left corner of the editor window (**Move, Rotate, Scale, Freeform**, etc.), scale down the UVs to resemble Fig. 3.16b.

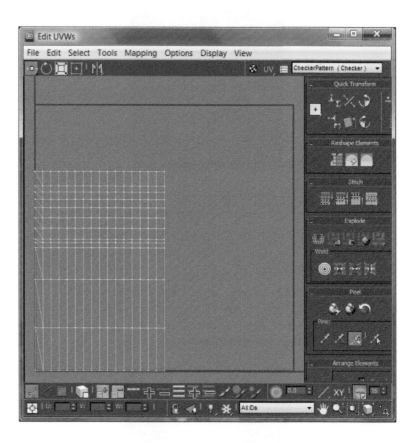

FIG 3.16b

Now, move the UVs outside of the center square (they will be repositioned later, so it doesn't really matter where you move them to as long as the area is empty). Now, select the horizontal elements and map those with a **Planar** gizmo. This time, add an **Edit Mesh** and do not sub-select. Now, add the **Unwrap** modifier. Notice now, the whole object is shown as you didn't limit the selection.

Scale the new UVs down and move the previous set into the square (as shown in Fig. 3.16c).

We now have the basis for the texture page for this model. This process now needs to be repeated with the remaining two parts. After this is completed, they can be reattached to the 'metal' part of the model. After this has been

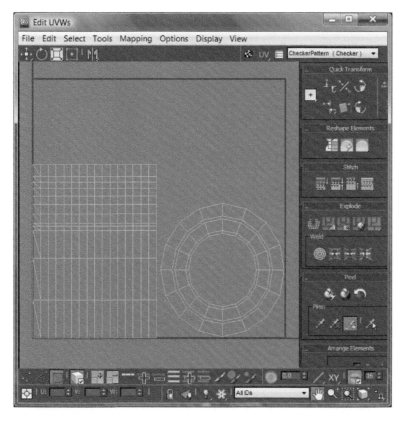

FIG 3.16c

done, add an Unwrap modifier. The resulting view will show overlapping UV sets in the same window. This needs to be tidied up before we continue.

Check the **Select by Element** UV toggle and rescale and position the UVs using **Freeform Mode** (Fig. 3.16d). Be sure to leave some space for the remaining parts of the model which are yet to be constructed (Fig. 3.16e).

The final parts of the model to be built are the handles, the prism, the lens, and the arm.

These can all be made from primitives. As you create the parts, reference the sketch for scale and rotation.

The Prism is basically half a cuboid. We can use **Box** mapping or **Planar** mapping for this.

The Lens is basically a cylinder with additional cap segments. Scale these in and extrude to model the glass part of the lens.

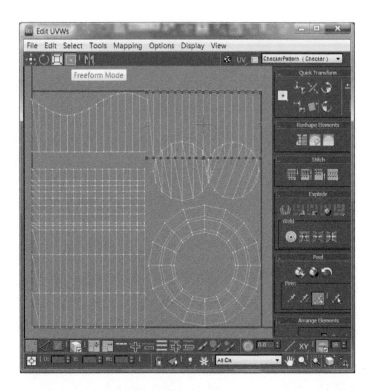

FIG 3.16d

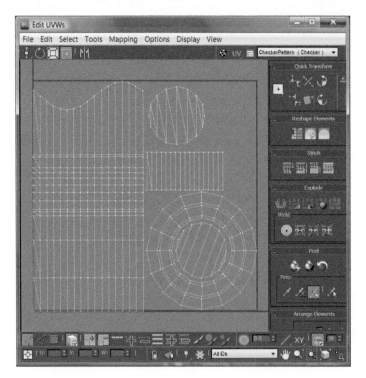

FIG 3.16e

FIG 3.17a

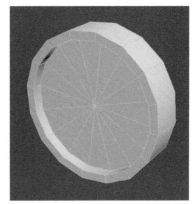

FIG 3.17b

Use **Cylindrical** mapping for the rim and **Planar** mapping for the glass and edges.

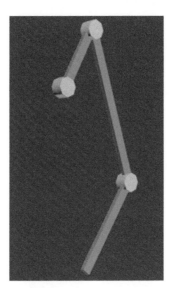

FIG 3.17c

For the Arm, use simple boxes and cylinders. Model and map one of each of the cylinders and arm components, then copy them to make additional joints. **Attach** together when complete.

Create the Handles by starting with a **Cylinder** and scaling it along the Y axis to flatten the shape. Provide enough segments to extrude out the middle area and then bend the top and bottom parts. Use an FFD modifier to pull in the top points, creating a vertical slant. The two connected base parts are simple cylinders – create one, map it and then copy it for the other one. When complete, **Rotate** around the main object at 60-degree intervals, then attach together.

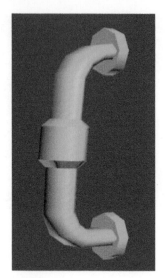

FIG 3.17d

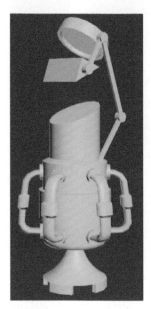

FIG 3.17e

After editing the base of the core object to properly match the concept, all the remaining parts can be attached to the main model. The UVs will need tidying up and may require a little rearrangement.

This will provide us with everything we need to make the texture. Using **Tools > Render UVW Template**, render out the UVs as a TGA image. This forms the basis of the texture page.

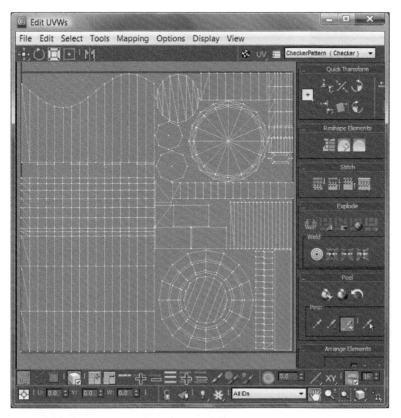

FIG 3.17f

FIG 3.18a

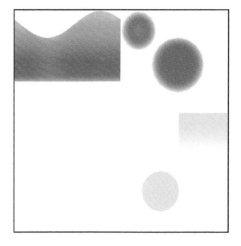

Using the UV render as a layout, create diffuse and opacity (alpha) maps. The opacity map is needed for the glass areas. Place the textures into the relevant slots in the Material Editor and apply them to the model.

FIG 3.18b

FIG 3.18c

Set up a basic rig and render the model to check the results. Edit the diffuse and opacity maps until you are happy with the results; also make sure the material is two-sided or the glass will look too transparent.

Note

As a finishing touch, try offsetting the top/cap vertices for the 'liquid' element in the **Y** axis (as shown in the render image Fig. 3.18b); this will help give the sensation of a liquid.

CHAPTER 4

Vegetation and Alpha Maps

Creating and Using Alpha Maps/Channels

In this chapter, we are going to look at the most common methods of creating various forms of vegetation used in the games industry.

As creating foliage and leaves still relies heavily on alpha maps or a texture with an alpha channel, I'll start off with a brief explanation.

An alpha map is a black-and-white or grayscale image, which controls the transparency of a surface when it's applied to a mesh using a shader. In the example pictured in Fig. 4.1, the alpha map is on the left, the diffuse texture in the middle, and the final result applied to the mesh is on the right.

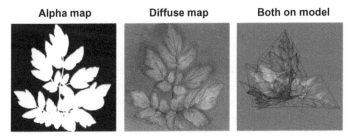

Alpha map   Diffuse map   Both on model

FIG 4.1

3ds Max Modeling for Games
© 2012 Taylor & Francis. All rights reserved.

53

This works because the shader is interpreting values of 100% white as being fully opaque; and values of 100% black as being fully transparent. Any gray tones between 100% black and 100% white will be interpreted as being transparent.

Now that we know what an alpha map is, let's look at how we go about creating them.

The first step is always the source image for the diffuse texture. Whether it is hand-painted or taken from a photo, you'll need to have this first before you create the alpha map. I'll use the previous example to demonstrate this.

This was initially taken from a photo and then modified using a mixture of Photoshop's blending modes and hand–painting tools.

Initially, I 'extracted' the leaves I wanted from the original photo, and then used them to create the alpha channel.

Source photo	Background removed	Alpha channel

FIG 4.2

There are a few different ways to do this.

I could simply create an alpha channel and start painting white around the leaves I want visible using the standard brush tool; but, this takes time and also means the background will remain. I wanted to remove this.

I started by creating a 512 × 512 image file. I then copied the source image into this file and scaled it to fit into the square texture page (**CTRL + T**). I then used the Lasso tool to create a selection around the area I wanted to retain.

I then inverted the selection by going to **Select > Inverse** on the menu bar. I then deleted the highlighted pixels. In a few key strokes, a large chunk of the unwanted image was removed.

For the remaining pixels around the leaves, we could either use the eraser, manually paint the pixels out, or we could use the magic wand tool to make pixel selections and delete them. The magic wand works best when the background is in a different color relative to the leaves, for example, silhouetted against a blue sky.

FIG 4.3

In the photo we are working with, there is a good level of contrast in the image; so we can use the magic wand tool. We need to keep the tolerance low, as the image is mainly green.

This time, I have decided to use the magic wand to quickly remove chunks of the image. I then finished off by removing the areas I didn't want by using the eraser to manually erase the final few stray pixels.

I also adjusted the levels and hue and saturation on the final version before starting work on the diffuse texture.

FIG 4.4

Now that we have separated out the area of the image we want to keep, we can quickly use this to create the alpha channel – or at least a good starting point!

Select the whole of the layer that the leaves are on by holding **CTRL + A**, then select the small thumbnail image on the left of the layer's name. This will select all pixels on the currently selected layer.

FIG 4.5

With this selection active, click on the Channels tab, go to the bottom right, and click on the new layer icon highlighted in Fig. 4.6.

FIG 4.6

This will create a new alpha channel in the texture file. Next, select the standard brush tool at 100% opacity and paint the selected area. The result is fairly good, but there are a few gray and white pixels around that will need painting over with 100% black (RGB 0,0,0).

When the alpha channel has been cleaned up, we can preview the results in Photoshop over the RGB image.

Do this by turning on the RGB channels by clicking on the box to the left of the RGB channel at the top of the channels list. This will show or hide these channels. The same applies to the alpha channel.

When the alpha channel is displayed over the RGB channels, it will only show the pixels under the white pixels of the alpha channel. In the next image, the entire purple area represents the black values of the alpha channel.

You can change the color and opacity of the alpha channels by double clicking on the alpha channel.

It's worth noting that you can still paint and edit the alpha channel while viewing all the channels simultaneously.

FIG 4.7

The last step is to save the final texture (once the diffuse map is complete), along with the alpha channel, so it can be used in 3ds Max. There are two ways to display the alpha channel or map in real time in the viewport.

The diffuse texture can be saved with the alpha channel inside the same file using a format that stores alpha information. Some formats that do this are .BMP, .PNG, .TIFF, .TGA, and .DDS.

This texture containing the diffuse and alpha channels will need to be assigned to both the diffuse and opacity slots in a material. When it is assigned to the opacity slot, the bitmap parameters will need adjusting. By default, the **Mono Channel Output** is set to **RGB intensity;** it will need to be changed to **Alpha** in 3ds Max.

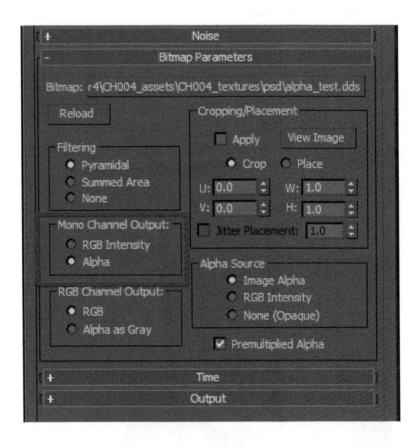

FIG 4.8

An alternative method of saving the Alpha texture is to save the alpha layer as a separate texture map.

This can be done by selecting the entire alpha layer by using **CTRL + A** while on the alpha layer to highlight it. Then, press **CTRL + C** to copy the selection and **CTRL + V** in the RGB Channels in the Layers tab to paste it as a new layer. Then, save the file as a separate texture file after flattening the image.

Then, we just need to assign this new texture map to the opacity slot in the 3ds Max material and assign the diffuse texture into the diffuse slot.

Both methods should display the diffuse map working with the alpha map in the viewport once **Show Standard Map in Viewport** is turned on in the material and the following display mode selected **Main Menu > Views > Show Materials in Viewport as > Standard Display with Maps** is also on.

This concludes our brief introduction to alpha maps. Next, we'll take a look at diffuse maps.

Creating the Diffuse Textures for Vegetation

In this section, I'll demonstrate how I created all the diffuse-texture maps in Fig. 4.9 .

FIG 4.9

The first aspect we need to look at is the layout of the texture pages. The bushes in the first two images take up the entire texture sheet. This was intentional, as I intend the bushes to range from a medium to a large size, so giving them more texture space; this will result in a higher resolution texture map. All the textures in this case are 512 × 512 pixels.

The texture sheet in the top right consists of four different types of leaves that will be used to create a variety of different plant models. This includes a horizontally tiling stalk section at the bottom that will be shared between the various plants. Each leaf gets around 256 pixels squared of texture space. These leaves are intended for small- to medium-sized plants.

The benefit of sharing many elements on a single texture sheet is that there are less individual texture files to deal with. In terms of real-time rendering in a game engine, the engine will also only have to call upon one texture map and not four, making it more efficient.

I also follow this concept of texture-sharing through on the smaller models shown on the bottom right image. This consists of a variety of grasses and small plants, which will be used as a cheap solution that we will use to fill our environment full of vegetation.

The texture on the bottom left will be used as the foliage for a tree. The leaves run diagonally across the texture sheet so that the space is used more efficiently. If we were to have it vertical as we have with the bushes, this would result in a top heavy texture with a lot of wasted, empty space at the bottom.

Let's move on to the actual texture creation.

The texture layout is the only real difference between all of these textures. The technique for creating the diffuse texture is largely the same for all of them.

I'm going to take the leaves used in the alpha map section to demonstrate this technique.

In the previous section, we extracted the leaves from the photo that are similar to Fig. 4.10 .

FIG 4.10

60

The first step is creating a background. Use the color picker to select two different green colors, one for each swatch. Make sure there is enough contrast between the values so we get a good result.

Then, create a new layer (**Shift + Ctrl + N**). We're going to use the clouds filter to create a random blotchy background. Go to the **Main Menu > Filter > Render > Clouds.**

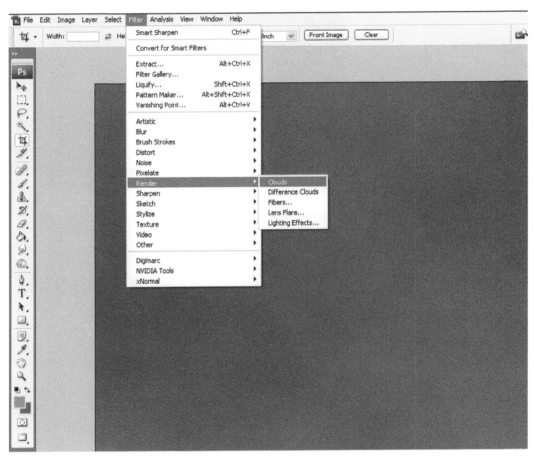

FIG 4.11

You may need to try adjusting the two colors a few times to get a good result. You should now have an image similar to the one in Fig. 4.12.

The layer the leaves are on has the blend mode set to normal. You could easily play around with all the different modes to see the results. One technique may not work every time. It all really depends on the initial reference photo.

The issue that I have with the leaves as they are now is that I don't like the varying colors and lighting from the photograph. In this instance, the color dodge blend mode worked really well to reduce these issues.

FIG 4.12

FIG 4.13

Obviously, now, the image is oversaturated; so we should use **Image > Adjustments > Hue/Saturation** to reduce this. Move the slider to the left to reduce the strength of the saturation. With the contrast reduced, I think we should reduce the brightness and contrast on this layer also a little bit. The results are shown in Fig. 4.14.

FIG 4.14

Now, copy the leaves layer (**CTRL + J**). Then, set the blend mode to normal. Then, use **Shift + CTRL + U** to desaturate the image. Then, type **Shift + Ctrl + L** to apply Auto Levels to the image. This will increase the contrast of the values in the layer, as in Fig. 4.15.

FIG 4.15

Set this layer blend mode to overlay. I also reduced the opacity to 46%. This will create contrast in the image. The previous steps have removed the contrast a little; so we are now putting it back in.

Just so that you can see the exact difference, have a look at both textures by comparing them side by side with each other, as in Fig. 4.16.

FIG 4.16

As you can see, my preferred texture on the right is softer, with lesser variations in color and contrast. As the grayscale layer set to overlay can also have its opacity adjusted, we can control the contrast easily.

Create two new layers and place them below the original layer of leaves and set to color dodge. We will use these to paint color variations back into the texture. I want to go through this process to add color details that were not in the original image.

For the first layer, I painted the stalks of the foliage brown and used a darker green with a little blue to paint some shadows. A lighter green was used to paint highlights. I used the standard Photoshop brush with a medium opacity. In Fig. 4.17, the new layer is on the left over the background and on the right, all the layers are displayed.

At this point, we can consider our texture as being complete.

Feel free to experiment with this process to create some really nice original textures. Figure 4.18 shows the second paint layer on the left over the background and the final result on the right.

I created the other three sets of leaves on the texture sheet in exactly the same way, using references from different photos. The horizontally tiling stalk

FIG 4.17

FIG 4.18

element running along the bottom of the texture sheet was created by using the **Rectangular Marquee tool (M)** to create a selection.

I then created a new layer and used the Gradient tool set to reflect the gradient. This applied a cylindrical style shading to define the stalk.

FIG 4.19

I then set this gradient layer to overlay. As it then looked too smooth, I copied a section from another image and stretched it out horizontally over the stem and set it to soft light. This was just to add a bit of noise and variety to the stem. This layer was also tiled horizontally using the Offset tool.

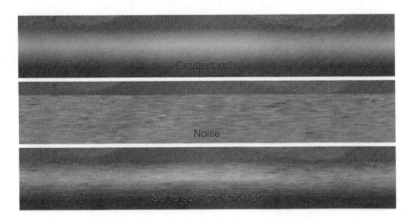

FIG 4.20

The other textures were created in exactly the same way. For the dry bush, I have extracted the sections of tree branches from a photo. I then duplicated some elements and moved them around to fill out the texture sheet to a greater extent. After this, the background was created. The texture was then adjusted afterward to blend in nicely with the other textures of the scene.

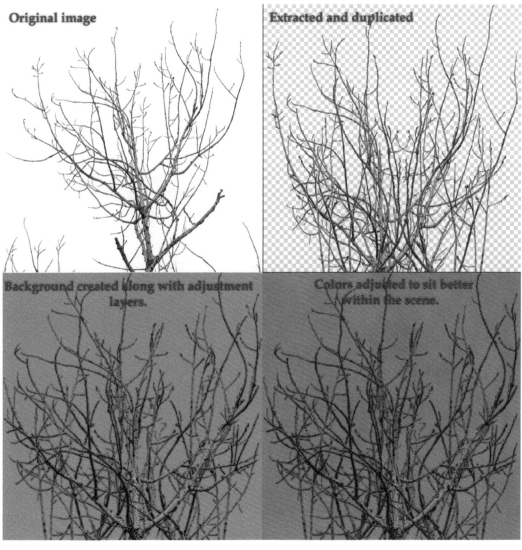

FIG 4.21

The tree branch and foliage were created by using the leaves from the earlier section and taking a section of the bush from the previous texture. Figure 4.22 shows the steps in creating this texture.

Various elements gathered.

Duplicated leaves to create the foliage.

Created a flat background layer.

Placed a blurred duplicate of the foliage beneath and a desaturated duplicate set to multiply on top.

FIG 4.22

First, the branch was rotated so that it starts in the bottom left corner. I then started to duplicate and move, rotate and scale the sets of leaves and place them all over the branch.

I tried to get as much variety as possible by tweaking the Lightness, Hue, and Saturation of some copies as I went along.

After I was happy with the result, I added a background. This time, the foliages blend mode was set to normal; so I did not use the cloud filter on the background.

The final steps were to duplicate the leaves and desaturate the image. I then set it to multiply to get some shading and contrast into the foliage. Another common trick that I do with foliage is to duplicate the final version and place this layer beneath the original. Then, I blur the copy. The reason for this is that if you use a file type or game engine that uses mip-maps, it will prevent the alpha and diffuse maps having issues like a 'white halo' effect on the textures.

Finally, there is a slightly different technique that I use for creating grass.

The two bottom sections of the grass texture were created by using photographs as a base, as in the previous examples. The other types of grass were created entirely in Photoshop.

First, create a new file with the dimensions of 512 × 512 pixels. Go to the **Main Menu > Edit > Preferences > Guides, Grid, Slices & Count.** Under the grid option, set the gridline to every 256 pixels. You can also change the color if you wish. I have set mine to red.

If the grid is not appearing, you can toggle it under **View > Show > Grid** or by pressing **CTRL + H.**

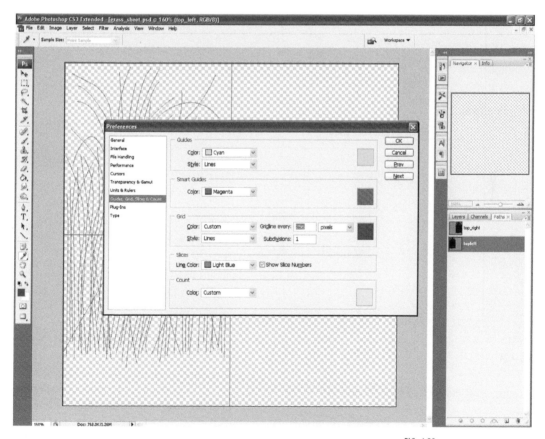

FIG 4.23

The grid should now be displayed over your texture, dividing it up into four sections of 256 pixels square. This tool is very useful when creating texture sheets as you can ensure that all the elements are of the correct resolution. I intend most of the grass to fit inside a 256-pixel square.

Then, using the **Pen tool,** lay out some curved paths that will be used to create the grass. I am trying to emulate the way grass grows with the flow of the paths. To use the Pen tool, simply left click on the image to start a path. Left click and hold elsewhere to create a new point. You can then adjust the curve of the line by moving the mouse. Then, repeat this process until you are happy with the number of paths. You can adjust the path's anchor points after they are created using the Direct Selection tool. This is in the same area as the Path Selection tool. Hold the LMB to access it.

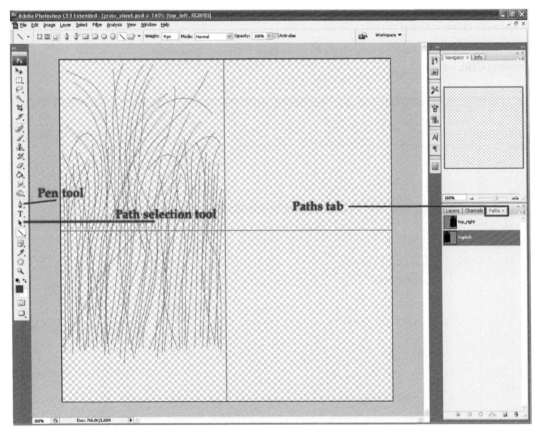

FIG 4.24

In Fig. 4.24, you will notice that I started the paths near the base of the bottom left quadrant. This was because when stroking the path, the **Simulate Pen Pressure** will be checked. This option will create a tapered line for the grass from bottom to top. The blades of grass should be thickest at the bottom and taper to a fine tip; so by starting the paths below the area we want to have the thickest will give the desired result.

To do this, select the paths with the Path Selection tool. Then, right click and choose the stroke path or go to **Edit > Stroke.** This tool takes the options from any tool in the drop-down list. For this, I used the Brush tool. Make sure that the **Simulate Pen Pressure** is ticked, then press OK. Figure 4.25 shows these options.

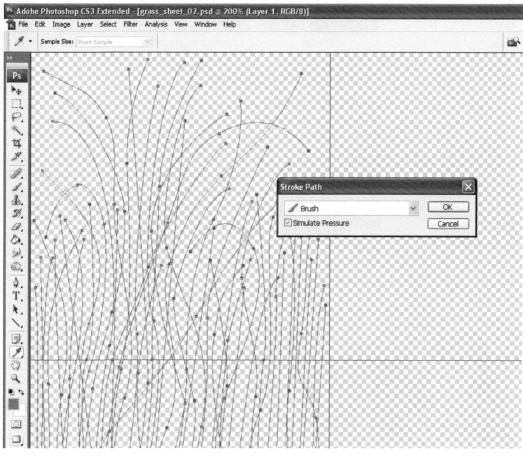

FIG 4.25

The end result should be similar to the grass on the left in Fig. 4.26. To finish off the grass, I used a soft airbrush with a low opacity to build up a gradient on the bottom of the grass. Then, with a standard brush on a medium opacity, I manually painted some highlights onto the blades of grass.

This completes our diffuse textures.

Always experiment using different methods, blend modes, and photographic reference.

Next, we'll have a look at modeling vegetation.

| Stroked | Airbrushed gradient | Standard brush highlights |

FIG 4.26

Modeling Vegetation

Creating vegetation for games using alpha maps usually means that the geometry can remain quite simple. You only need a group of planes with some simple modeling, letting the textures do all the work.

A good approach to creating vegetation models is to look at the "flow" of the plant, or how a plant or tree grows. In addition, pay attention to the overall silhouette of the plant. This will determine the form of the mesh and how the components will be placed together to create the overall shape to achieve a realistic, natural look.

In Fig. 4.26b, I did a quick paint-over of a variety of trees to show how they differ in the way they grow. The blue lines represent the 'flow' of the foliage or how it grows on the branches. The red lines are the growth patterns of the trunks and branches. I use this approach to break down the shapes into simpler forms before I begin modeling the tree.

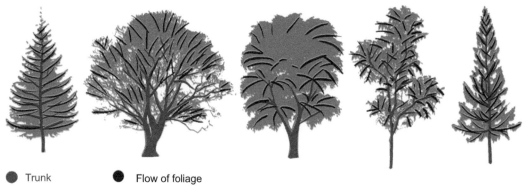

● Trunk   ● Flow of foliage

FIG 4.26b

This approach of breaking a complex object down into simpler parts also works well for plants. In Fig. 4.26c, I demonstrate this. On the left is the reference and in the middle are some quick sketch attempts at breaking down the shapes of the leaves and the growing patterns of the plants. Finally, silhouetted images of the final models are on the right to show how this technique has been applied.

Plant silhouettes

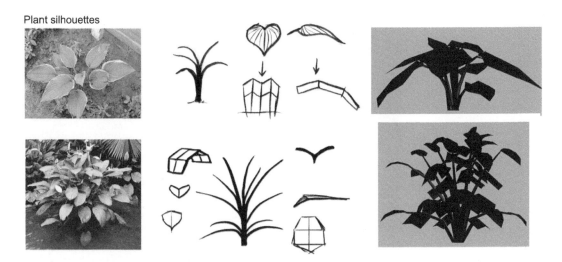

FIG 4.26c

We'll start with the grass models.

Create a square plane and apply the grass texture sheet to it and planar map it. Then, using the Slice Plane tool, divide up the different grass elements, as shown in Fig. 4.27. Then, duplicate the plane four more times. The idea is to delete all except one grass element on each plane. The end result will be that each mesh consists of only one type of grass. You should end up with five types.

FIG 4.27

In Fig. 4.28, on the top two grass meshes, I duplicated the polygon and rotated it 90° to create crossed planes. Then, the two planes were combined into one mesh (using Attach). This is the most common and basic grass model used in games. It is very cheap and can be duplicated a lot within a scene to quickly create dense areas of grass.

FIG 4.28

I then made a couple of more elaborate and interesting versions of this model, as shown in the bottom two examples in Fig. 4.28. Slice Plane was used to add in some additional edges to the plane; then, these new edges were used to add some bends to the polygons. The example on the right is a combination of this method and the crossed-plane method to create a really dense patch of grass.

You can make the grass models as complex or detailed as you like, by using a few different textures or adding extra edges to create smoother more detailed shapes. In current games, the methods shown here are usually enough.

The more details you add, the less efficient the models will be when they are placed down thousands of times within a scene.

In Fig. 4.30, I have cut around the texture to reduce the amount of unused transparency on the mesh.

This is a widely used optimization technique as unused transparency on the surface of the mesh will often still be calculated by the game engine when rendering, even if it is not visible.

In Fig. 4.29, the area highlighted in red is the area I have removed. This makes the mesh more efficient to render, especially when there are a lot of instances of the model in the scene.

I then used these extra vertices to add depth to the model by pulling them back. The meshes were then duplicated and positioned to act like crossed planes.

FIG 4.29

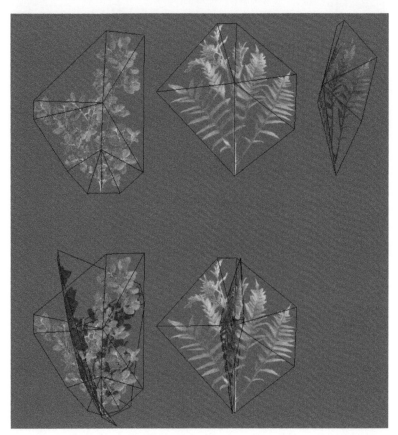

FIG 4.30

The next models are a selection of smaller plants. They are very simple models and designed to be cheap, so that they can be used many times in a scene. These models were created in the same way as the grass was, although three of them also have stems. These were created by moving, rotating, and scaling the vertices of a three-sided cylinder. You could start with a cylinder with a few height segments or use slice plane to add in some edge loops as you need them.

The leaves on the far right plant have more modeling detail on them. The cut tool was used to add extra geometry. The vertices were then adjusted to create a central crease in the leaf.

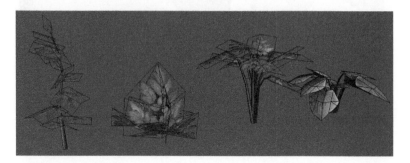

FIG 4.31

The next models created were the bushes. The starting point was a square flat plane. Another plane was added along with some extra edges, and the central vertices were moved out to create some depth.

I then built the bush out from a central point on the ground using duplicates of these two meshes. The model on the right (Fig. 4.32) is much cheaper and intended for use on the edges of the scene.

I could have cut around the bush as an optimization from the initial state before I duplicated them, as mentioned earlier, to reduce the surface area of unused transparency.

FIG 4.32

As an example to show how flexible vegetation meshes are, I have assigned the dry bush texture to this model. It looks a lot different from the green leaf version, even though it is the same mesh. This is easy to do as a texture swap as long as the texture layout is similar; this will mean you won't need to remap anything.

FIG 4.33

The final model we will look at in this chapter is the tree. First, we need to start with a cylinder and delete the polygons on the top and bottom. Then using the slice plane tool, we add some edge loops.

Next, use these to shape the bottom of the trunk. Duplicate the mesh, scale it, and position it high up on the original mesh. This will form the basic shape of a branch. These steps are shown in Fig. 4.34.

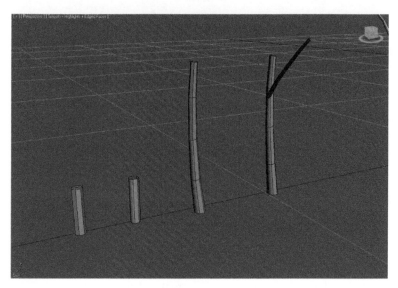

FIG 4.34

Duplicate the trunk and branch meshes a few more times and use them to create the rest of the tree structure. Figure 4.35 shows the final version of our basic tree model.

After positioning all of the branches, I spent a few minutes modeling a few more branches to create some variety in the model.

The next step is to combine all the meshes together using Attach and then to stitch the branches into the main trunk mesh. Use the Cut tool to create the edges on the trunk to match the branches. Delete the faces on the trunk where the branch will connect. Then, use weld or target weld to stitch the vertices of the trunk and the branches together.

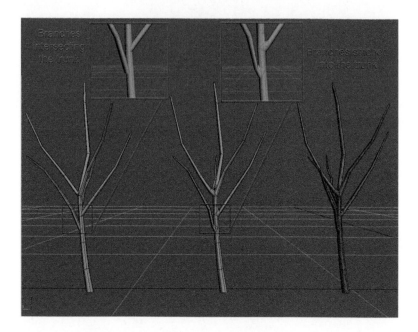

FIG 4.35

Attaching the branches to the trunk is a personal preference of mine as I prefer to have the branches and trunk as one solid mesh. It is ok to leave the branches intersecting the trunk, as shown in the version on the left of Fig. 4.35. I just prefer the look of the lighting and shading on the stitched version in the center.

When you are satisfied with the tree model, next we need to unwrap it.

Cylindrical mapping is the easiest technique to use, paying close attention to keeping the seams facing inward into the tree so that they'll be hidden by foliage later.

Figure 4.36 shows the final unwrap of the trunk and branches. I tried to have as few UV shells as possible. There is one for the trunk and one for each branch.

Now that the tree itself is complete, it's time to look at the foliage.

Just as we did before, I created a flat plane and one with some extra detail. I then used lots of duplicates of these to fill out the foliage on the tree, placing them around the branches. I move, rotate, and scale as I go. Figure 4.37 shows the two foliage meshes used on the left and the final tree on the right.

FIG 4.36

FIG 4.37

When the foliage was complete, it was attached to the trunk to create one mesh. The pivot point was then centered to the object and snapped to the bottom vertices at the base of the trunk. This will allow for easier placement of the tree in the environment later.

As it is still not possible to build current game environments full of thousands of trees, many cheaper solutions are used to make environments seem fuller than they actually are. One of these methods is the use of tree walls.

Tree walls are flat planes or simple meshes used on the edges of an environment. They usually consist of one texture that repeats (tiles) along one axis. Figure 4.38 shows a flat plane with the texture applied.

FIG 4.38

Figure 4.39 shows a similar mesh, but a section of a cylinder has been used to give the model more form.

FIG 4.39

As always, this method of construction can be taken further. I would personally use the previous tree-wall methods if they were to be placed a good distance away from the game play area. They are great background fillers, but they don't hold up well to close inspection if a player is beside them.

FIG 4.40

One solution is to fill out the tree wall with other meshes and create a more expensive version that will sit well just off to the side of the game play area behind other assets. Figure 4.40 shows a good example of this method.

It was created from most of the meshes created in this tutorial.

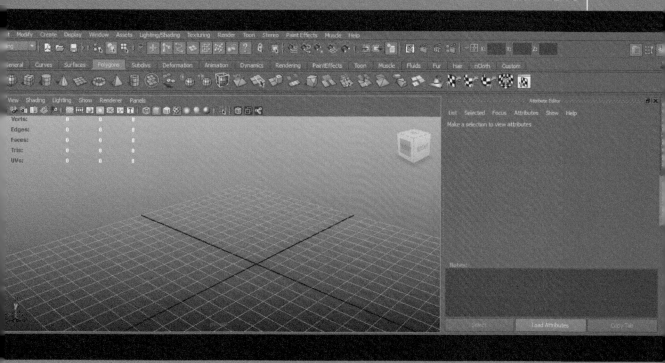

CHAPTER 5

Introduction to Maya

Tutorial Overview

This is a basic modeling workflow for a simple trashcan prop created in Maya. Despite the simplicity there will be a lot of techniques discussed and multiple ways of accessing various important tools and menus.

The tutorial is aimed at someone with a brief understanding of Maya. However, if you have just opened up the application for the first time, a brief understanding can easily and quickly be acquired using the Learning Movies that are supplied with Maya. These can be accessed usually at start up or using the **F1 Help** function or going to **Help > Learning Movies** .

Here is a brief overview of the interface to help you get started.

At the top we have our main menus, these contain **File, Edit, Modify**, and so on.

Immediately below this is the **Status Line**, you can see on the left that this holds a pull-down menu that is currently set to **Rendering**. This is where we can select different menus that will appear on the top menu bar. Below this are our **Shelves**, currently this is set to **Polygons** and beneath these are all the icons contained in that shelf.

The main central space that contains the grid is our main work area panel. The menu and toolbar icons for this can be seen immediately above the space. For example, we can change what is viewed in the work area panel by selecting **Panels >** and then any one of the many options.

Going up the left side is the **Toolbox** with the main **Translate** tools. If you are working on a larger monitor, you will probably see just below the toolbox the quick layout buttons. These are the same options found on the Panel menu as mentioned above.

On the right-hand side is one of the most important areas, the **Attribute Editor** and the **Channel Box**. We will be using this area extensively. At the very right edge you can see where you can toggle between the **Attribute Editor** and the **Channel Box**. These can also be toggled using the icons at the very right side of the **Status Line** .

Of course there are other features and areas within Maya but for our purposes this overview should suffice. Remember, never be afraid to check up any details using the F1 Help within Maya.

For this tutorial, I have preferred to keep the figures quite low and simple. The scale of this prop will therefore actually be quite small in reality. We start with a radius of 25 cm. However, this can be simply scaled up to fit any scene in one simple scale operation at the end.

Many of the images have corresponding Maya scenes. These were created using Maya 2012. In order to view these on previous versions, go to **File > Open Scene**… and make sure under the general options that **Ignore Version** is checked.

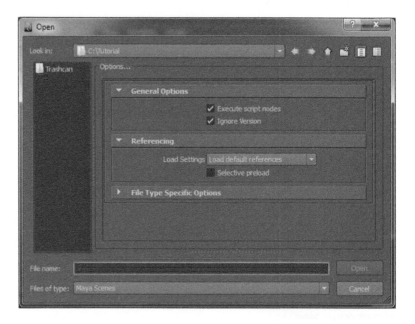

FIG 5S.00

Setup

Let's put some safety measures in place, select **Window > Settings/ Preferences > Preferences.** Highlight **Files/Projects** in the categories column and check the **Enable Autosave** box and ensure the interval is set to 10 min.

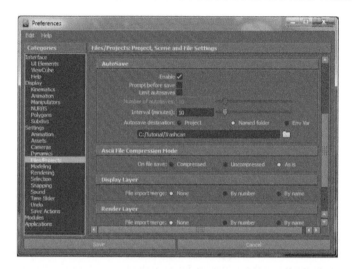

FIG 5S.01

From the same categories column select **Undo**, then switch from **Finite** to **Infinite**. Also, under the **Settings** category, make sure the **Linear Working Units** are set to **Centimeters**. As well as the **Up Axis** is set to **Y** .

Next we will enable the **Incremental Save** function. This will preserve a copy of the file with an appended incremental number to the end of the file you are working on within an automatically created folder. This means that the last 20 times you saved your scene will all be accessible as individual files should something have gone wrong.

Click the **Option** box (the square to the right) of **File > Save Scene** ..., check the **Incremental Save** box and the **Limit incremental saves** box setting it to 20.

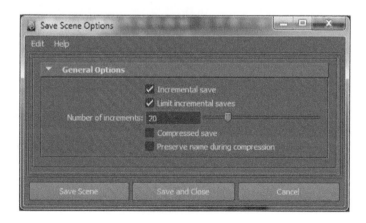

FIG 5S.02

Next, we'll turn on the polygon count display that we will find useful to have in the top left of each panel. **Display > Heads Up Display > Poly Count**.

This will give us the amount of vertices/edges and so on for each selected object as well as a total on screen.

For the purposes of this tutorial it will be also handy to turn off the interactive creation. Go to **Create > Polygon Primitives** uncheck **Interactive Creation** . This means whatever the values are for each shape (which can be found by opening up the Option box – the squares on the right) will be automatically created at the origin. Maya's origin is the very center of the grid, in coordinates this is represented as X, Y, and Z = 0.

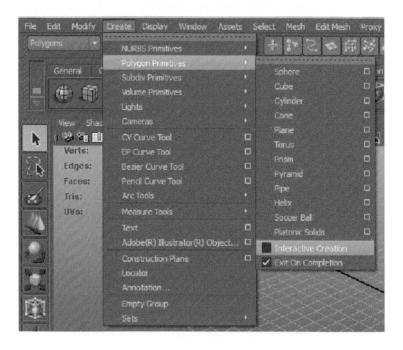

Finally, we will need to ensure that the menu bar is set to **Polygons** . This will affect options available to us in the menu bar. **File** through to **Window** will remain constant throughout all the available options.

Also switch the **tool shelf** to **Polygons**. This will give us a shortcut to most of the tools we will be using. I would encourage you to create your own custom tool shelf in time by CTRL and Shift clicking items in menus.

In any case, I will be showing you several ways to reach these tools.

FIG 5S.05

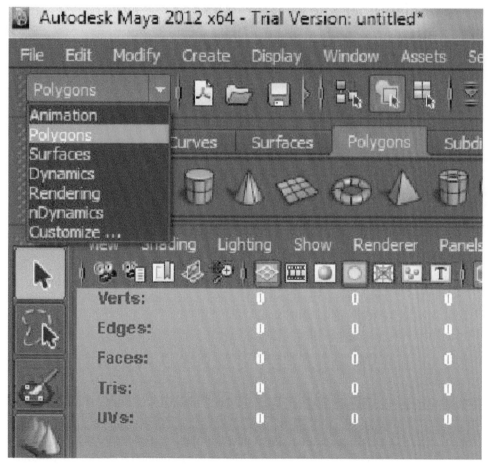

FIG 5S.06

Creating the Trashcan

First we'll create a cylinder which will be the main body of the trashcan. Go to **Create > Polygon Primitives > Cylinder**.

There are two different main viewing modes that we will be using, these can be toggled between by pressing numbers 4 (wireframe mode) and 6 (textured mode).

On the right side of the screen you will find the **Channel Box** and the **Attribute Editor**. This will be where we can alter and tweak settings at any stage in the creation process. If you can't see this, the shortcut to toggle it on and off is to press **CTRL + A**.

In order to change the settings of this cylinder now scroll down in the channel box and click on the polyCylinder1 that we just created under inputs.

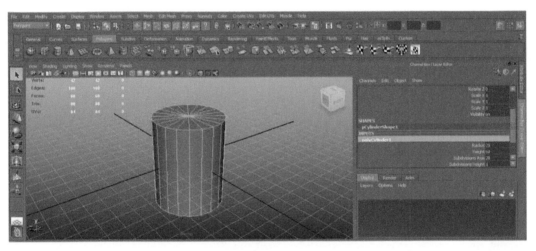

FIG 5.1

Change these settings to radius = 25, height = 60, and subdivisions are 20 (the idea behind having a 20 sided cylinder, is that it is divisible by 4, making it easier to slice in half later.

Rename this object from **polyCylinder1** to something more meaningful like **Trashcan**. This is done by double clicking on where you can see the name at the top of the channel box.

Next, we need to move the pivot to the base of the cylinder. Select the **Move** tool (shortcut W). Navigate the camera so we can see underneath the cylinder, **Press D** and hold it, this causes the arrow heads of the transform gizmo to disappear. Next, while still holding **D**, hold down the **V** key. This will allow us to snap the pivot to a vertex. This is done by middle clicking and then moving over the desired vertex. In this instance this is the vertex in the center at the bottom of the cylinder.

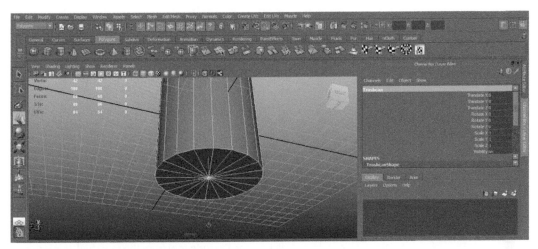

FIG 5.2

In the top right corner of the screen on the status line you will see three black boxes with X, Y, and Z next to them. Press the icon to the left of these to ensure that the **Absolute transform** is selected. This will allow us to place an object exactly where we want it in 3D space.

FIG 5.3

Then, key 0 for the value in the Y axis. This will place our trashcan properly at the origin, with the base of it sitting on the grid. Right click on the object and select **Vertex** from the radial menu. Select the center vertex at the base of the cylinder. Hold the **CTRL** key and then **right click** over the object. This will bring up another radial menu, this time allowing us to convert the selection to another component type. Select **To Faces** and then when the next sub menu appears again **To Faces,** hit **Delete** .

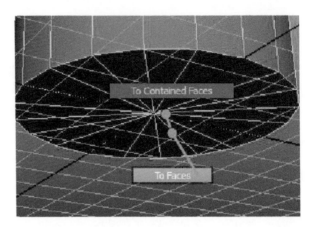

FIG 5.4

Next, we will **Extrude** the top faces of the cylinder. **Right click** the object and select **Vertex** from the menu. Select the center vertex and then **CTRL + right click** to change the selection to **Faces** as in the previous example. With these faces selected click on the **Extrude** tool from the tool shelf, this is the icon that looks like this…

In the channel box there is a new **Extrude Node** that has just been created, scroll down to the **Local Translate Z** option and key in 8. Further down under **Divisions** enter 2.

FIG 5.5a

Right click the object and select the **object mode**. Note that each time we do a command it appears as a node in the **channel box**. If we scroll down, we can see all of our commands so far under the **inputs** heading, with our most recent commands on top.

We can still click and change any of these settings at any time.

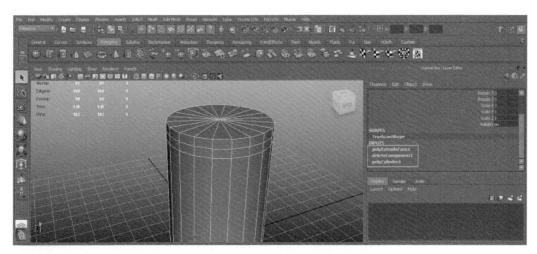

FIG 5.5b

There are several ways to select various loops in Maya, one of the most convenient is to select a **face** and then press **Shift + double click** the face next to it in the direction you want it to go. We will do this now in order to select the top loop of faces.

Right click the object and enter **face** mode. Select one of the faces that make up the top loop (see Figure 5.5c). Then hold **Shift** and then **double click** the face to the left or right, see Figure 5.5d. This will give us the loop of faces shown in Figure 5.5e .

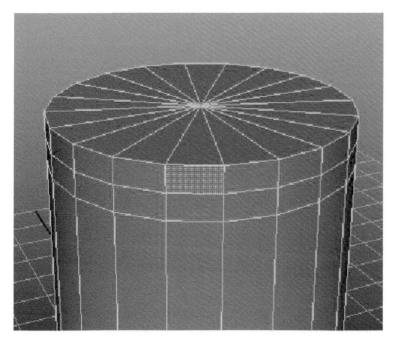

FIG 5.5c

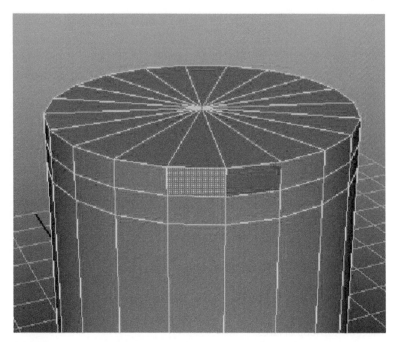

FIG 5.5d

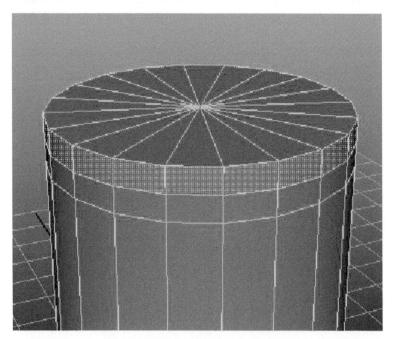

FIG 5.5e

With this loop of faces selected, go to **Edit Mesh > Transform Component**.
In the channel box key in 1.1 for the scale values of x and z.

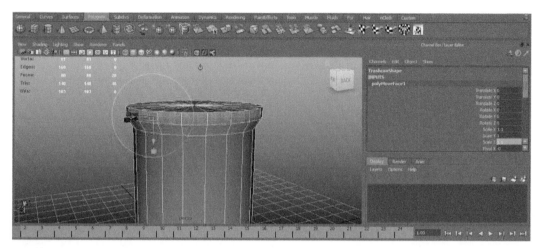

FIG 5.6

Select the top edge loop by **right clicking** on the object and by selecting
Edge mode .Then **double click** one of the edges of the top loop. Hold the
space bar and then **left click** to bring up a menu that will allow us to swap to
the side view. Press **F** to **Frame** up onto our selection.

Press **W** to use the **Move tool** .**Left click** the Y axis of the gizmo (the green handle)
and drag down a little. This will make the lid of the trashcan slightly convex.

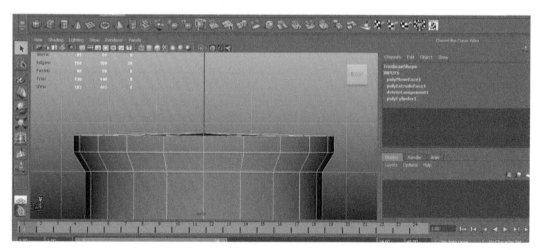

FIG 5.7

Next, select the edge loop below the top loop and lower this in a similar way.

Note that although we have made a couple of movements to the geometry no
additional inputs have been made in the channel box. If we had instead selected
the **Transform Component** option, as we did a few steps ago, we would have
created these as inputs and been able to alter them later on if we chose to.

It is standard modeling practice to do most of the shaping and moving using the gizmo in the panel as we have just done. Many tweaks are usually performed in this way and to record these actions in the input nodes would simply make the list get bloated and convoluted. I wanted to make sure you were aware that not everything will appear there. However, almost every action is recorded in the **undo** history should we want to try and revert back to a previous point.

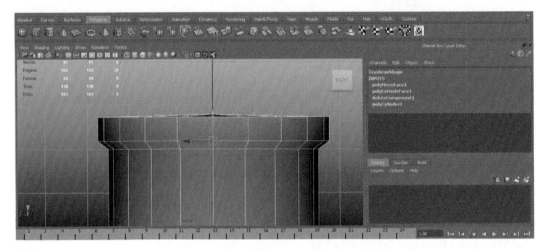

FIG 5.8

Switch back to the perspective view by holding down the space bar and left clicking to bring up the panel menu.

Go to **Edit Mesh > Insert Edge Loop Tool**. Click somewhere along one of the edges that makes up the main shaft of the trashcan. This will create an edge loop across the can and an input node called polySplitRing. For precision, let's go to the channel box and key in 0.15 for the weight value.

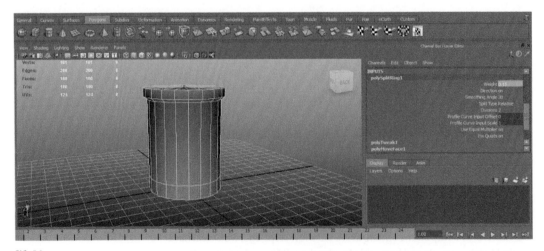

FIG 5.9

Select this edge loop by entering **Edge mode** and then double clicking on one of the edges. Go to **Edit Mesh > Bevel**. In the channel box this has created a new input node called polyBevel. Change the offset to 0.15 (make sure the segments are set to 1).

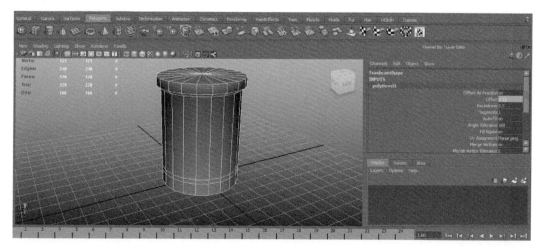

FIG 5.10

Select the bottom loop of faces by clicking on one of them then **Shift** and **double click** on the face to the left of right. Go to **Edit Mesh > Transform Component**.

In the **channel box**, change the **scale** settings for the X and Z axes to 1.1

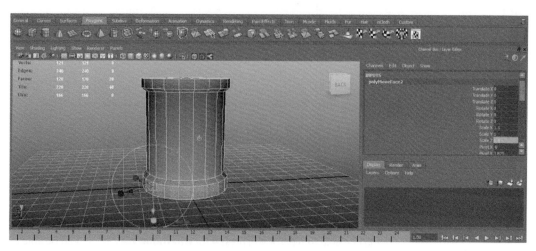

FIG 5.11

95

Go to **Edit Mesh > Insert Edge Loop**, and then click an edge somewhere in the middle of the main shaft of the trashcan. Change the weight of this in the channel box to 0.4.

Select this new edge loop (double click on one of the edges) go to **Edit Mesh > Transform Component** – change the scale on the X and Z to 0.95.

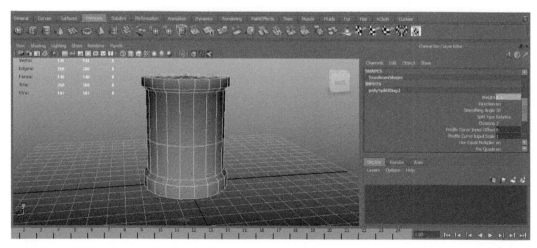

FIG 5.12

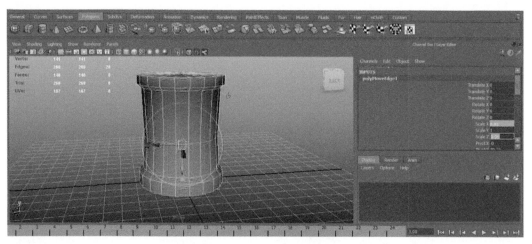

FIG 5.13

We've now finished creating our basic low poly shape. Let's now add some quick handles.

Go to **Create > Polygon Primitives > Cube**. This will be created at the origin as the cylinder was. However, if we are in textured view by pressing **6** then we won't be able to see it. If you press **4** for **wireframe** view, we should be able to see the small cube that was created. Make sure it's selected.

Rename it to HandleSide. In the polyCube input node, in the channel box, change the width, height, and depth to 1.5. Also, while we are in the channel box, change the scale of the x axis to 8.

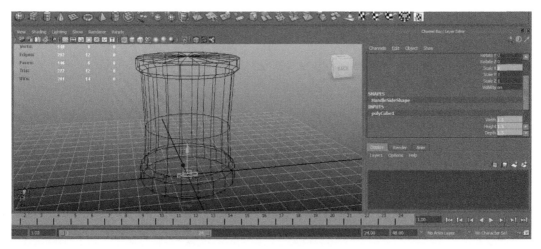

FIG 5.14

Enter **Edge** mode, select one of the long edges and hold down **CTRL + right click** to bring up a radial menu, move the mouse to the **Edge Ring Utilities** and from the submenu select **To Edge Ring and split**. This will create a loop around the center of the handle.

> **Note**
>
> There are many ways to do the same thing in most modeling applications, we could have also entered the Edge Loop tool and selected a weight of 0.5 to achieve the same effect.

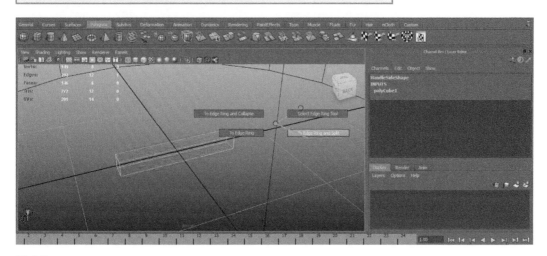

FIG 5.15

97

With this new loop selected, go to **Edit Mesh > Bevel**, select the offset to 0.75 in the channel box.

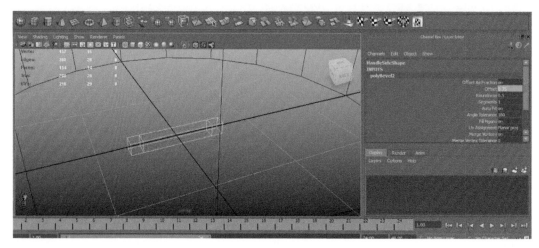

FIG 5.16

Select the two underneath faces and go to **Edit Mesh > Extrude**. In the channel box set the Local Translate Z value to 4.

Then **delete** the two selected faces.

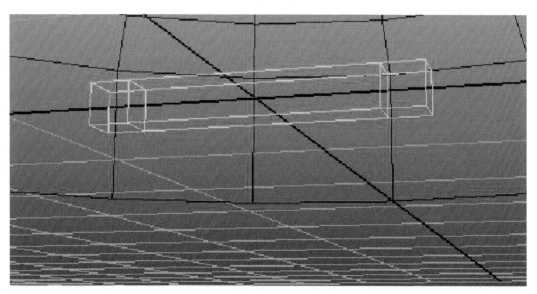

FIG 5.17a

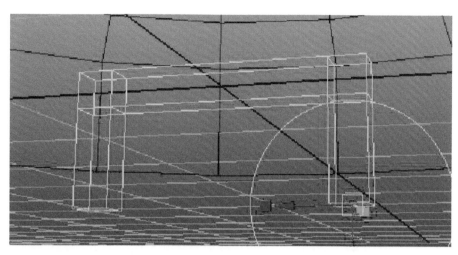

FIG 5.17b

Next, we need to move the selected edges that can be seen in Fig. 5.18a into their respective corners.

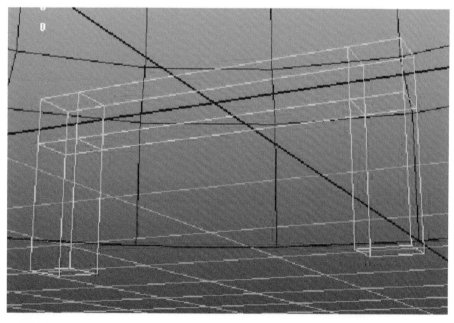

FIG 5.18a

We've already seen vertex snapping at work when moving the pivot points, and the same technique would work by moving the vertices instead of the pivot point. However, we will snap with an edge selected instead.

Select one of the four indicated edges.

Ht **W** to make sure you are in the **Move** tool. Left click the green Y axis of the gizmo. This constrains any of our movement to affect only this axis (as indicated by it turning yellow). Hold the **V** key to snap to a vertex and then middle click and move the mouse slightly on the desired vertex of the edge we would like to snap to. Repeat this with the other edge in this corner.

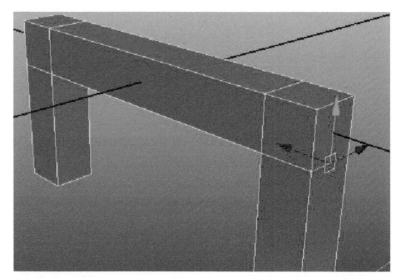

FIG 5.18b

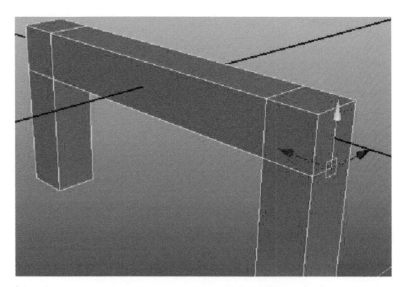

FIG 5.18c

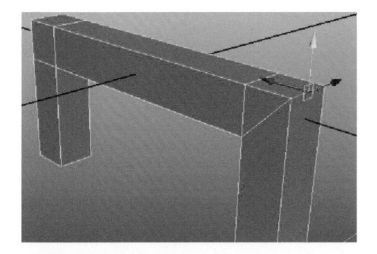

FIG 5.18d

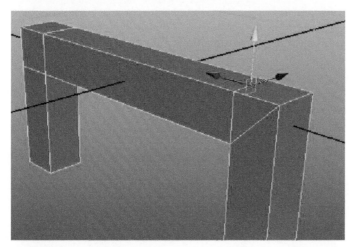

FIG 5.18e

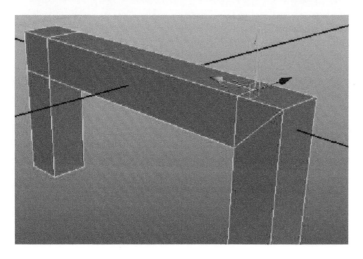

FIG 5.18f

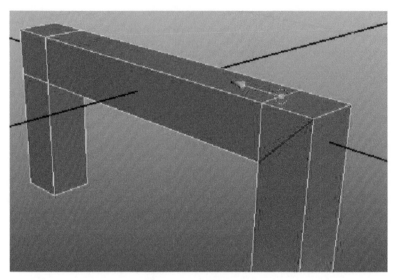

FIG 5.18g

Repeat this for the other corner. Select all the vertices of the handle and then go to **Edit Mesh > Merge**. In the polygon count heads up display notice the vertex count drop by 8.

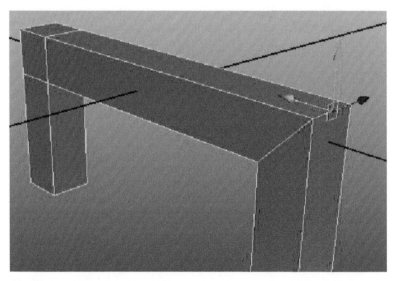

FIG 5.18h

Select the two edge loops that make up the corners and go to **Edit Mesh > Bevel**. In the channel box set the offset to 0.15.

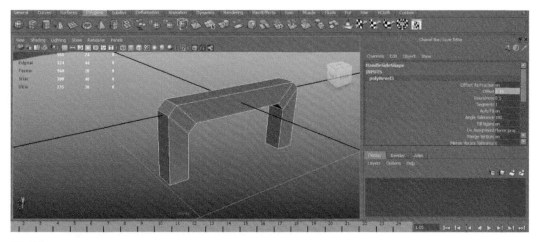

FIG 5.19

At this point, we will **duplicate** the object by selecting **CTRL + D**, name it HandleTop and translate it about 80 units along the Y axis. We will fine tune the location of this when we come back to it in a moment.

Reselect the HandleSide object and then **right click** the object and enter **face mode**. Double click any of the faces, this selects all the faces attached to that face, which in this case means all of them.

Click on the **option box** (the little square) of the **Duplicate Face tool** that can be found under **Edit Mesh** on the pull-down menu. Uncheck the **Separate duplicated faces** checkbox.

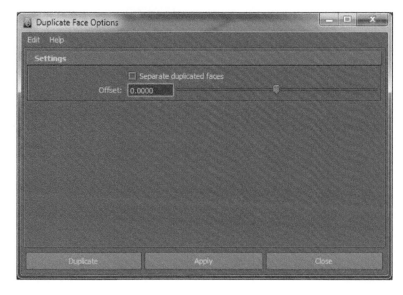

FIG 5.20a

Then select **Duplicate**. This will create a node in the inputs of the channel box called "polyChipoff". Change the value for the Rotate Z to 180. Change the translate Y value to 9.5.

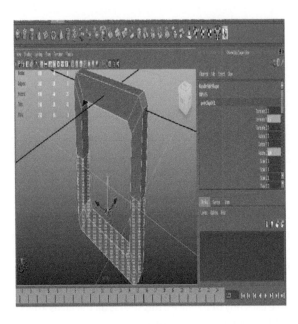

FIG 5.20b

Enter wireframe mode by pressing 4. Left click and drag across the middle vertices and then go to **Edit Mesh > Merge**. This will take the vertex count of the selection down to 8.

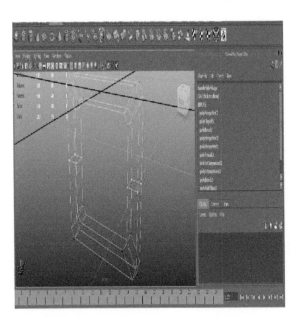

FIG 5.20c

Now that we have merged the vertices of those two loops we can delete them. Select the two edge loops and then go to **Edit Mesh > Delete Edge/ Vertex**.

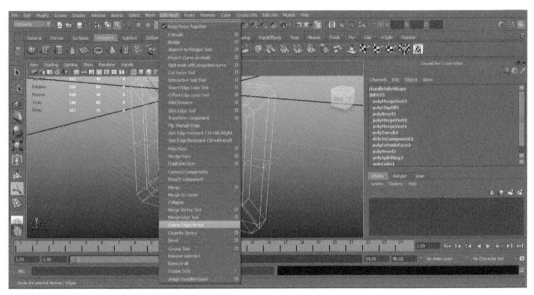

FIG 5.20d

This will leave us with a clean four-sided low poly handle.

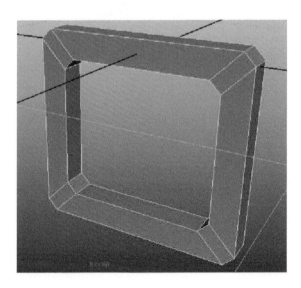

FIG 5.20e

That's the low poly handles now done, now let's move them into position. Select the HandleSide object and then translate it, so that it fits the upper side of the can, hovering just in front. I've rotated round and angled it slightly. You can see the translation and rotation settings in Fig. 5.21a.

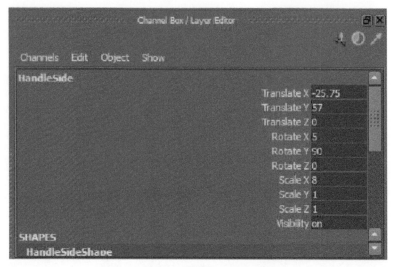

FIG 5.21a

The same goes for the HandleTop object, the translation settings can be found in Fig. 5.21b .

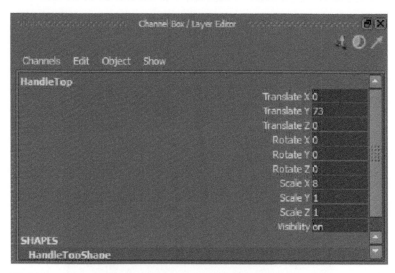

FIG 5.21b

The reason the handles slightly hover above and away from the trashcan at this stage is that during the upcoming baking process we limit any strange artefacting we might get. The handles can be moved into a slightly tighter position into the can once the baking has been completed.

The final locations can be seen relative to the trashcan in Fig. 5.21c.

FIG 5.21c

Highlight the two handles and the trashcan, and then go to **Mesh > Combine.**
This will make everything one object.

Now make a couple of last minute checks and clean up our low poly trashcan.

Make sure the pivot point of the object is still at the bottom of the mesh.
Now we need to delete all the nodes that we created along the way. Go to
Edit > Delete by type > History .

Now rename the object "Trashcan", which was reset during the combine
operation.

We also need to make sure all the edges are softened. In edge mode,
click and drag across the entire object to select all the edges then go to
Normals > Soften Edge. Now repeat the step where we deleted the history.
Go to **Edit > Delete by type > History**.

FIG 5.22

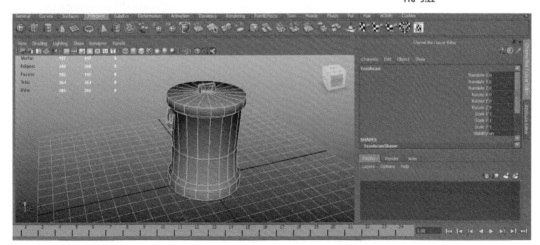

UV Unwrapping the Low Poly

Now it's time to unwrap the model. We will need to open up the UV Texture Editor for this.

This can be found by going **Edit UVs > UV Texture Editor**. First let's select all the UV's and then move them out of the way of the main area to help us see what's going on properly.

In the **UV Texture Editor, right click** in the main window and select **UV** . Then make a **left click** selection across them all. Press **W** to enter the move tool and then **left click** the center of the gizmo and move them off to the side.

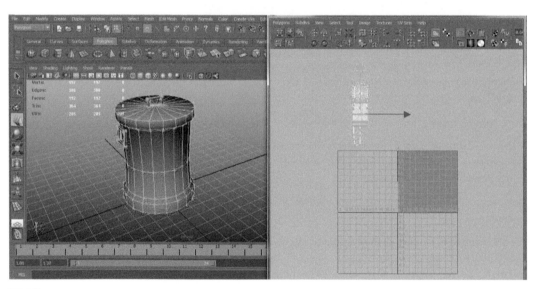

FIG 5.23

Select all the faces of the trashcan base. Go to **Create UV's > Cylindrical mapping**.

This has produced a new input node called polyCylProj. In the channel box change the Rotate Y to 90.

This is aligning the UV's so that we can later delete the right half of the base without it creating any seams. This will allow us to maximize the UV space and not need to find space for the whole base just half of it.

In the UV Texture Editor press **CTRL + hold right click** which will bring us a radial menu, select **To UV** .

Then go to select the option box of **Unfold** which is found under the **Polygons** pull-down menu. Make sure that **Pin UV's** is set to **unselected UV's** . Also select the **unfold constraint** to be **vertical** .

Then select **apply** and **close** .

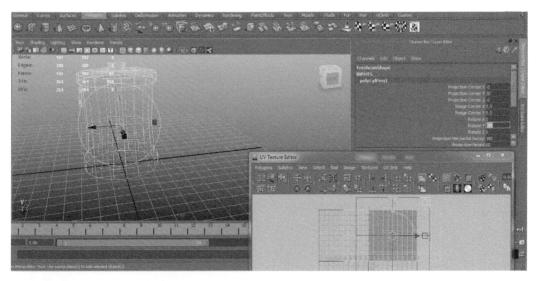

FIG 5.24

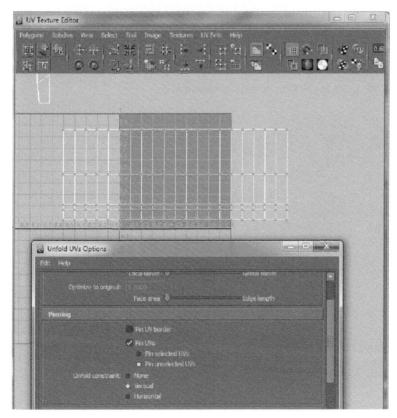

FIG 5.25

Next in the main perspective 3D panel select the right half faces of the trashcan base and **delete** them. We will copy the half we unwrap back later.

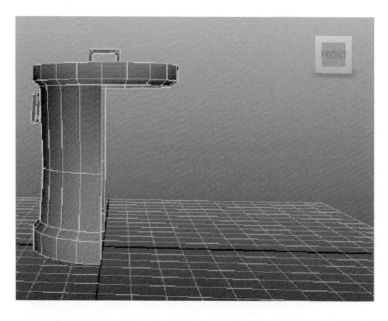

FIG 5.26

Scale and **move** the UV's using the **R** and **W** hotkeys, respectively, so that the first column of UV's are half way between 0 and 0.1 on the Y axis. And the other end is at 0.8. And the bottom edge is at 0.

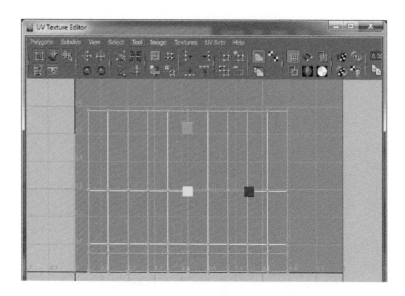

FIG 5.27

We will now fine tune this by selecting the farthest from left column of UV's and entering them in as 0.05 and the farthest to the right column as 0.8.

I've highlighted the necessary boxes in blue in Fig. 5.28a. The horizontal and vertical refers to the numbers that can be seen on the axes of the UV space.

While we're here, let's make sure the bottom rows are definitely at 0 by selecting them and entering 0 into the second box.

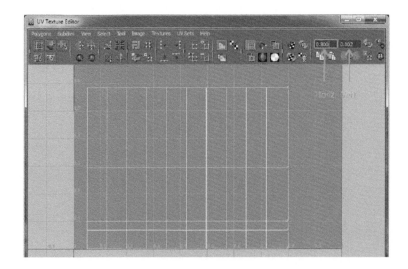

FIG 5.28a

Now select the inverse UV's of the UV shell or island that we just created (a UV shell or island are simply different ways to refer to a connected series of UV's, you will most likely come across other terms).

Go to **Polygons > Unfold** choosing the option box again and switching it to being a horizontal unfold constraint. This will iron out any distortion with the horizontal spacing of the UV's in that shell. Then **apply** and **close** .

FIG 5.28b

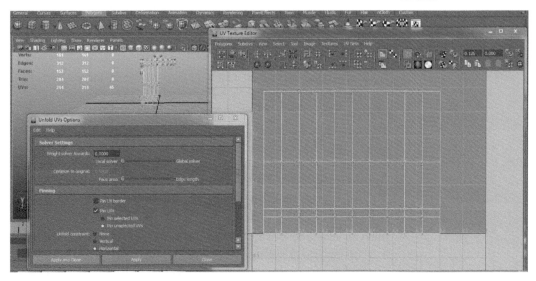

Select the top two loops of faces that make up the sides of the trashcan lid. Then go to **Create UV's > Cylindrical mapping**. This time we aren't concerned with the location of where the split in the UV's are so convert the selection to the UV's and unfold constraining along the vertical.

Then rotate these UV's 90 degrees using this icon in the UV Texture Editor.

Move and **Scale** these into position so that the tops and bottoms touch the top and bottom of our UV space.

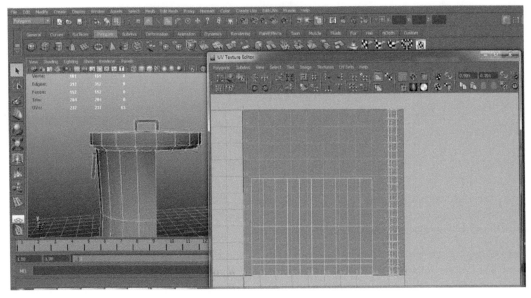

FIG 5.29a

Let's fine tune this, keying in 0 and 1 for the bottom and top rows of UV's, respectively. I've highlighted them in blue.

Again select the internal UV's of this shell and deselect the top and bottom rows that we've just put into place. Then **unfold** with a constraint on the **vertical** axis to correct any nonuniformity.

Let's move this shell of UV's so that the left edge is at 0.9. **Double click** the **move** icon in left-hand side ToolBox, to bring up the tool settings. Check the **Retain component spacing**. I've put a blue ring around the move icon in Fig. 5.29c. In the **UV Texture Editor**, hold down the **D** key, this will take the arrow heads off our gizmo to show that we can now move our pivot point.

Then by holding down **V** at the same time as **D** we can snap this to a vertex point, or in this case a UV point. Then middle mouse button press the center

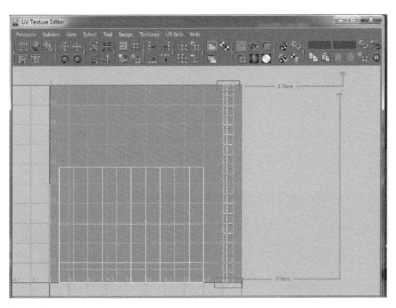

FIG 5.29b

FIG 5.29c

of the gizmo now with everything still held, move it over to any of the UV's along the left edge.

When you let go, the gizmo should now have its arrow heads back and remain where we just put it.

Now when we hold **X** to snap, we should be able to move the whole UV shell with the shell intact.

Without the component spacing all selected UV's would have flattened along this edge at the 0.9-mark.

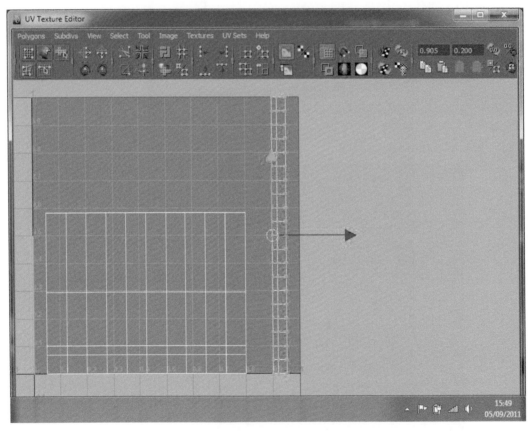

FIG 5.30

After we have finished with maintaining our component spacing uncheck it again in the tool settings.

Next, let's take a look at the top lid of the trashcan.

Select the central vertex and then hold **CTRL** and **right click** to convert that selection to faces.

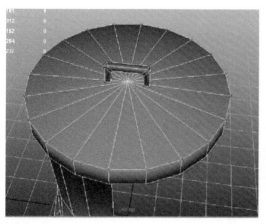

FIG 5.31a

FIG 5.31b

Go to **Create UV's > planar mapping**, in the option box make sure that it is
set to project from Y. Then **apply** and **close** .

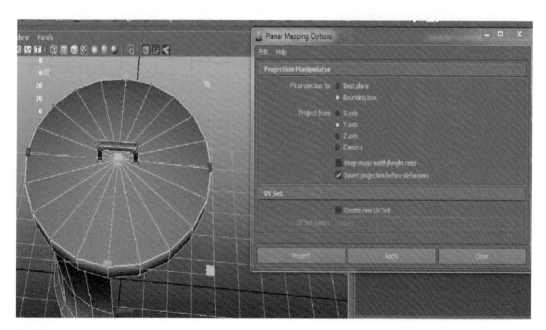

FIG 5.31c

In the **UV Texture Editor** convert the current selection of **faces to UV's** .

Move and **scale** to the upper left corner of our UV space giving ourselves a
little bit of space around it.

115

Now we just need to unwrap the handles.

Select all the faces in the top handle and go to **Create UV's > Automatic Mapping**. Convert the selection to UV's and move them off to the side so we can see a little clearer what we are doing.

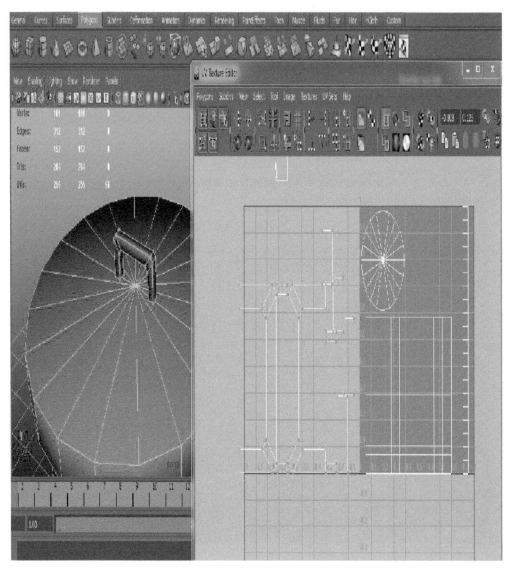

FIG 5.32a

Select the edges of what is the very top of the handle and then go to **Polygons > Move and Sew UV Edges**.

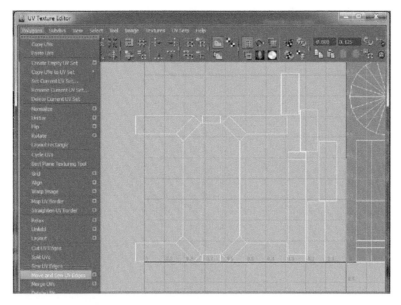

FIG 5.32b

Now select the top and bottom UV edges of the piece we've just sewn together and then select **move and sew** .

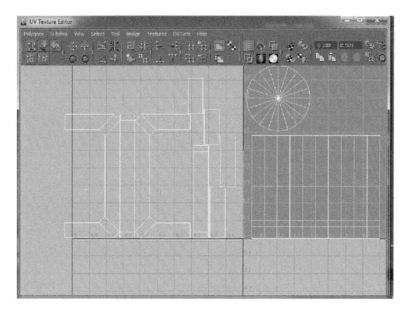

FIG 5.32c

Select all the horizontal edges of what we have left from this handle and then move and sew them together.

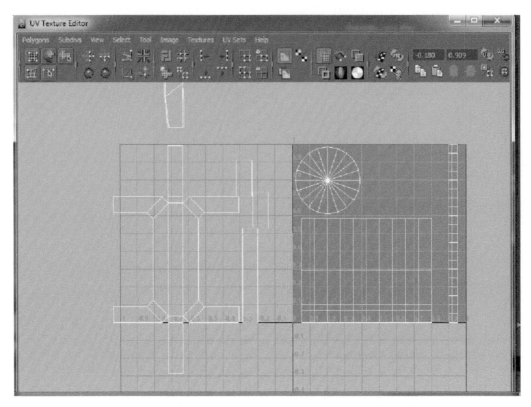

FIG 5.32d

Making sure that no unfold constraint is active, unfold all of the UV's in the handle. Finally move them into position in the main UV space.

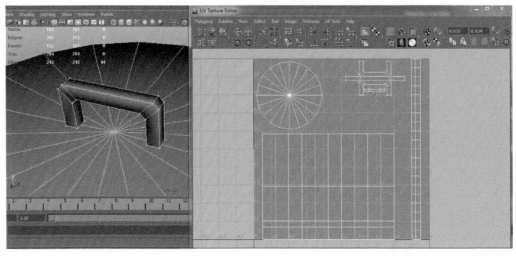

FIG 5.32e

Using the same techniques as the first handle try unwrapping the side handle.

Go to **create UV's > automatic unwrap**. Then **Unfold** the main faces of the handle.

If you find you have a UV shell that is slightly rotated, just snap one side to the grid (rather than hold down V for vertex hold down X for the grid) then unfold the other side. If things are still uneven at that point, then unfold the whole shell one last time. Scale and move into position.

I've reduced the size of the side that we can barely see, to fit inside the other. This will save a little space should we ever decide to add more details on the model.

Then simply move and sew the inner faces and outer faces, and place them as shown in Fig. 5.33 .

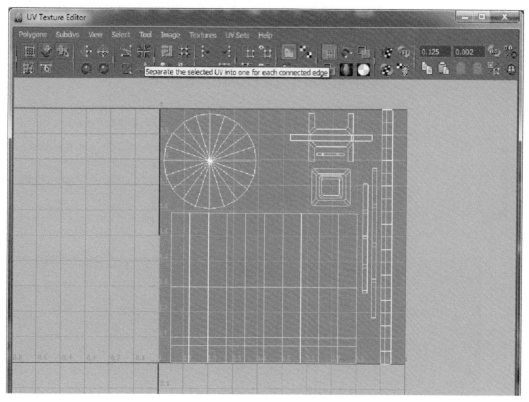

FIG 5.33a

We have now finished unwrapping the model. What we need to do now is to take a snapshot of the UV layout so that we can use it in an image editing program for the texturing process.

Go to **Polygons > UV Snapshot**. Change File name and location to something sensible. Set the X and Y size to 1024, make sure the color value is black and that the image format is **.PNG.** Then select **ok.**

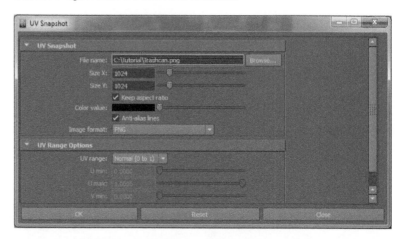

FIG 5.33b

High Resolution Object Modeling for Normal and Occlusion Baking

Rename our existing trashcan model to TrashcanLowRes. Duplicate the object with **CTRL + D** and move it off to the side. We will call this TrashcanFinal.

Select all the faces of the base of the trashcan and the side handle and then hold down shift and right click. This will bring up a radial menu with most of the common modeling tools (we will be relying on this menu now more heavily as the workflow speeds up).

Select **Duplicate Face** from the list, then in the polyChipOff input node in the channel box, enter 180 for the Rotate Y.

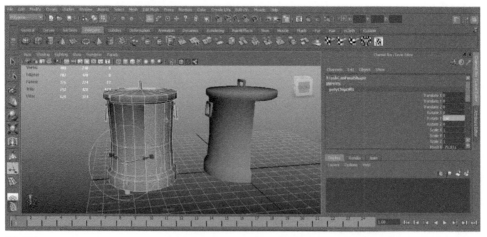

FIG 5.34

120

Enter face mode and then select all the faces of the trashcan base not including the handles, convert this selection to vertices **(CTRL + right click)** , then hold Shift and right click to bring up the radial menu and then select **Merge vertices > Merge vertices**.

Double click any face in the model to select the whole trashcan area that we've just merged together and then convert the selection to edges. Then hold Shift and right click to bring up the context radial menu and select **Soften/Harden Edge > Soften Edge**.

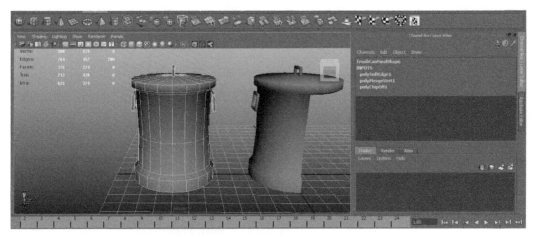

FIG 5.35

Finally delete the history go to **Edit > Delete By Type > History**.

Duplicate this object (Trashcan Final) and then move it to the other side. This will be the start of our high resolution modeling. Rename it TrashcanHighRes.

We will break down the high resolution sections into subcategories – screws, a plate for the screws and handles, general bevels and lid details, and reinforced side indents.

Bevels and Lid Details

First we will bevel most of the edges to soften them up. Select the object TrashcanHighRes and select these loops from the main trashcan as shown in Fig. 5.36a and the four main loops that define the handles as shown in Fig. 5.36b .

Hold shift and right click and select **bevel** from the radial menu. Set the offset to 0.4 and the segments to 3.

Sometimes during a bevel operation Maya can lose the material on the newly created geometry. This has the appearance of being completely transparent

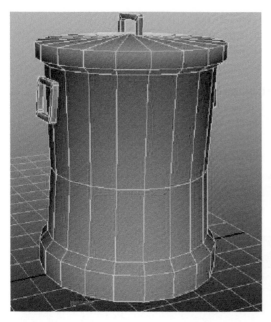

FIG 5.36a

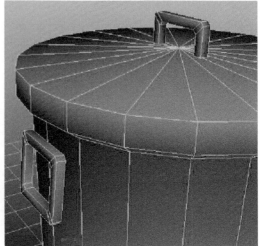

FIG 5.36b

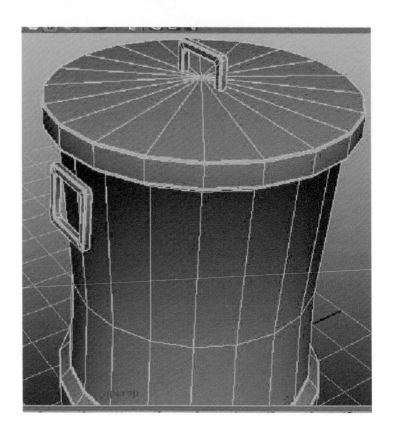

FIG 5.36c

in those areas. To resolve this, simply right click the object and select **Assign Favorite Material** and then select **Lambert** from the list.

Next, select the loop of edges under the trash can lid and then hold shift and right click and select **Soften/Harden Edge > Harden Edge** from the menus.

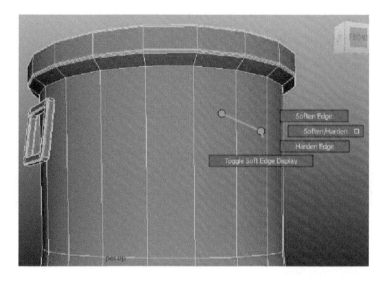

FIG 5.37

Next, let's do the ridges for the top of the lid.

Select the top vertex and then hold **CTRL + right click** and select **To Edges > To Edges**. Then hold **Shift + right click** and select **Connect Components** from the list.

FIG 5.38

Create another loop in between this new loop and the outside loop by holding **CTRL + right clicking**, selecting **Edge Ring Utilities > To Edge Ring** and **Split** .

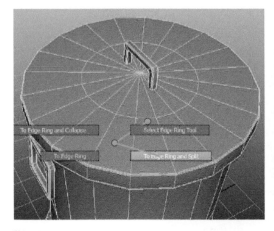

FIG 5.39a

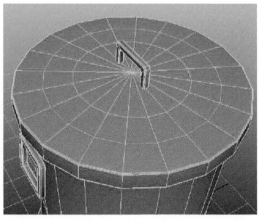

FIG 5.39b

Once again, select the center vertex of the trashcan lid and this time, convert the selection to faces.

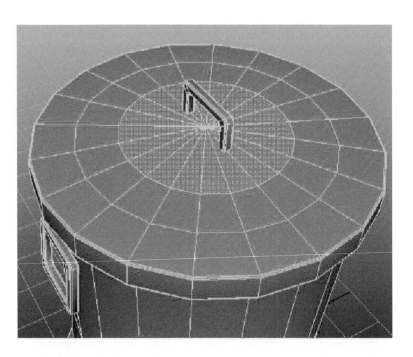

FIG 5.40a

Then press the > symbol on the keyboard, to **grow** the selection into the next loop of faces.

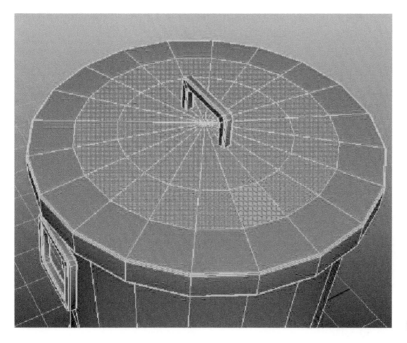

FIG 5.40b

With these faces selected, **extrude** and in the channel box set the Local
Translate Z to 0.4. Now **shrink** the selection by pressing the < symbol and
then extrude again changing the Local Translate Z to the same 0.4 value.

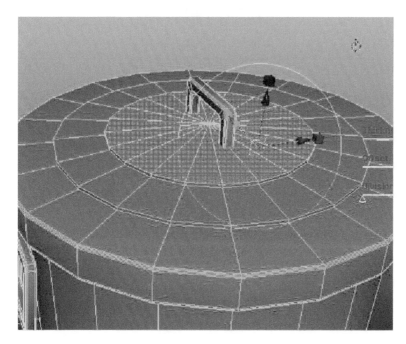

FIG 5.40c

Select these two new edge loops and then **bevel** them with an offset of 0.4 and changing the segments to 3.

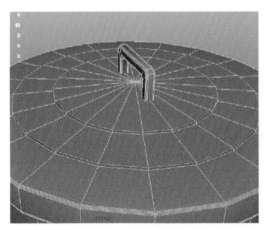

FIG 5.41a

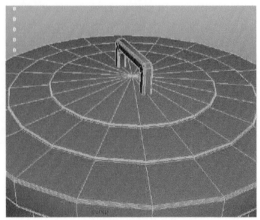

FIG 5.41b

That's it for the bevels and the lid. The trashcan should now look something like Fig. 5.41c .

FIG 5.41c

If you run into any problems you may need to make sure that there are no transparent faces as discussed earlier. Also you may need to soften some edges and harden others to make sure the model shades correctly.

Handle Plates

Create a new cube with the dimensions, width = 6, height = 1, and depth = 14.

Move the cube to the topmost point of the lid just under the top handle.

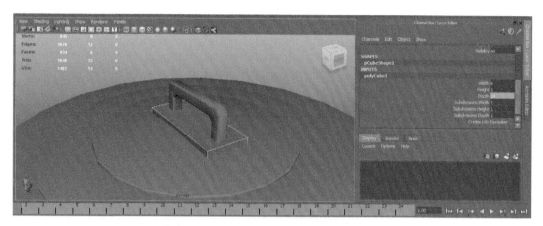

FIG 5.42

Bevel the four corners with an offset = 0.2, and segments = 6.

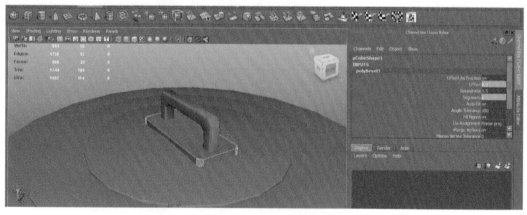

FIG 5.43

Select the top four edges as seen in Fig. 5.44a and **delete** them.

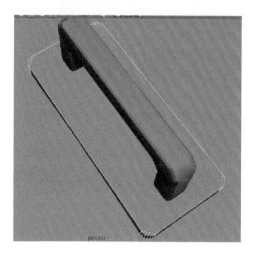

FIG 5.44a

127

Select the top face and then convert the selection **To Edges > To Edges**.

Now **Bevel** this edge loop with an offset = 0.3, segments = 3.

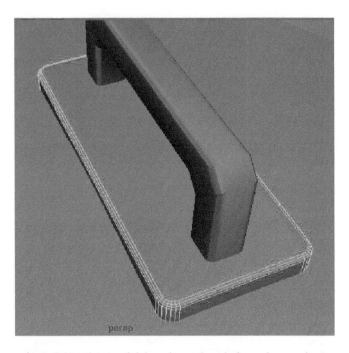

FIG 5.44b

Next, soften all the edges and delete the underside faces that we don't need.

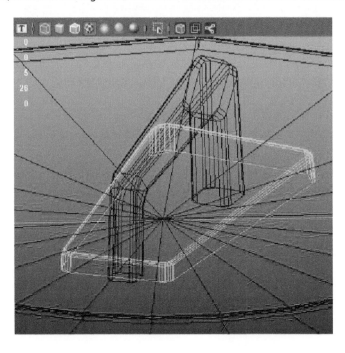

FIG 5.44c

Create a **sphere,** with the subdivision axis and height set to 20. Change the radius to 0.8.

Move this into one of the corners of the handle plate. Have just the top half showing.

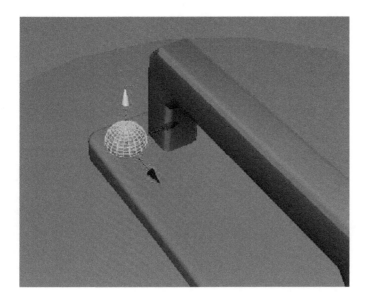

FIG 5.45a

Next **create** a **plane**, move this just on top of the sphere. Change the subdivisions of the plane to height = 1 and width = 0.3. **Extrude** the edges of the plane and set these to 0.2 for the Local Translate Z value. Then **extrude** these edges, change the scale of them on the x to 1.3 and change the scale of the z to 1.1.

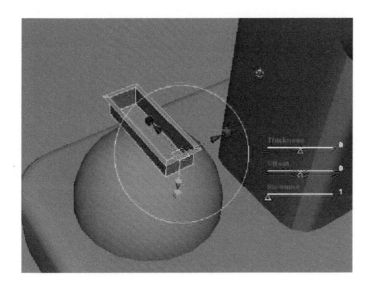

FIG 5.45b

Select all the edges. Then **shrink** the selection using the < symbol, then **bevel** the remaining edges with an offset value of 0.3 and with segments = 3.

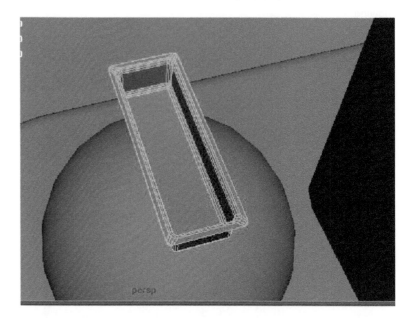

FIG 5.45c

Then **delete** the outer two loops of faces so we don't have any flat surfaces at the top.

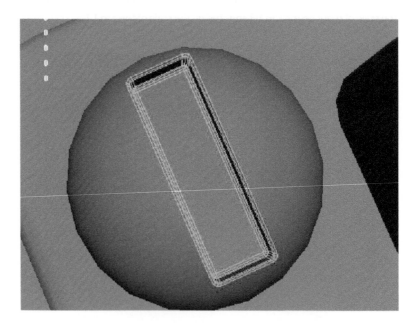

FIG 5.45d

Copy the **sphere** and **cube** that make up the screw into the three remaining corners of the plate. **Rotate** the cube using the E hotkey to get different angles.

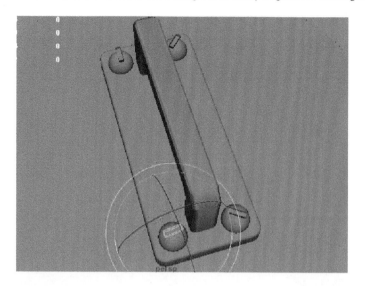

FIG 5.45e

Indents

Select two vertical faces that make up the main body of the side of the trashcan.

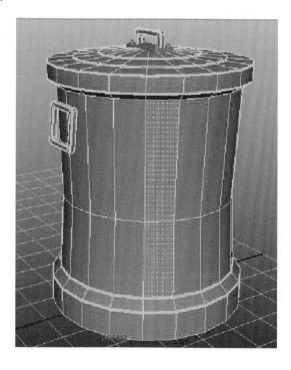

FIG 5.46a

Select **duplicate face** from the context radial menu. Then hit **W** and then move the faces away and **delete** the middle edge again using the Radial menu.

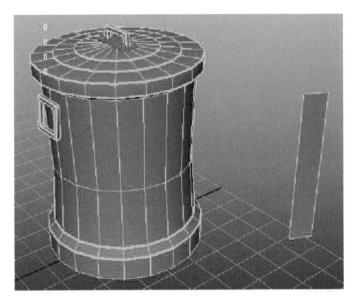

FIG 5.46b

Make it so that this face has six vertical faces by selecting the face and then holding Shift and then right clicking and from the menu select the option box for **Add division to faces.**

This should allow us to change the add division settings to be **linear** instead of **exponential.** This will open up the **linear controls** at the bottom. Change the divisions in V to 6.

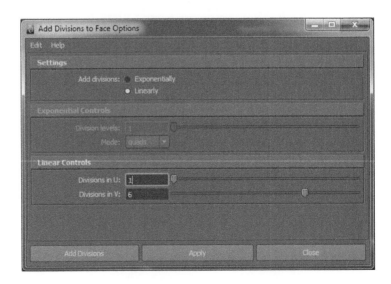

FIG 5.47a

Select one of these vertical edges and then hold **CTRL + right click** to bring up the **Edge Ring Utilities.** Select **Edge Ring and Split.** Change the polySplitRing Weight value to 0.8.

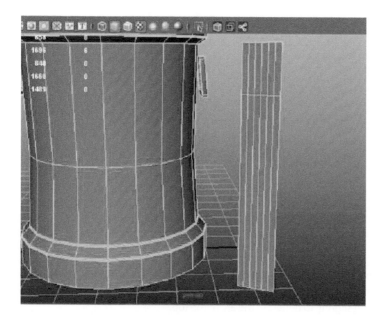

FIG 5.47b

Perform another **Edge Ring and Split** operation on the lower half of these edges and then change the weight setting of the splitRing input node to 0.25.

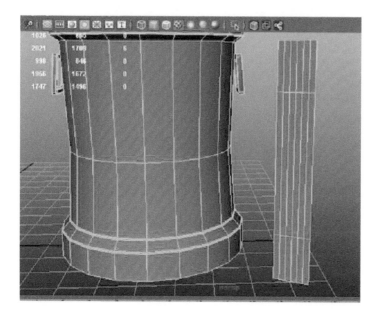

FIG 5.47c

Bevel these two newly created horizontal loops of edges with an offset value of 0.1.

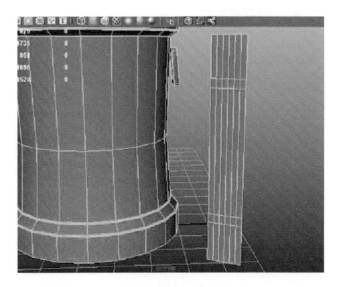

FIG 5.47d

Next, select the two second most outer vertical edges that will make up the basic shape of our indents. Press **R** to enter the **Scale** tool and then scale them down slightly to generate the arc of the top.

Repeat this again with the next set of edges in.

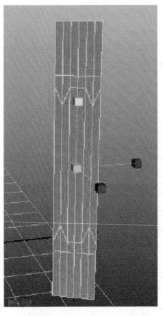 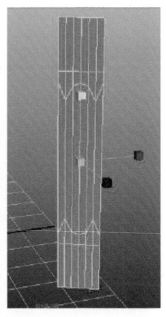

FIG 5.48a   FIG 5.48b

Next, select the four innermost faces and then **extrude.** Set the Local
Translate Z value to −1.5 and the offset value to 0.1.

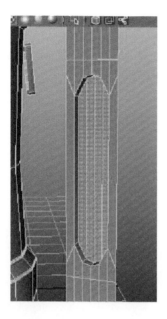

FIG 5.49

Select the loops of the edges that make up the inner and outer flat parts
of the indent and then **bevel** the edges, use an offset value of 0.25 and
3 segments.

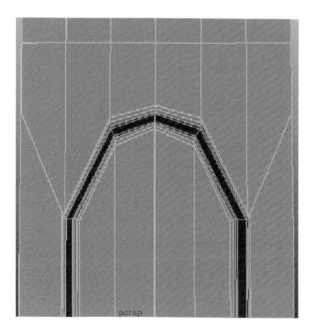

FIG 5.50a

135

The bevel has created some triangles that we don't want. Select the innermost vertex, and then snap it to the outermost vertex by holding down **D** and **V** and then middle click moving the mouse over the vertex you want to snap to.

The heads up display should show we have two vertices selected. Merge them so that this number is reduced to 1. Repeat this process with the other triangles that were just created.

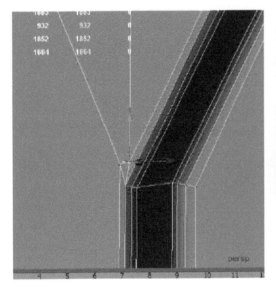

FIG 5.50b

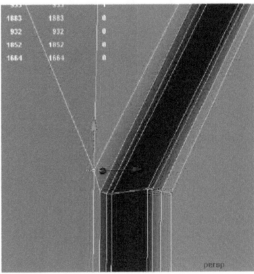

FIG 5.50c

Select all the edges and then set them all to **Soft Edges** .

Next we need to separate this indent that we have created from the main trashcan object.

Select all the faces then select **Mesh > Extract.** Select both the trashcan and the indent and go to **Edit > Delete By Type > History.** Now we can rename the objects back to TrashCanHighRes and call the new object indent.

With the indent object selected, press **3** to turn on **smooth mesh preview.** This will greatly increase the polygon count on the object and make it appear much smoother.

Finally go to **Modify > Convert > Smooth Mesh Preview to Polygons.** Then again delete the history.

Lastly we need to create a piece of geometry that we will be baking the indent onto so create a **Plane** and change the subdivisions to 1.

Enter vertex mode, snap each vertex to the corner 4 vertices of the indented panel.

Select a vertex, hold down **V** to snap to vertex, middle mouse and click onto the desired vertices new position.

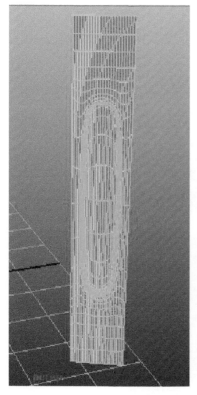

FIG 5.51
FIG 5.52

Enter the **UV Texture Editor**, select the newly created plane and then enter **UV mode**, select all and then select **unfold**. Shift select the TrashcanLowRes, then select the newly unfolded UVshell.

Scale this down to a manageable size if necessary, in order to be able to comfortably snap the four UV's to the corners of one of the panel sizes of the trashcan. In Fig. 5.53, I am just about to snap the four UV's over the panel to ensure it bakes to the right part of the UV's.

With the simple plane that we have just snapped into position select the face. Hold down the **W** key and left click. Select **normal average** from the radial menu. This will allow us to then move it back exactly behind the indent.

Then go to **Modify > Center Pivot**. That's it for the indent. For the seam simply use a cylinder that has been rotated onto its side.

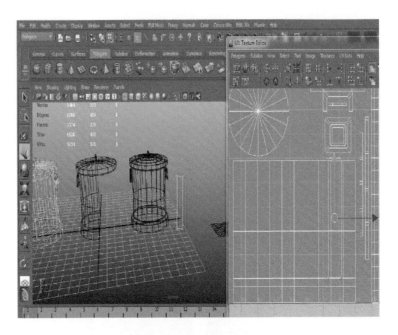

FIG 5.53

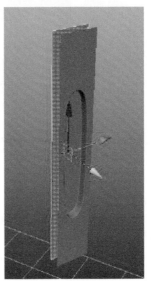

FIG 5.54

Transfer Ambient Occlusion and Normal Maps

First let's generate the normal map from the bevelled TrashcanHighRes model that we made.

Select the TrashcanHighRes model and ensure it is at the origin. In the exact same place as the TrashcanLowRes model.

Using the pull-down menu, just below the main menu bar on the left, switch from **polygons** to **rendering**.

FIG 5.55a

From the menu select **Lighting/Shading > Transfer maps** ...

First select Clear All in both the Source Meshes and Target Meshes options.

Select the TrashcanLowRes shape (the one with just half the base) and add this as selected in the Target Meshes.

Select the bevelled TrashCanHighRes shape. Add this as selected in the Source Meshes.

The distance of the search can be changed using the **Search Envelope** slider, setting this to **1** or **2** should be sufficient for our needs in this instance.

To be able to see the search envelope under Target Meshes, switch the display drop-down box to **Envelope.** This will then show in the main view panel as a red object.

FIG 5.55b

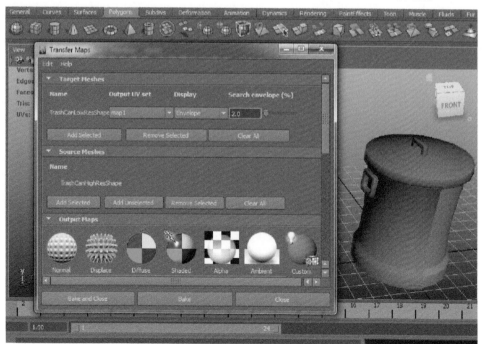

Under**Output Maps**, select the first on the left option **Normal** by selecting the image of the sphere. This creates a new **normal map** panel area for us to change some settings within.

Set the first parameter under **normal map** to a sensible location and set the file format to .jpeg.

Uncheck the **use Maya common settings** box. This will allow us to create individual texture resolutions. Change the map width and height to **1024** .

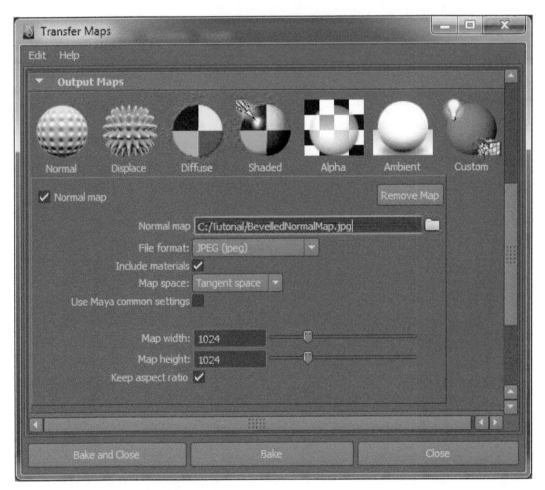

FIG 5.55c

Then hit **Bake**, wait a few moments for it to generate the normal map, then navigate to where you set the destination of the map to check you are happy with the outcome.

Please note that in order to get the cleanest normal map generation in this instance it may be worth moving the handles slightly farther away from the main trashcan body on both the high res and low res meshes, then moving them back once the normal map appears clean.

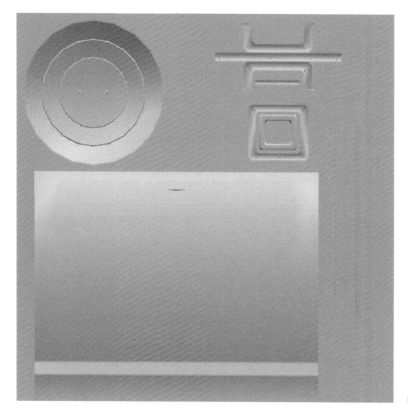

FIG 5.55d

xNormal

For the ambient occlusion bake, I would like to quickly go over a very handy application called xNormal.

This is free to use, commercially or otherwise which is a standalone application dedicated to generating the type of map that we are generating now.

Sometimes Maya can generate unusual artefacts in an ambient occlusion bake, and for this reason I want to show you an alternative method for baking/transferring, should you run into any issues.

Once xNormal is installed we will need to export our objects from Maya into xNormal. To do this we will export them out in the .obj format.

Go to **Window > Settings/Preferences > Plug-in Manager.** Scroll down to find **objexport.mll** and then ensure both of these boxes are checked.

To ensure you get smooth results both inside and outside of Maya it will be useful to delete the history and freeze the transforms of the objects involved. **Edit > Delete by Type > History and Modify > freeze transforms**.

Also make sure that both objects occupy the same world space. In other words, they look like they are sitting right on top of each other in the viewport.

Select the TrashCanHighRes version go to **File > Export selection, Files of type > obj**, change location to something sensible and name as highRes.

Repeat the same with the low resolution version saving as LowRes, respectively.

Now it's time to launch xNormal.

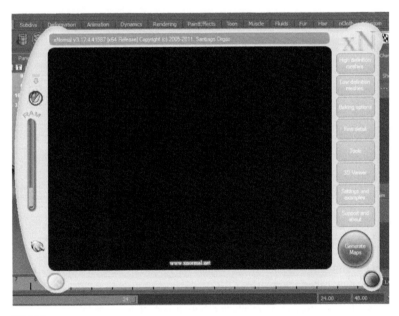

FIG 5.55e

Make sure the High Definitions button is highlighted on the right side. Right click under the file and select add mesh. Navigate to our highres.obj. Select the low definition meshes button on the right side. Set the maximum frontal ray distance to 0.1. Right click under the file and select add mesh. Navigate to the lowres.obj. Select the baking options button.

In Output file give this a sensible location. Set the size to 1024, edge padding 2. We want to render out an ambient occlusion map so let's make sure the check box is checked.

FIG 5.55f

Then simply hit **Generate Maps**.

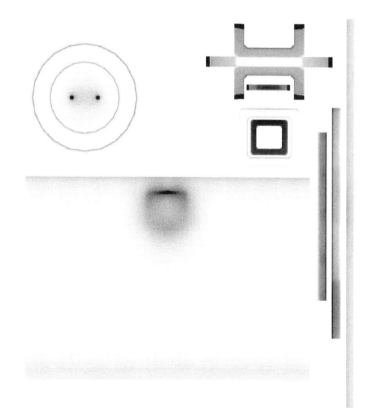

FIG 5.55g

With that complete, we can close xNormal.

We will now return to Maya and transfer the ambient occlusion and normal maps for the indents that we made.

Name both of these objects something sensible so it's easy to keep track of them. I have decided on **IndentHighRes** and (the simple plane) **IndentLowRes** .

Again open up the transfer maps options. Select the low resolution object for the target mesh, and select the high resolution object for the source mesh. Change the display from **Mesh** to **Envelope**, and increase the search until it hovers in front of all the necessary detail.

Select a **normal map** and an **AO** map. Change the path for the maps to be generated into something sensible. Change the file format to .jpeg and make the map width and height 1024.

For the ambient occlusion map keep the **optimization for single object** and the occlusion rays to 128, ensure this map will also render out at 1024. Then simply hit **bake**.

Repeat these same principles for the remaining objects (panels/screws and seam) and bake out normal and occlusion maps for these too.

For simplicity, I have moved the panel and screws off to one side and will bake these together. The plane that will be baked onto is just a simple square plane. This comes with readymade UV's so there is one less step to prepare.

Texturing in Photoshop

First let's quickly set up a grid that will mimic the UV Texture Editor grid in Maya. This will help us snap to any of the same grid lines we were snapping to in the Texture Editor.

Go to **Edit > Preferences > Guides, Grid & Slices**.

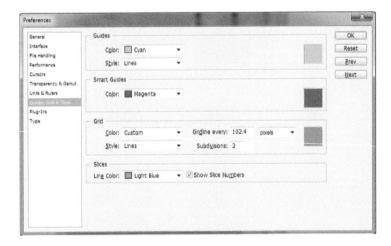

FIG 5.55h

Here I have set the gridlines to be every 102.4 pixels and the subdivisions to 2.

First we will create the diffuse texture which will be our basic color information for the shader we will set up later in Maya. We will also be creating a normal map which will hold the high resolution geometry details and finally a specular map which will contain how shiny the surface of the object is.

Open up the UV snapshot image that we saved off earlier and then lock the layer. Keep this layer on top of all the others.

Create a new layer – this will be our base metal texture. Fill it with a flat blue-gray.

Next go to **Filter > Noise > Add Noise**.

Then go to **Filter > Blur > Motion blur**. An angle of about 45 degrees and a distance of 50 pixels should do it.

I've then reduced the contrast of it slightly and then used the burn and dodge tools to create dark and light areas.

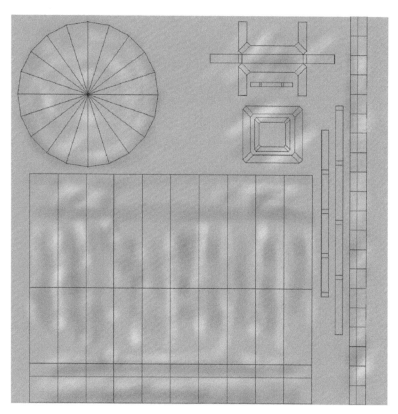

FIG 5.55i

Next, open up all the ambient occlusion bakes from Maya and xNormal. The AO bake isn't perfect so we'll correct a couple of details first.

Select that layer and soften it by selecting **Gaussian Blur** by 2 pixels. Set these layers to **multiply** and copy the details into the necessary areas – highlight both the normal and occlusion layers and then move them at the same time. This way it will be easier to line everything up.

Note that some of the occlusion layers have had the opacity settings slightly reduced. Also most of the normal layers have been set to overlay except the base texture (as there isn't anything to overlay it onto).

FIG 5.55j

Note that it is at this stage that I decided to stretch up the indents in the texture slightly.

Next take a light brush and scuff up the edges to add in little scratch details, set this layer to **screen** and set the opacity to the desired value.

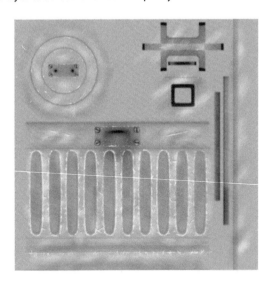

FIG 5.55k

FIG 5.55l

Next create a new layer and then alter the foreground and background colors of the brush to some rusty hues and then go to **Filter > Render > Clouds.** Then change the **Blend If** settings in the layer styles options to only blend over the top of the underlying darker areas.

By double clicking on a layer it is possible to bring up all the effects for it. At the bottom in the center there is an area called **Blend If**. Note that it is set to blend only if the underlying layer is between the black and the mid grays. This causes the rust to show through only on the darker bits. To split the arrows to give a nicer fade, click **Alt** when dragging one of the arrows.

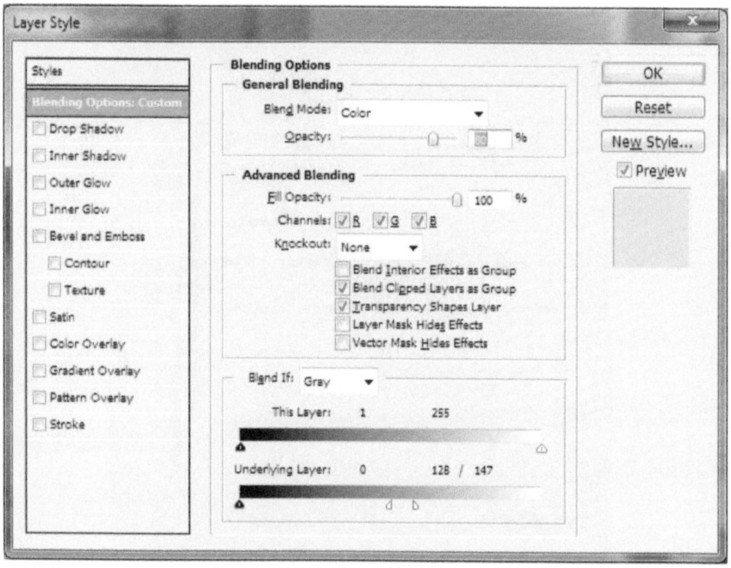

FIG 5.55m

Next, try painting more rust details on an additional two layers and then set the layer style to include an emboss. Next, experiment with the settings to make the effect quite subtle.

We don't want to have too much shadow detail in a diffuse texture as that might fight against what the normal map is trying to do visually.

Finally, create another couple of dirt layers. One as rendered clouds, the other as a noise layer which is first filled white, then use **Filter > add noise**.

Use **Gaussian blur** 0.5 and then adjust the contrast. Set this as **multiply** and use the **Blend if (red)** options, using the underlying layer. This noise will mostly affect the rusty colors.

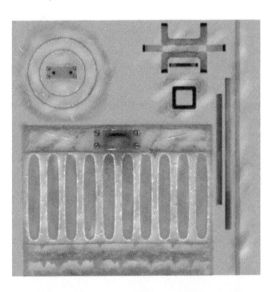

FIG 5.55n

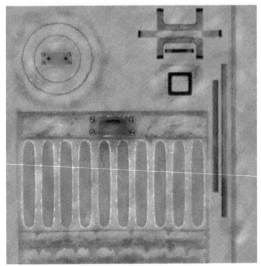

FIG 5.55o

Next we will create the normal map texture. Most of the details should be now set up from the ambient occlusion setup of the diffuse texture.

The normal map of the base of the trashcan didn't come out cleanly as it is trying to bend round the model. We need the left side to be the same as the right side on the trashcan so it can tile correctly. Simply choose a very thin section of this section of the normal map and stretch it out along the horizontal to fit over the old version of the normal map.

FIG 5.55p

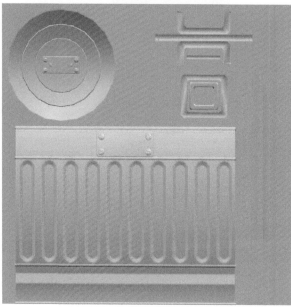

FIG 5.55q

The rest of the details are added and overlaid. Next take some of the diffuse rust layers and desaturate them and lighten them up and merge them over a flat black layer. This gives us an image that we can then process through a normal map filter.

Nvidia have a free one to go with Photoshop that I will briefly outline here.

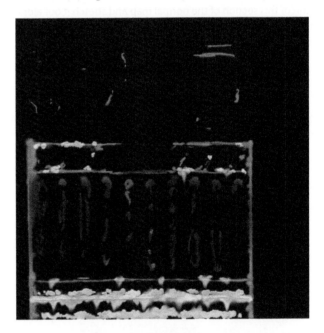

FIG 5.55r

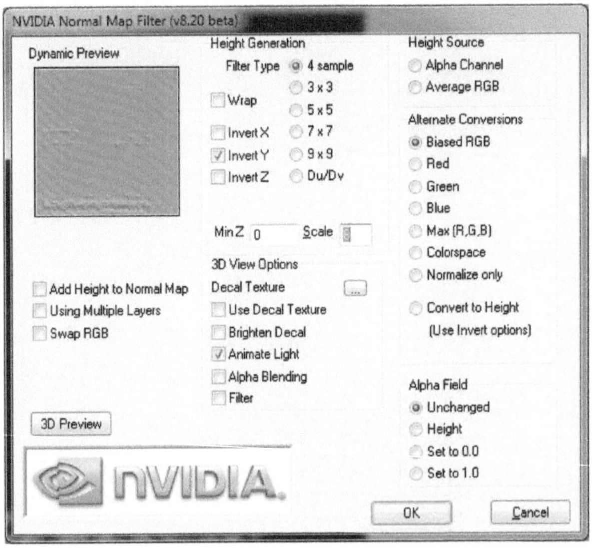

FIG 5.55s

The Nvidia plugin can be found under **Filters > Nvidia Tools > NormalMap Filter** … Change the settings to match what I have entered here. Then hit ok.

Try experimenting with the **scale** setting to generate more or less intense results. This layer can also be then set to overlay and have the opacity lowered to whatever you like.

FIG 5.55t

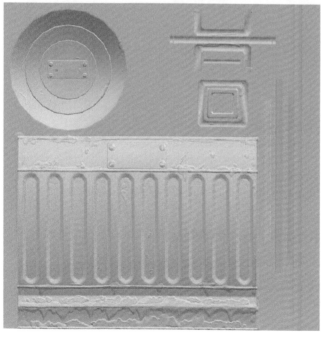

FIG 5.55u

Finally, we need to set up the specular map.

This can be generated by creating a new layer and then copying the whole diffuse canvas as one layer (**CTRL + A** to **Select All,** then **CTRL, SHFT + C** to copy all layers, then to paste, hit **CTRL + V**).

Once we have this layer, **desaturate** it and then experiment with the levels and contrast until you get something where the very shiny areas will be quite bright and the dull dirty areas are darker.

Also use certain individual layers of the diffuse map like the rust, scratches and indents and copy them into the specular folder and desaturate them. Again, experiment with the opacity settings to get something that works.

Remember, the simple premise of a specular map is that the light areas of the texture are the shiny areas on the model. Black means no shine at all.

FIG 5.55v

Save out the textures as .jpegs – full quality named **Trashcan_d ,Trashcan_n,** and **Trashcan_s** for diffuse, normal, and specular, respectively.

Basic Rendering in Maya

In Maya we will create a new shader and assign our textures to it.

Right click our TrashcanFinal object, select **assign new material**, and select **phong** from the list that pops up.

The Attribute Editor for the material will open up on the right side.

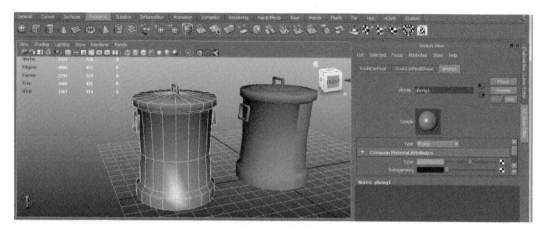

FIG 5.56a

In the Attribute Editor, click the checker icon next to **Color**, then select **File** .

Click the folder icon at the end of **image name** and navigate to the diffuse texture. In the example files, I have placed these textures in a folder within a "TrashCanTutorial" folder in the root of the C:\ drive.

It is no longer necessary to be able to see the other objects so I have hidden them.

The hide and show options can be found as part of the Display options in the menu bar. The shortcuts are **Alt + H** to hide everything except what is selected, it is also possible to press **CTRL + H** to hide the selected.

Next click the bottom arrow next to the file which will take us back to the previous menu. I've circled this in the Fig. 5.56b.

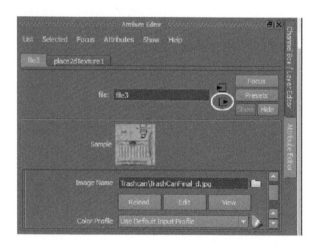

FIG 5.56b

Repeat the same process for the specular file clicking on the checker next to **Specular color**. This time, insert our specular map.

In order to be able to see the specular and normal map show up in the viewport we will need to turn on **high quality rendering**.

153

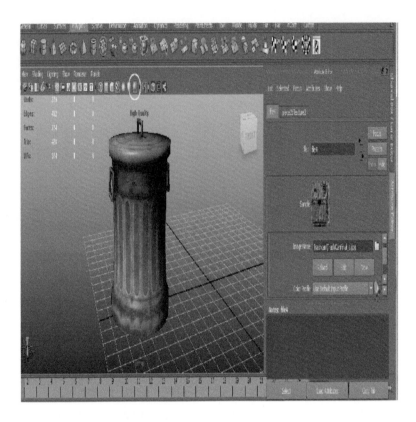

FIG 5.57a

Next we will set up the normal map.

Click the checker icon next to the bump mapping option of the phong shader in the Attribute Editor. Under the 2D bump attributes change the drop down menu to use as **tangent space normals**. Then select the arrow next to the bump value.

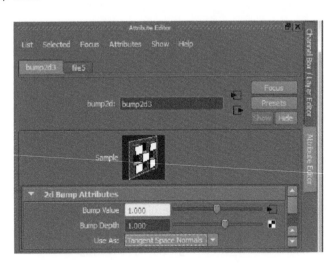

FIG 5.57b

154

Click the folder icon at the end of **image name** and navigate to the normal map texture. Click the bottom arrow next to phong which will take us back to the previous menu.

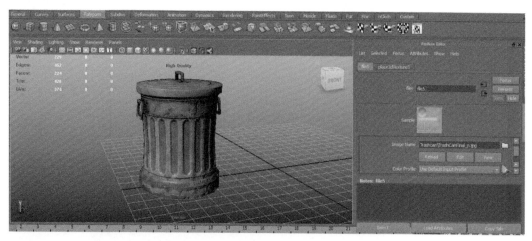

FIG 5.58a

Now that we have set the shader up, we will quickly alter some basic rendering settings. These can be accessed by selecting the circled icon in fig. 5.58b .

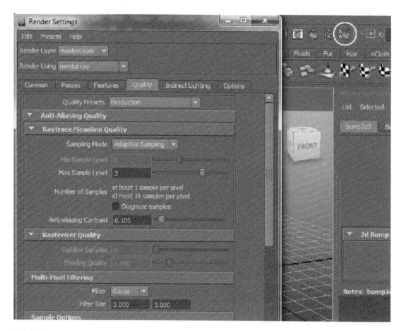

FIG 5.58b

In the **Render Using** pull-down menu select **mental ray**. If this doesn't appear as an option, do the following. Go to **window > settings > plug-in manager**, ensure that **mayatomr.mll** boxes are checked.

Back in the render settings, once mental ray is selected, go to the Quality tab and change to **production** from the pull-down menu.

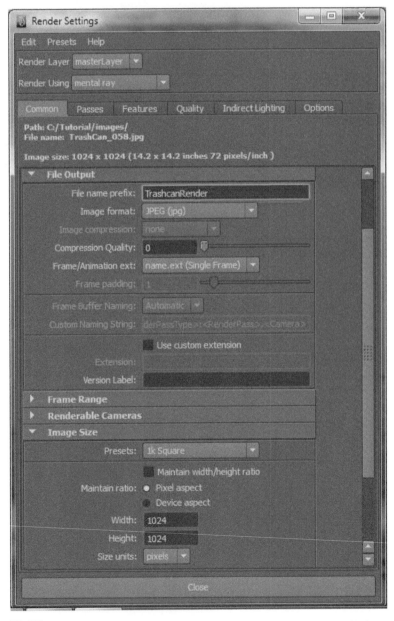

FIG 5.59a

The image size can be changed under the Common tab, **image size** – width and height values. Finally under file output, give it a name. Change the image format to jpg.

There are some other settings that will affect the render that can be found in the **Camera Attribute Editor** found under the **Panels View menu.**

In the **Attribute Editor** scroll down to the **Environment** section and change the background color to something that isn't pure black or white.

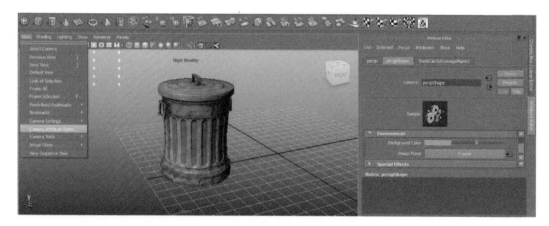

FIG 5.59b

FIG 5.59c

A pure black or white background will most likely confuse the silhouette details of the model by blending with the edge shadows or highlights.

Congratulations! We're at the end of the tutorial. You have now used some of the most useful techniques and tools for one of the most powerful applications in the industry. There's a lot more to know (there always is) but you've already come this far so enjoy the ride!

CHAPTER 6

Modeling the Robot in Maya

Welcome to the robot modeling tutorial. This will give you a taste of modeling in Maya and will hopefully help to broaden your understanding of the software.

Let's take a look at the concept sketch of the robot to see what we are building.

FIG 6.1 The robot concept art.

To start off with we will start shaping the first cylinder for the block-out. We should be paying attention to the overall shapes and forms at this point rather than the finer details of the model.

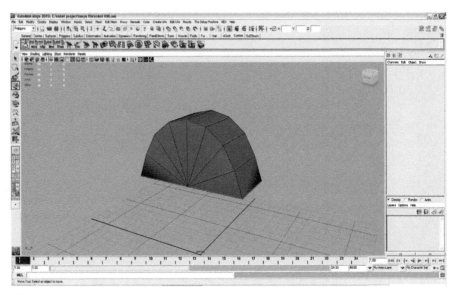

FIG 6.2

We will continue by blocking out the pelvic area and leg. The concept art is a little vague here so we may need to experiment with a few shapes before getting something that works well.

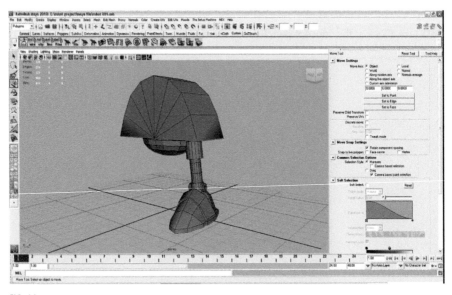

FIG 6.3

Next, we can **mirror** the legs and build the head. Model one half then **mirror** it and position it.

Make sure that the head is interesting from all angles and remember not to just concentrate on only the front.

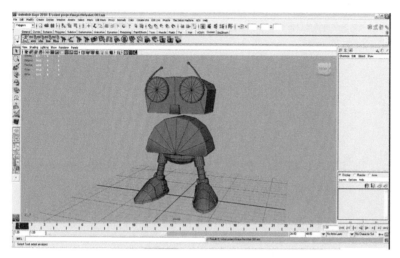

FIG 6.4

Next, we need to get the arm assembled and the proportions tweaked to match the overall design of the robot. The hips are an issue at the moment and we will probably need to tweak them a little more as we get further into the process.

I am looking at correlations between the mass of the character to get the overall form as close as possible to the concept art.

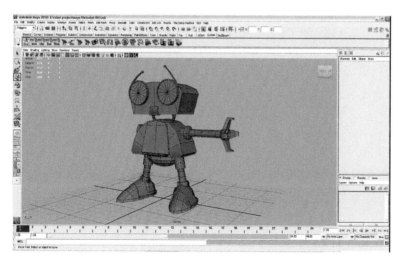

FIG 6.5

161

With the block-out now completed, we can start to look at specific details. I'm
a little unsure about the feet at the moment, especially where the ankles join.
We can make a note of this and refine them further when we get to the high
poly stage. I'm sure we will come up with something that works.

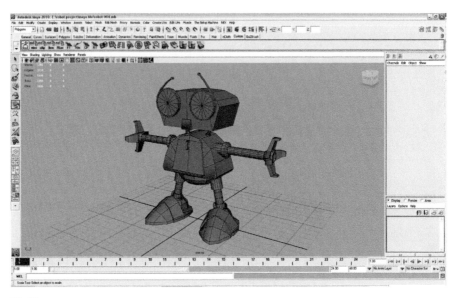

FIG 6.6

Next, let's have a look at the silhouette to check that the block-out is looking
good so far.

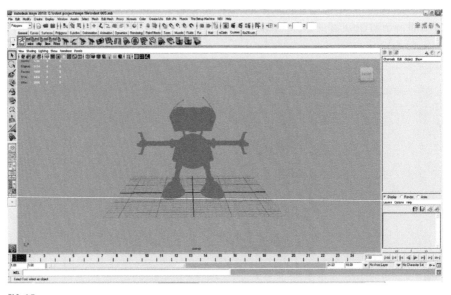

FIG 6.7

We will now make a copy of the head mesh as this will serve as a base for the high poly head mesh.

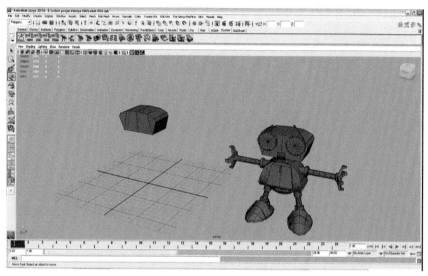

FIG 6.8

We now need to add supporting edges for subdivision. If we don't do this, we will lose the overall shape when we subdivide the model to create the high poly version. We do this with a mixture of **beveling** and adding **edge loops** . We need to constantly check the **smooth preview** (hotkey 3) to make sure that the object will smooth cleanly once subdivided.

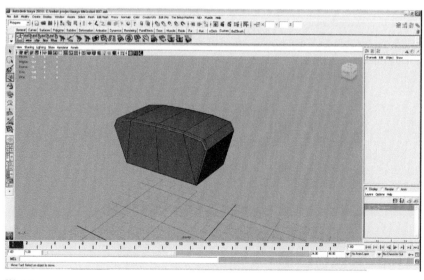

FIG 6.9

163

Next, the basic edges are added for the groove detail at the back of the robots head, the faces will then be **extruded** inward to create the panel lines in the concept.

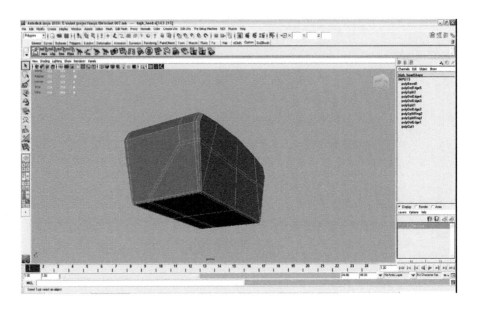

FIG 6.10

With the supporting edges complete, I then **duplicate** the object and place it on a new layer so that I have all presmoothed components. I do this in case I need to change something later and I need to go back to the original safe model I'm happy with.

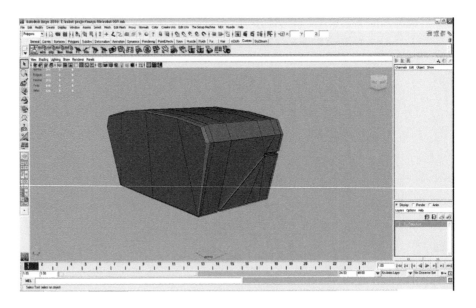

FIG 6.11

164

I'll now apply the smoothing to the head object and give it a quick visual check over for any smoothing errors like pinching. If you find any, just revert back to the lower detail, make sure you have enough edges to support the smooth, and smooth once more.

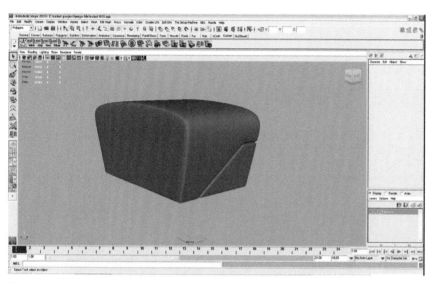

FIG 6.12

We start the mouth piece in the same way as we did with the head. We add supporting loops and ensure that they are spaced nicely to achieve the correct curves of the corners.

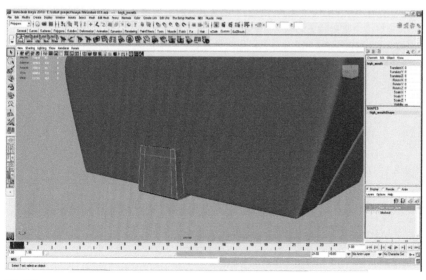

FIG 6.13

The dimples on the mouth piece are made by floating an array of dish-shaped objects above the body of the mesh. Once baked, these will appear to be cut into the mouth piece rather than floating above it. This removes the need for creating complex geometry, while giving the same effect on the normal maps.

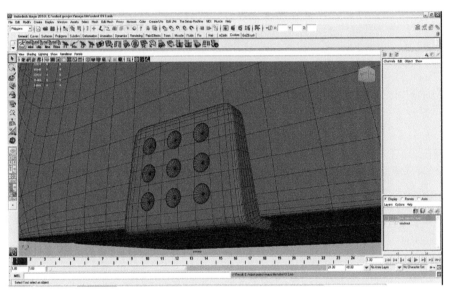

FIG 6.14a

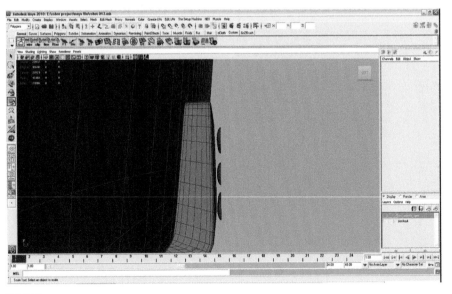

FIG 6.14b

Because I intend to cut an area into the side of the eye for the wiper mechanism, I start with an 80-sided **cylinder**, this will give me enough geometry to keep a smooth profile for the eye. This is then given supporting edges, just as we did before.

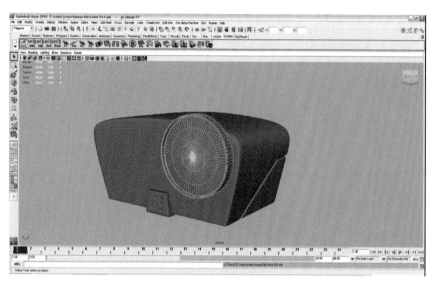

FIG 6.15

The hole for the wiper pivot is now cut into the eyepiece. Next, we can turn our attention to the wipers themselves.

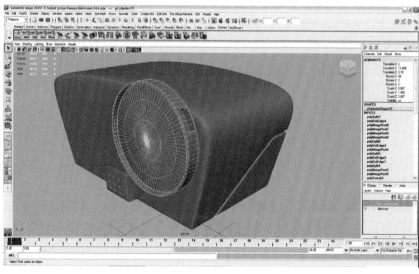

FIG 6.16

Extra loops are added to the block-out piece, along with an **extrusion** for the pivot area at the base of the wiper. Once this is **smoothed**, this will complete the high poly work for the head. I'm not duplicating the eye and wiper across as we shall be mirroring them at the low poly stage once they share the same texture.

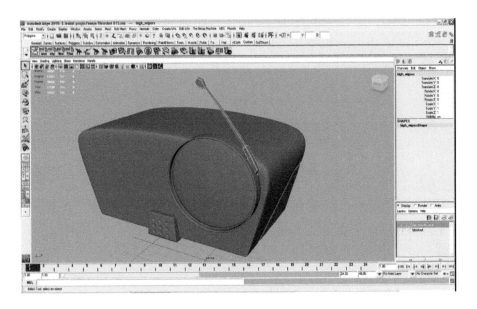

FIG 6.17

Next, we move onto the torso section, following the same process as the head object. Create the simple form, and add the supporting edges so that we achieve the correct shape once smoothed.

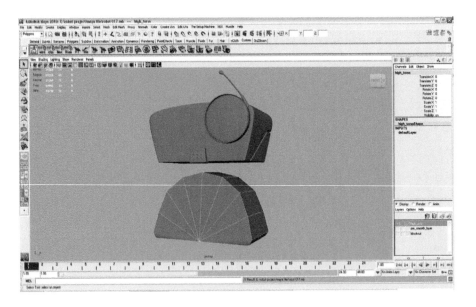

FIG 6.18

With the main shape of the torso in place, we can move onto the compartment door. Once again, I start by duplicating the original shape from the block-out layer and I move it into position. I will keep the external edges from this piece, but rearrange the internal edges so that we can achieve the extra panel detail in the surface.

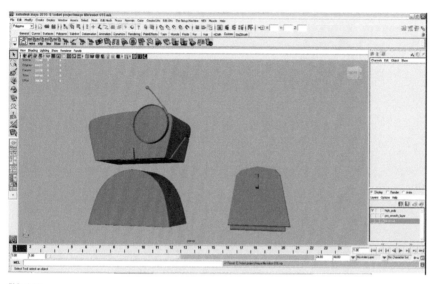

FIG 6.19

Now we have our front panel before smoothing. Even though we won't see the back faces they will need to be left in place, otherwise the border edge that they create will not be affected by the smoothing when we apply it.

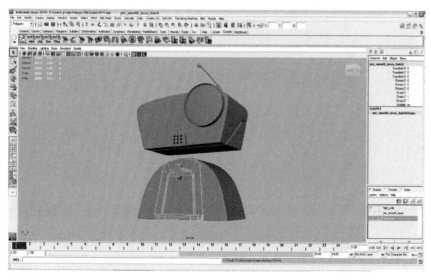

FIG 6.20

Next, we need to make an L-shaped piece of geometry, with a profile similar to a trough. This is then positioned floating above the main torso to replicate the groove in the concept. The floating geometry will work in the same way as the dimples do for the mouth area when we bake the texture out.

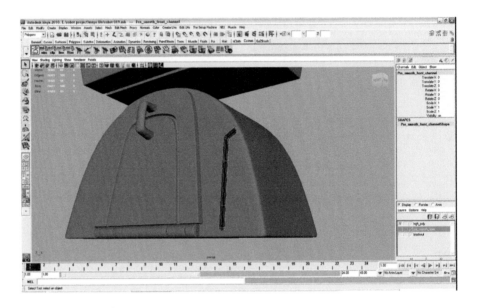

FIG 6.21

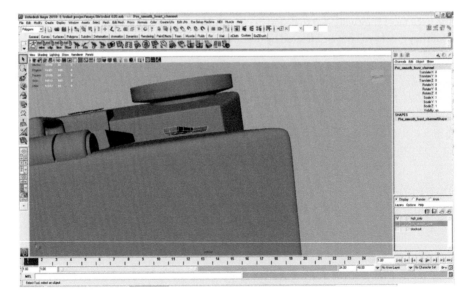

FIG 6.21a

Next, we will move onto the shoulder. I've cut it in half while the arm connection is modeled, and will mirror it back across, once it's finished.

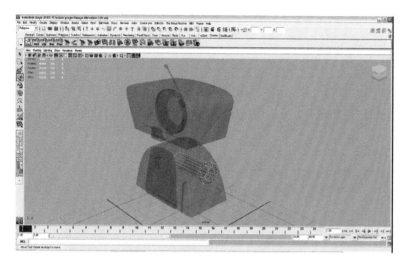

FIG 6.22

I've added a little more detail to the shoulder in the form of a small groove, giving the appearance of two components fixed together. Next, the cylinder that will form the arm is added.

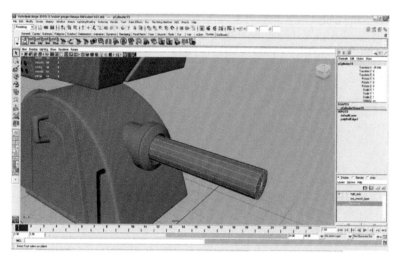

FIG 6.23

Edge loops are added to the cylinder using the **multiple loop** setting. I've added 10 loops in this instance.

While the selection is still live, the loops are beveled and adjusted to an appropriate thickness. First we extrude outward slightly. We do this so that once they are subdivided, the edges will be crisp. We will then **extrude** inward to make the corrugated surface. The extrusions are repeated at each point that a supporting loop will be required. Once this is complete, the edge caps of the cylinders are deleted.

171

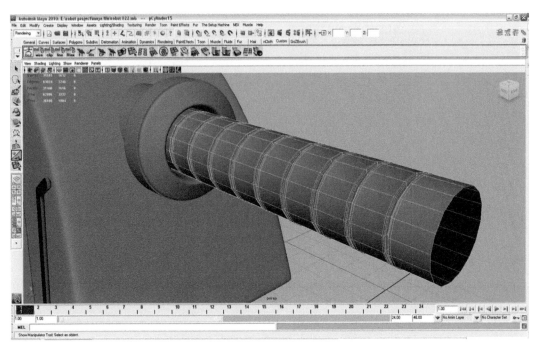

FIG 6.24

The hand block-out is added back in to be used as a guide for modeling the high poly version. I find using the block-outs as guides an easy starting point for the geometry. It's a good habit to get into.

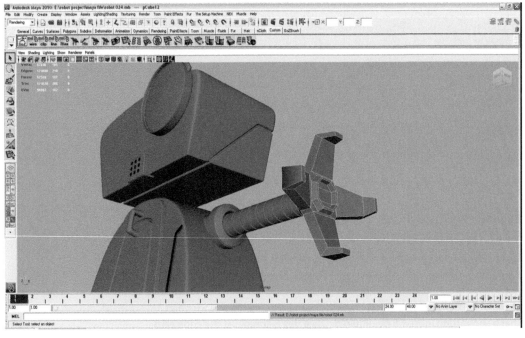

FIG 6.25

I'm using a mixture of **bevel** and **extrude** to begin to get the right shape for the high poly palm. I'm following the basic shape already established in the block-out.

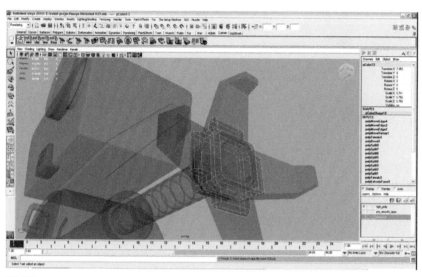

FIG 6.26

Further supporting loops are then added to the palm object. All the time I am checking that everything will smooth OK with smooth preview.

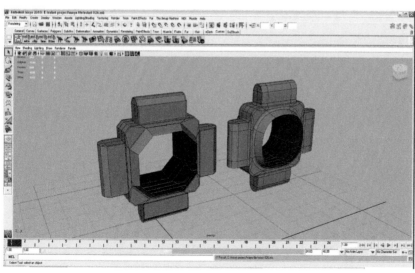

FIG 6.27

Next, bolt holes are created in the four hinges of the palm. First we will start off by selecting the vertices at the center point of the hinges.

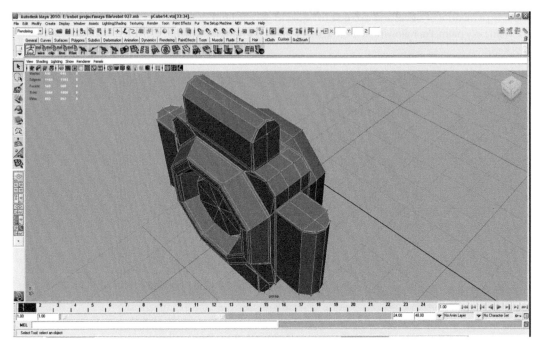

FIG 6.28

These are then **beveled**, and the vertices shown are **merged** .

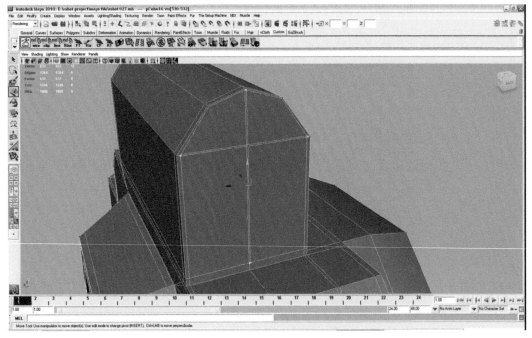

FIG 6.28a

The center face is then **scaled** up with the **Transform Component tool** .

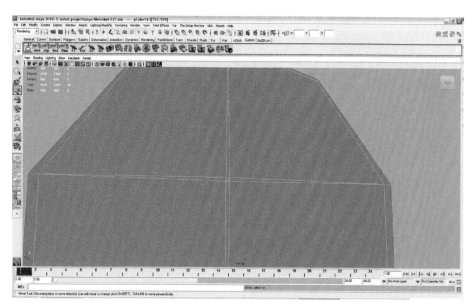

FIG 6.28b

The same face is then **extruded** twice to create the supporting loops for the edge of the hole.

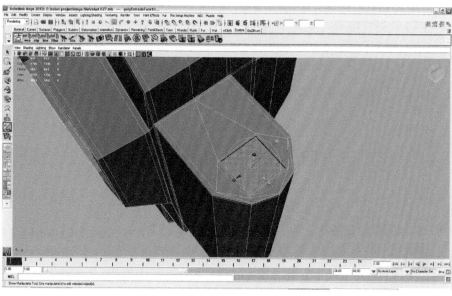

FIG 6.28c

Before being **extruded** so that the two opposing faces touch, the selection is converted to vertices.

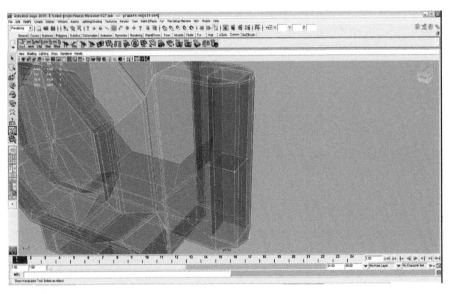

FIG 6.28d

These vertices are then **merged** and the faces that join them are **deleted** .This will have to be done separately for each hinge plate. You should then just be left with a single internal loop in the hinge that can be deleted as you see fit.

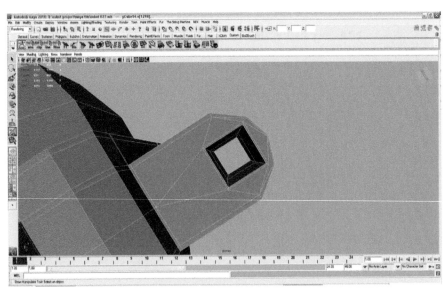

FIG 6.28e

Here's how the resulting palm should look once smoothed.

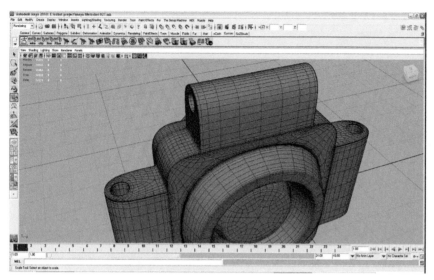

FIG 6.29

For the "fingers," we will start by extracting some of the faces from the block-out mesh, to give us some starting geometry.

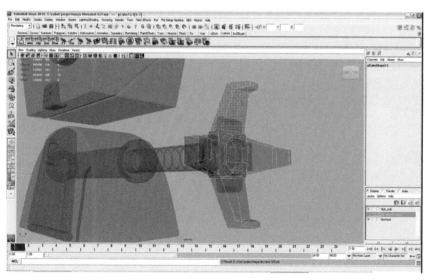

FIG 6.30

We need to add the extra **edge loop** that runs right round the finger and add the extra detail for the hinge. With the geometry for the finger completed we need to **rotate** it around the palm. Firstly **move** the **pivot** of the finger object to the center point of the palm object.

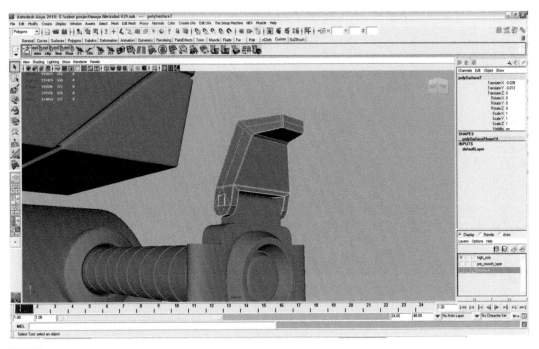

FIG 6.31

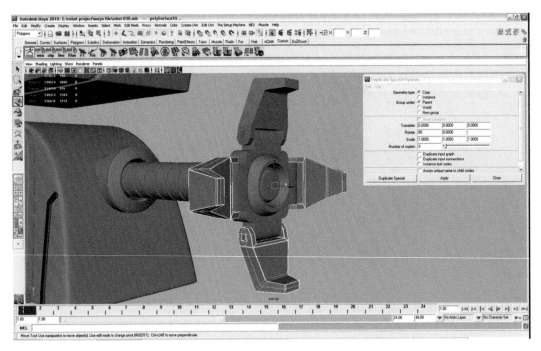

FIG 6.32

Now, with the object selected, open the **duplicate special options box** and **rotate** the object around the x axis by 90 degrees. Make sure that the number of copies is set to 3.

A basic bolt is then made and then rotated around the palm, using exactly the same process as we used on the finger objects.

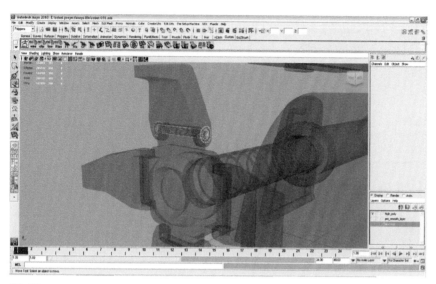

FIG 6.33

Moving down the character, let's now have a look at the area around the groin. This area isn't particularly clearly described in the concept art, which gives us a little freedom in this area.

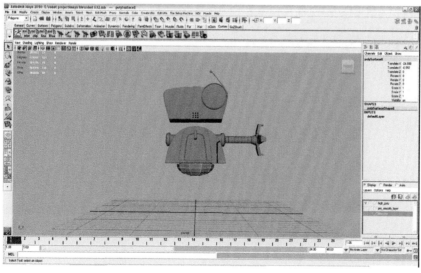

FIG 6.34

Thinking about the model and how I thought the robot would work
functionally, this time I've decided to start with new geometry rather than
using the existing block-out. I feel that the semi-circular shape didn't quite
belong to the model, so let's go with something a little more angular.

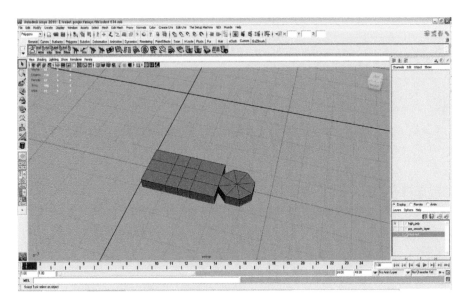

FIG 6.35

The first component for the groin is progressing well. I've modeled the
basic shape and the geometry has been merged. I've added the required
supporting edge loops and I have created a little detail to make it a bit more
interesting.

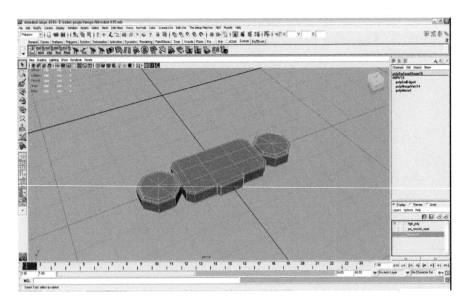

FIG 6.36

For the second part of the geometry in the groin area, I have created a half cylinder shape, to reference the shape of the torso.

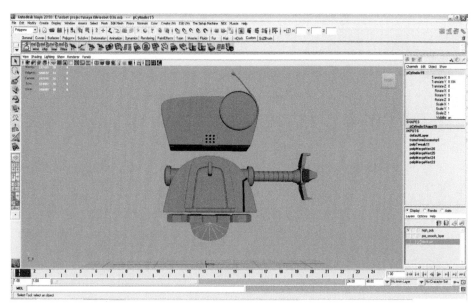

FIG 6.37

I have **extruded** a small recess in the front and an area for extra cabling is extruded and given supporting edges at the back.

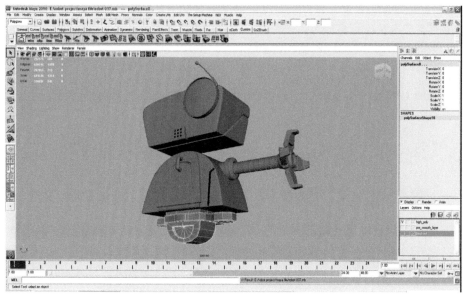

FIG 6.38

To make the cable at the back, we first need to create a CV curve following the path that we want the cable to take.

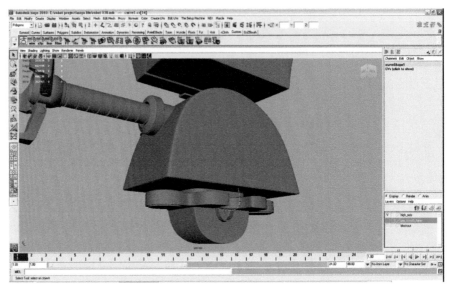

FIG 6.39

Then, I create a **cylinder** and **delete** everything except for one of the end caps, which I then position at the origin of the CV curve.

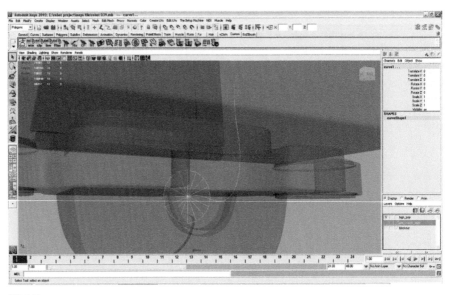

FIG 6.40

Next, select the cylinder, shift select the CV curve and hit **extrude** .The cylinder will stretch to the end of the CV curve and a dialogue box will appear in the right of the viewport.

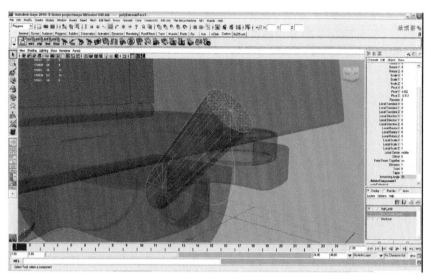

FIG 6.41

Next, we need to adjust the number of divisions until you have something that you can work with – here I started with 10. Sometimes you might need to tweak some of the edge loops a little, or move the points of the CV curve to get the shape you are looking for.

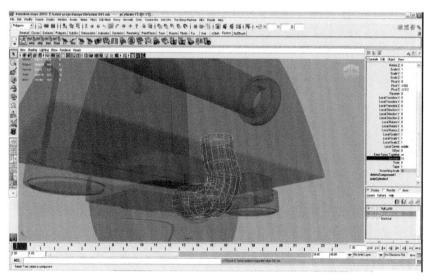

FIG 6.42

Now we just need to **delete** the cylinder end caps, and if you are sure that you are happy with the position of the cable, delete the object history and then select and delete the CV curve. Then we need to select the edge loops and **bevel** them.

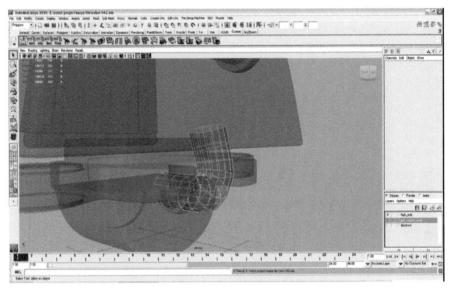

FIG 6.43

Now we can select the newly created loops of faces and **extrude** them inward, to create some interesting surface detail, which can then be smoothed.

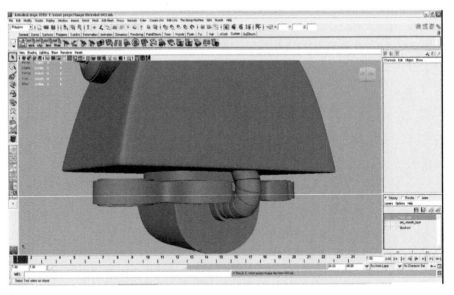

FIG 6.44

The legs are simply a duplicate of the arm component, which we have rotated, scaled slightly, and moved into position. We can use the block-out of the feet as a guide to get the correct angle and position.

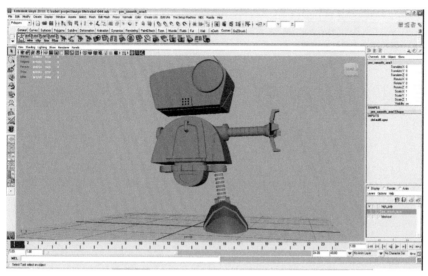

FIG 6.45

A cylinder is then created and moved into position at the joint between the hip and the leg. This is then shaped and has the supporting edges added before smoothing.

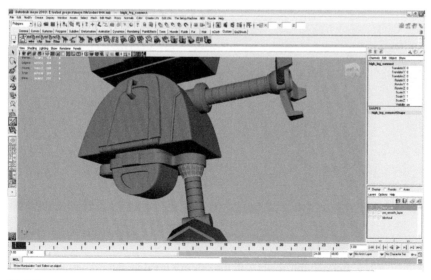

FIG 6.46

Next, we will look at working out how the ankle area should look over the top of the block-out foot. We should try to make sure that we develop something that can actually articulate well while staying true to the concept art.

FIG 6.47

The ankle begins to take shape by starting with the rough forms of the ball joint like mechanism. These can now be worked into further to refine the shape and to try to give a good sense of the way that the foot would articulate.

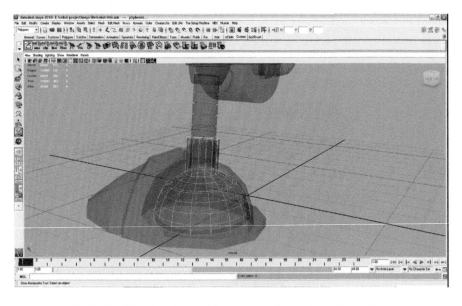

FIG 6.48

While checking the object with the **smooth preview**, it looks like we can improve the back of the heel, and give it sharper lines.

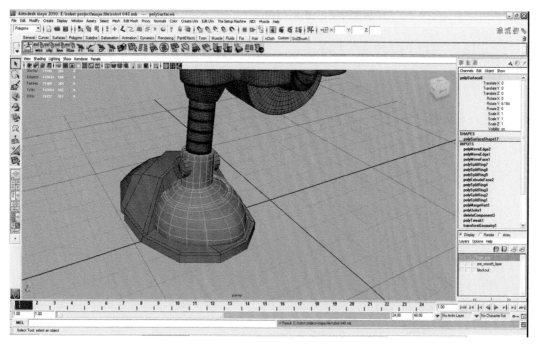

FIG 6.49

Let's start by selecting the lower vertical edges on the back of the heel.

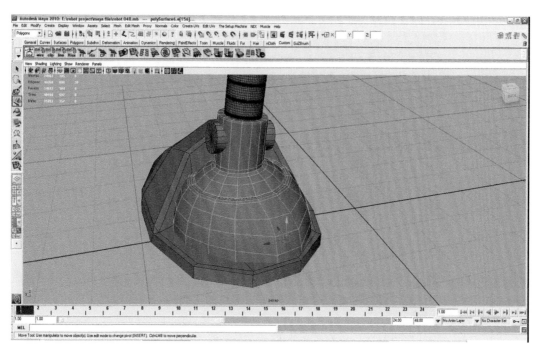

FIG 6.49a

Now let's bevel them with two segments selected.

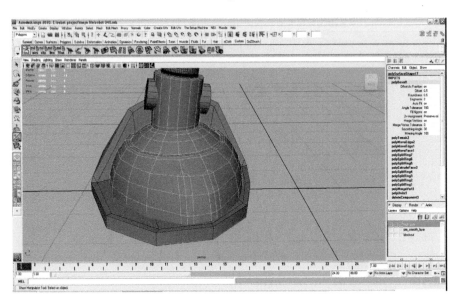

FIG 6.49b

Next, we need to join the top vertices on the bevel (the top tip of the triangle) and merge them with the vertices directly above them. We need to do this for both bevels.

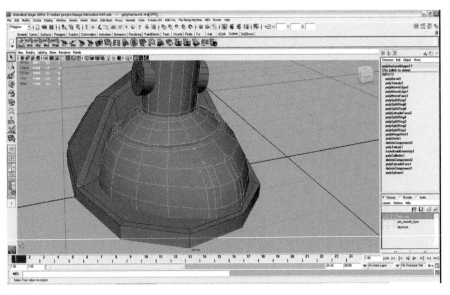

FIG 6.49c

Then we need to select the edges to the sides of each crease and adjust them slightly until we are happy with the severity of the edge.

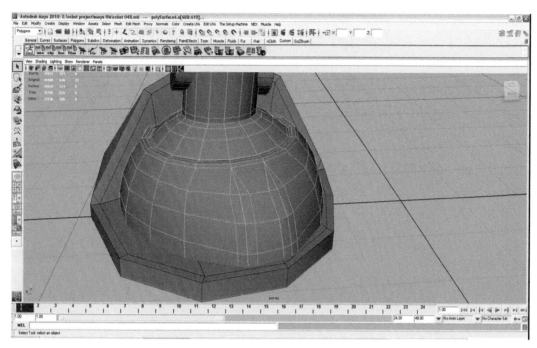

FIG 6.49d

Let's have a look at the result, with a smooth applied.

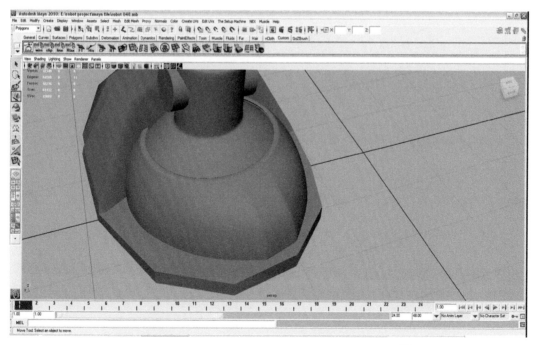

FIG 6.49e

Ok, I'm happy with the back of the heel, so let's move on to the rest of the foot. We will start with the block-out geometry minus the heel area, which will be re-build in a style closer to the ankle.

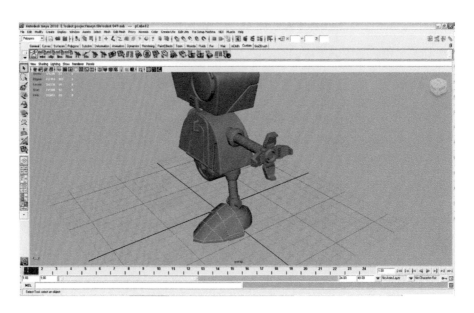

FIG 6.50

To begin with, let's start by **extruding** a new heel, and extracting the toe part of the foot from the main object.

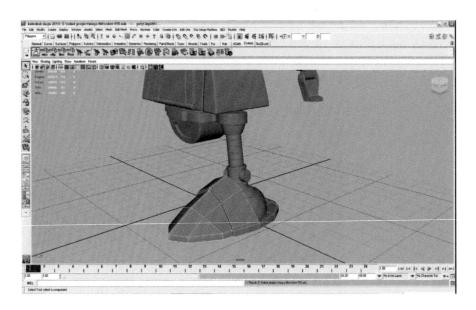

FIG 6.51

We can now add the supporting edge loops and do a quick smoothing check.

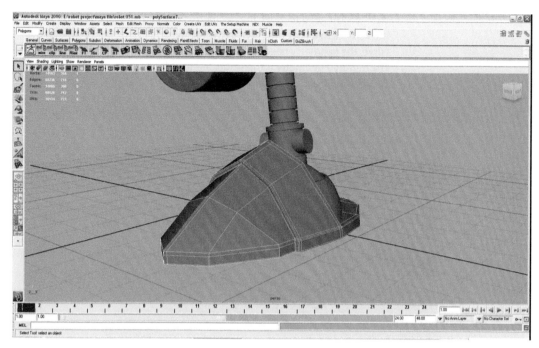

FIG 6.52

Next, we need to create the geometry for the floating details on the toe.

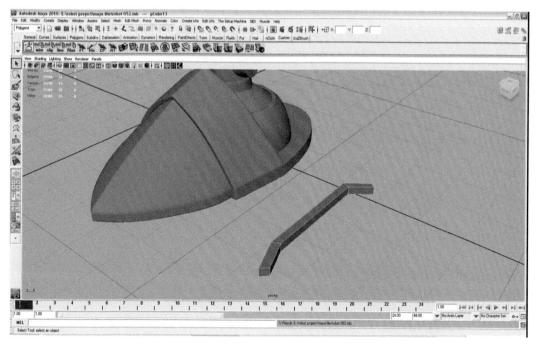

FIG 6.53

We then just need to move the geometry to its approximate position, aligning the vertices to follow the curve of the toe mesh. Once we're happy with the curve, the geometry needs to be mirrored over to the other side of the foot. The mirrored geometry is then adjusted to fit that side, and then combined with the original.

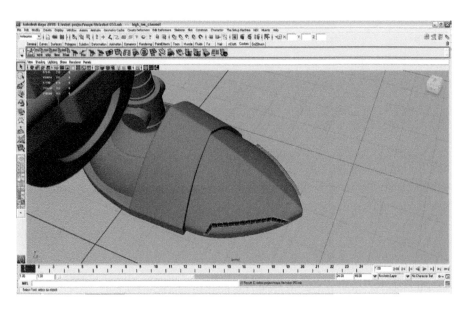

FIG 6.54

Then, the components of the foot are grouped together and the pivot point is changed to the center of the heel. We do this so that we can rotate the foot to a more natural position.

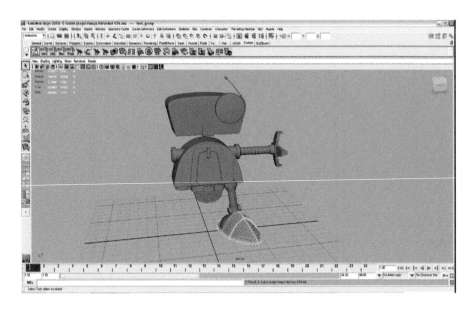

FIG 6.55

Let's now turn our attention to the bolt mechanism at the top of the ankle. We will do this by starting with a cylinder.

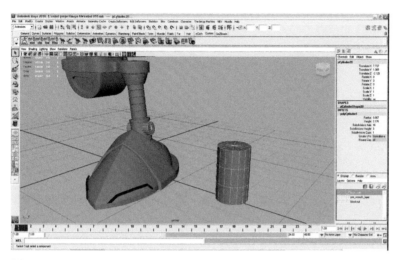

FIG 6.56

The bolt is simply made by using **extrude** to create an interesting center detail. Then we **scale** the individual surfaces and move them into position. Finally the block-out geometry is deleted.

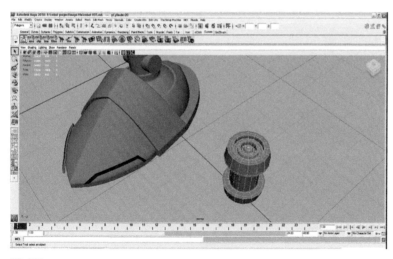

FIG 6.57

The final parts to be modeled for the high poly version of the robot are the neck cables. The starting point for these will be the arm cables. As before, they are duplicated from the presmoothed copy that we already have. We just need to copy them, then move and scale them into place.

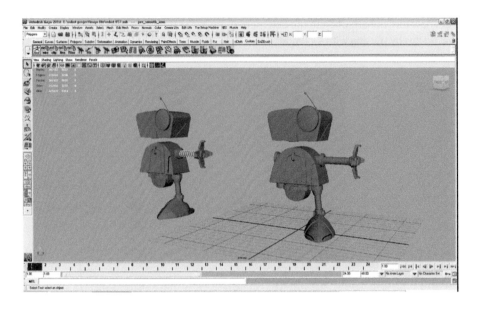

FIG 6.58

Up to this point, the neck cable is kept vertical so that it is easier to model and position the two end caps. Once you're happy with the size and position, the whole assembly needs to be combined and rotated to fit the robot.

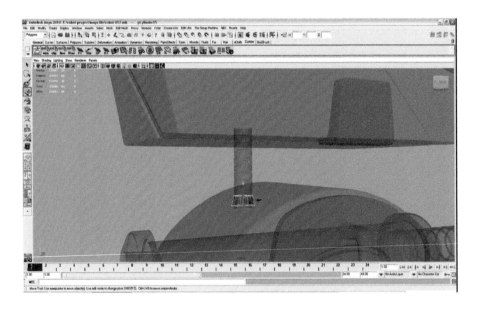

FIG 6.59

Here's my version of the neck cable – feel free to do what you like with yours – as always there is no right or wrong way to model this stuff – just get it looking the way you like it.

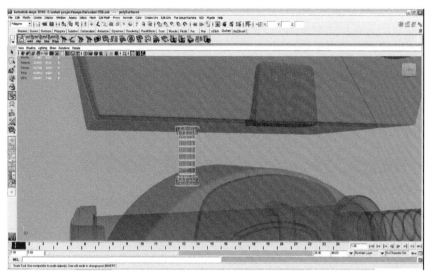

FIG 6.59a

To get the final look, just right, I'll apply a **lattice deformer** so that we can position it a little more accurately. Remember – the number of divisions in the deformer can be edited in the **channels box**.

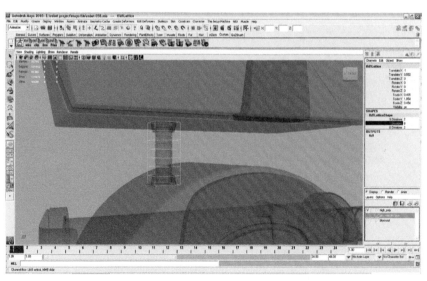

FIG 6.59b

Once you have the **lattice deformer** set, you can manipulate the deformers' lattice points to adjust the geometry contained within it. Have a play until you achieve the desired result.

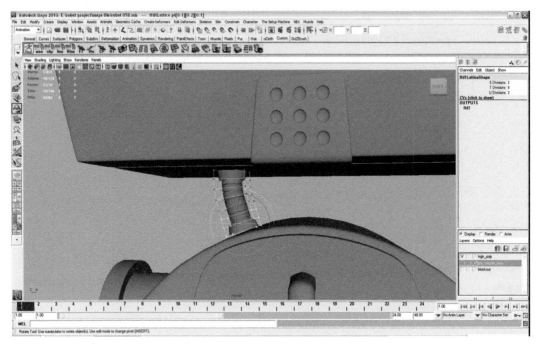

FIG 6.59c

As soon as you are happy with the deformation, select the object and **delete its history** to remove the deformer.

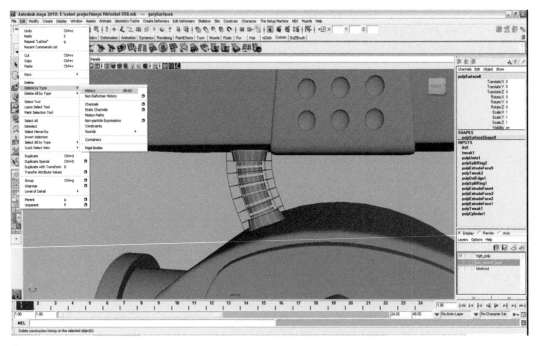

FIG 6.59d

That pretty much wraps up the basic modeling of the robot. In the penultimate image in this part, you should see the three different versions of the robot. On the left we have the presmoothed model, then in the middle the high poly model and finally on the right the original block-out.

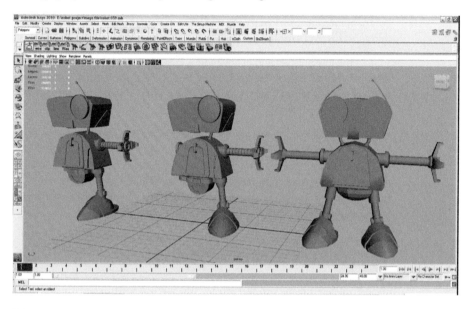

FIG 6.60

Finally, here we have the high poly robot with each of the relevant parts mirrored across.

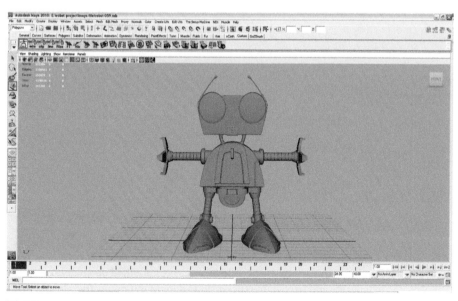

FIG 6.61

Modeling the Low Poly Version

Now that we have our high polygon version of the robot, we need to move on to building our low polygon version. We build two versions of the mesh so that we can take the details from the high poly version and "bake" them onto the low poly game version. Don't worry too much about this process if you've not been through it before, I'll explain it all for you once we have the low poly version built.

To start the low poly version of any model, I usually use a lot of the existing geometry from the presmoothed model. Support edges are usually removed from the basic geometry and I will usually add extra edges on the curved surfaces to smooth them out a little.

We should try to keep the geometry as quads where possible, so that we can keep everything readable and neat. Most game engines will triangulate the mesh but it does help when making subobject changes (vertices, faces, etc.). When creating the low poly topology, try to avoid long triangles, as these don't deform well when the model is animated. Even if you are not planning to animate the mesh, creating good topology is a very good habit to get into.

Ok, let's start off where we left the high poly build. We should have our smoothed and presmoothed high poly model.

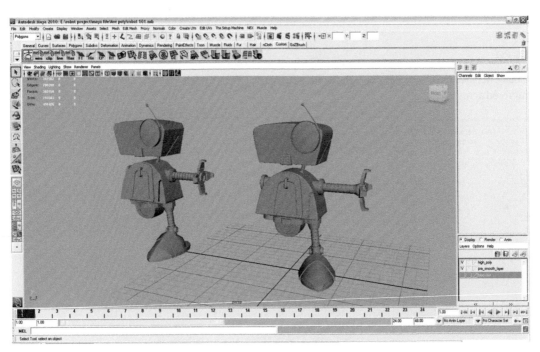

FIG 6.62

Starting with the foot, we need to take the presmoothed geometry, create a duplicate and remove the supporting edges as this geometry will not be subdivided.

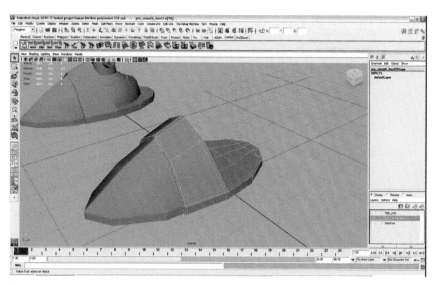

FIG 6.63

Take the foot components and remove all supporting edges. We also need to fill in the hollow of the heel. Next, prepare the toe cap to be attached to the heel by **deleting** any faces that would be on the inside of the mesh.

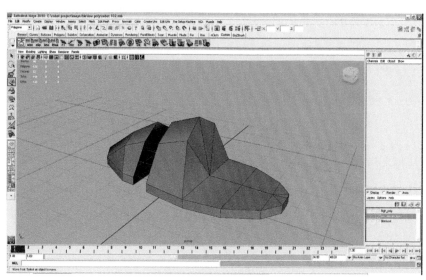

FIG 6.64

The next step is to position our low poly geometry in the same space as its high poly counterpart. Maya's **x-ray** feature is great for this. I will sometimes use the **Make Live** function on the high poly mesh too, at this stage it's simply to help see the high poly shape a little more clearly.

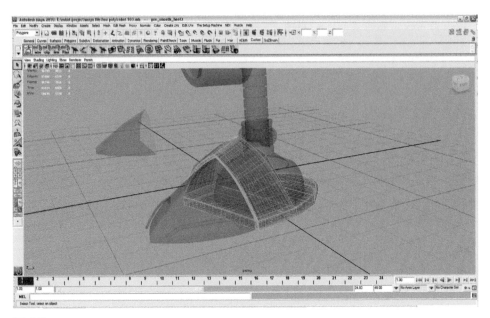

FIG 6.65

Let's add some extra edges to the arch of the top of the foot to improve its shape a little. They can be placed in the center of the existing faces by checking **Multiple Edge Loops** in the **Insert Edge Loops options box** ,and setting the number of loops to 1.

FIG 6.66

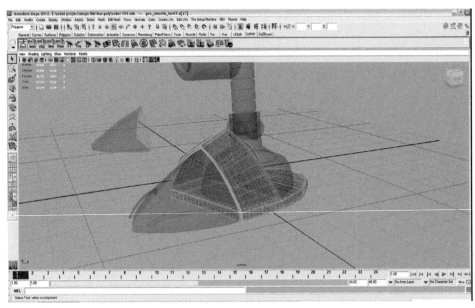

The vertices are then moved to better positions to follow the high poly shape a little more closely.

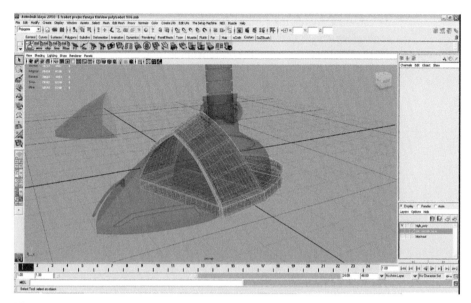

FIG 6.67

Now, let's have a look at the toe. Follow the same process as before by moving the vertices to match the high poly shape. Remember that this piece and the low poly heel shape will be joined together after this step.

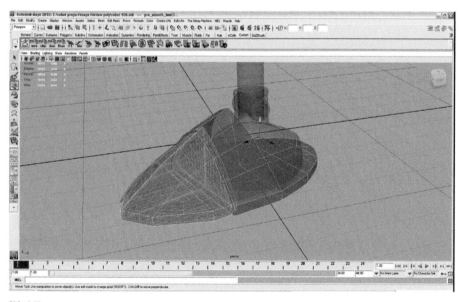

FIG 6.68

Having refined the shape of the foot object, the vertices that are to be **merged** are **snapped** into place (hold **V** while using the **Move** tool). This leaves us with several edges that need to be resolved. There are two choices. We can either merge the vertices at the join point, or we can continue those edges down the toe. I think I will go for the second option, as the extra edges will help define the curve of the bottom of the foot.

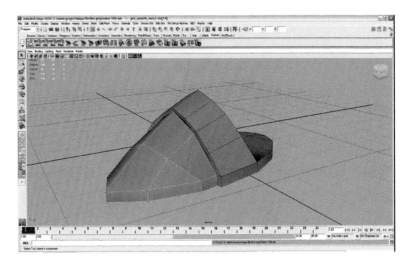

FIG 6.69

The extra edges are moved into place making use of the high poly object. Being "live," the low poly vertices can be moved along the surface of the high poly object by either using the tweak setting in the move tool options box, or by grabbing the central circle of the move tools manipulator rather than any of the axis.

The next step will be to combine the two objects and merge the vertices along their join to create a single foot object.

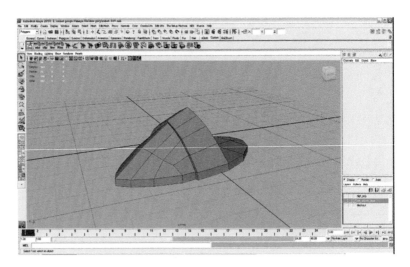

FIG 6.70

The faces at the back of the foot are then extruded to create a few extra faces.
This will give us a starting point to build the ankle component.

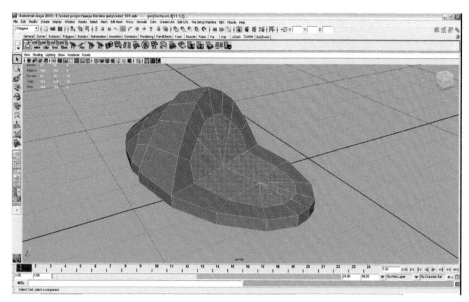

FIG 6.71

The center faces are **deleted** and the edges are redistributed across the "live"
high poly shape.

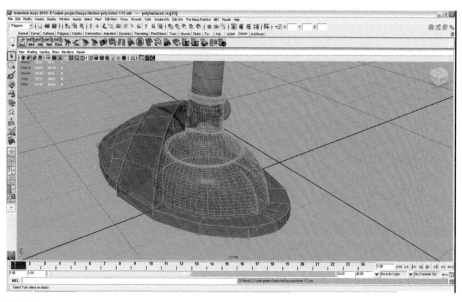

FIG 6.72

The edges shown are then extruded.

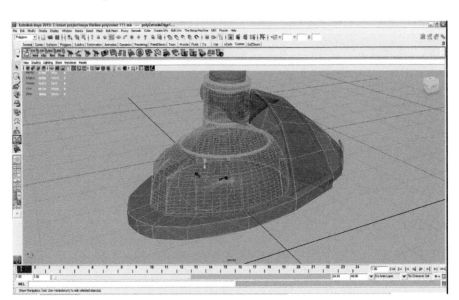

FIG 6.73a

Then the vertices shown are merged using the **Merge Vertex tool**, and the other vertices are **moved** into place over the live mesh.

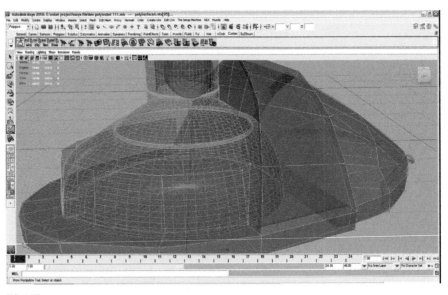

FIG 6.73b

The edge extrusion process is repeated, and once again, the vertices are adjusted before a third edge extrusion is done.

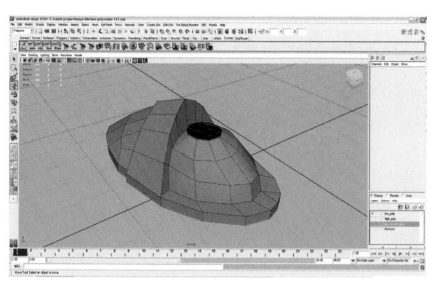

FIG 6.73c

Now we need to add some extra edges to help define the shape at the back of the ankle.

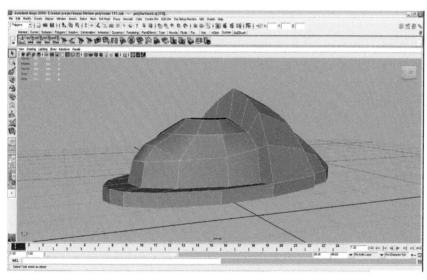

FIG 6.73d

Next, **create** an eight-sided **cylinder** and move it into position at the top of the ankle. Once there, snap the vertices of the ankle to its base. At this point, we will need to bring several edges together to reduce our geometry down to the eight sides needed. Once done we can then combine and merge the ankle to the cylinder.

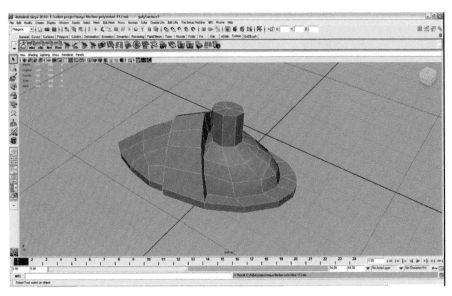

FIG 6.73e

Now we need to tidy up the edge flow around the ankle a little. We do this by moving vertices over the live surface of the high poly and deleting any unnecessary edges that we find.

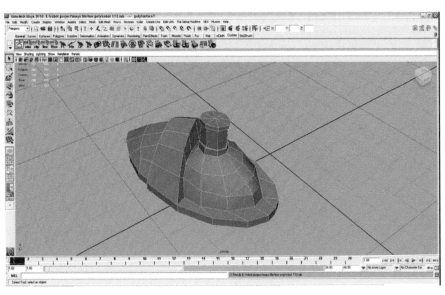

FIG 6.74

To create the leg we just need to perform a simple **extrude** from the top of the ankle, to which we add four edge loops to mimic the bands on the high poly version.

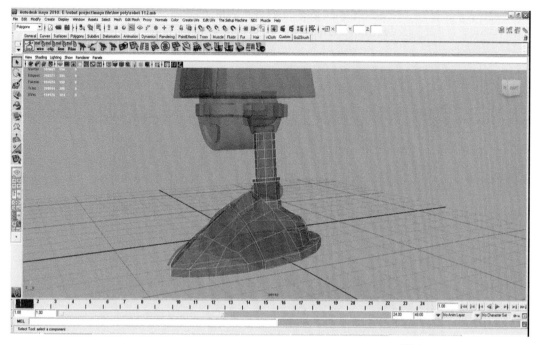

FIG 6.75

We then take the top edge of the leg and **extrude** it several more times to make the joint of the hip.

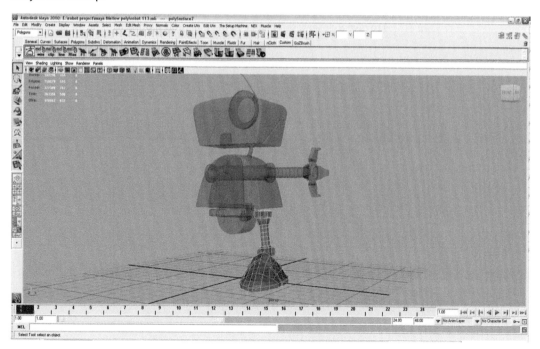

FIG 6.76

Select the innermost face and **scale** along the Z axis. The resulting edges are **extruded** to make the shape needed for the upper groin area.

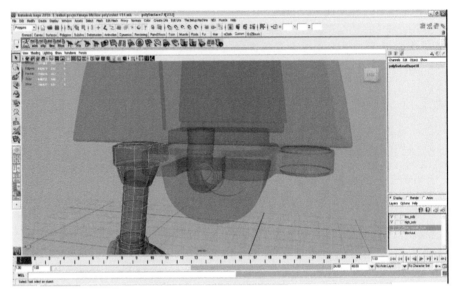

FIG 6.77

The corners are then **beveled**. By clicking **polyBevel** in the **channel box** you can access the **bevel options**. In this case, change the number of segments to 3 to give a closer resemblance to the high poly model.

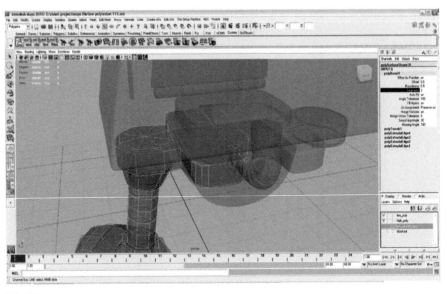

FIG 6.78

Now we can rearrange the edges created by the bevels using the **Split Polygon tool** .

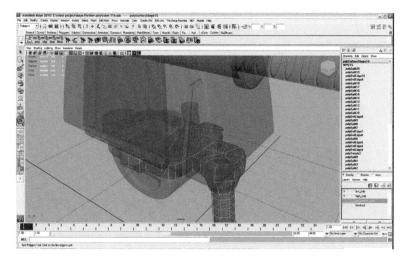

FIG 6.79

To make the waist connection, grab the faces shown in Fig. 6.80, **extrude** them, scaling inward so that we create a second row of faces around the selection.

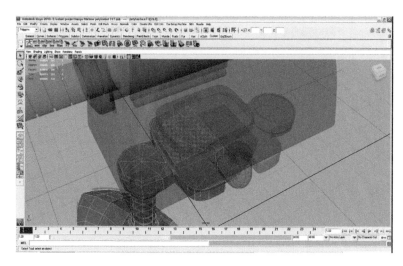

FIG 6.80

Next, **delete** the selected faces, this will leave you with a border edge which needs to be lined up with the high poly waist. We then need to **move** the vertices over the live high poly mesh until they sit at the bottom of the waist connector. We can then select this row of edges and **extrude** upward to create the waist.

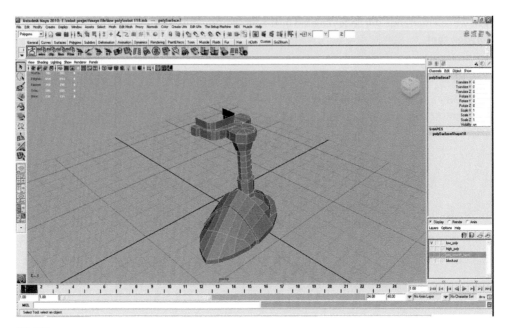

FIG 6.81

We make the lower groin area by simply stripping the support edges from a duplicate of the presmoothed object.

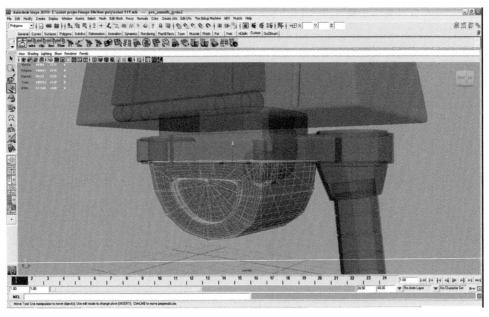

FIG 6.82

The front edges are then **beveled** and then the vertices are repositioned as necessary with the aid of the "live" high poly model.

The tail pipe is derived from the presmoothed pipe and converted for use by deleting edges, reducing down the sides from 16 sides to 8 and by removing the cut-in detail.

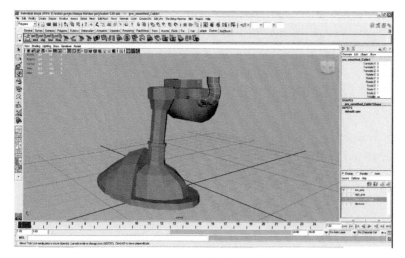

FIG 6.83

The torso is next to be modeled. Starting with geometry from the block-out torso, the front faces are **deleted**, and the resulting border edges are shaped to allow an edge extrusion for the door.

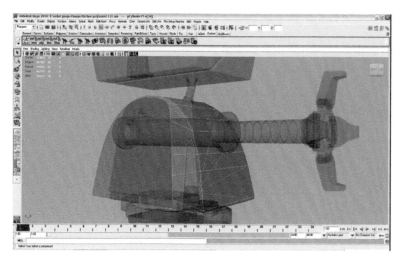

FIG 6.84

Those edges are then **extruded** and **scaled** to a point to create the hatch. Then rearrange the edges a little to avoid too many triangles in the center of the torso.

211

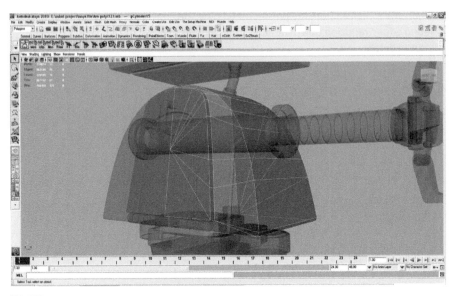

FIG 6.85

The front hatch is now modeled. Notice that I have also altered a few edges on the front of the torso itself.

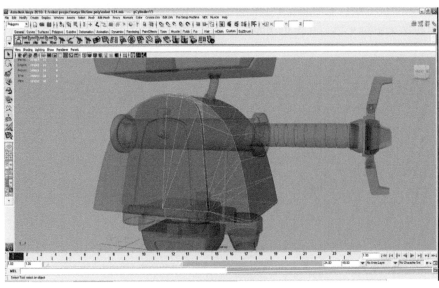

FIG 6.86

The hinge is created by duplicating the presmoothed version of the object. We just need to **delete** the cut-in edges, and reducing the number of divisions to 8, by deleting every other division. The faces shown are then **deleted** as they will not be seen.

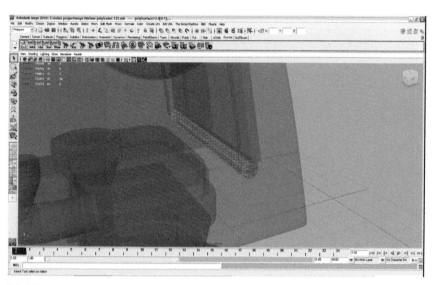

FIG 6.87a

The handle is just a duplicate of the presmoothed object. Just move the
vertices slightly and add a single loop to match the shape of the high poly
version.

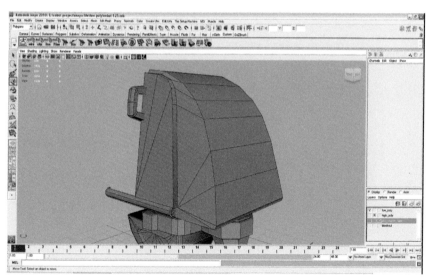

FIG 6.87b

Again, the shoulder component is just a duplicate of the presmoothed model.
Reduce the divisions and moving into place. The same process is performed
on the arm, making sure that we have a loop at each of the high poly
corrugations, so that he will deform in a way similar to the high poly model
when animating.

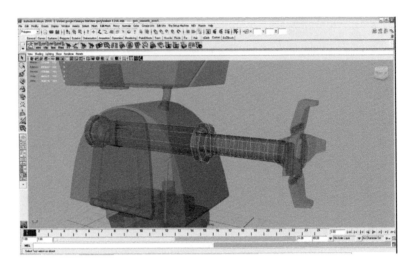

FIG 6.88

To build the hand we start with new geometry. A **cube** provides the base on which to extrude the area of the palm. We then **bevel** the corners, adding three segments to keep the curve of the high poly.

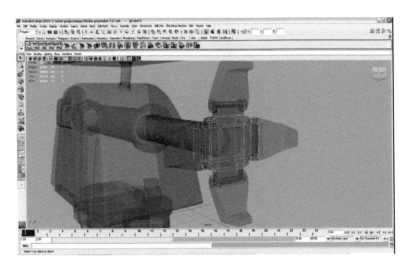

FIG 6.89

Next, we duplicate a single digit from the presmoothed version of the hand, which then has the supporting edges deleted. The remainder are moved to match the high poly shape.

A simple cylinder is added to give the bolt a little definition in the silhouette, and then the digit is duplicated and once UV'd, we will duplicate and rotate the digit three more times using the same **Duplicate Special** method used to create the high poly versions.

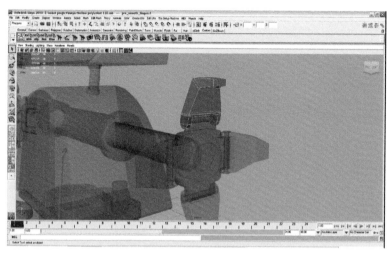

FIG 6.90

The center of the palm is now created with a cylinder. Keep this to10 sides so that it will match up with the palm component. The vertices are merged to form a single object, which is then combined with the palm component.

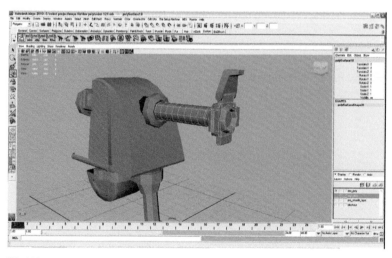

FIG 6.91

The head is modeled using the block-out geometry. As there are large amounts of supporting edges on the presmoothed head shape, it will be easier to start with a more basic shape. First we **delete** one half of the head (as it will be mirrored). Next, we **bevel** two edges to give the head a more rounded appearance, and finally we add a few edges so that we have the faces needed to extrude the mouth.

215

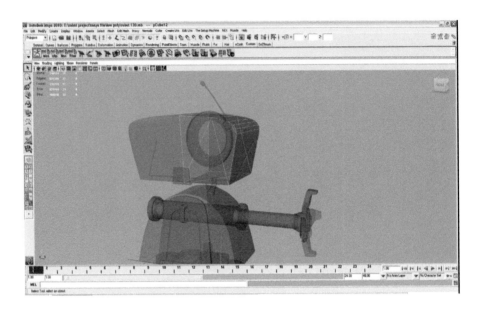

FIG 6.92

The mouth piece is **extruded**, then, with all of the center line vertices selected, the move tool options box is opened. Check **Move Axis: World** ,and uncheck **Retain Component Spacing**. Then by holding SHFT + X, **snap** the vertices to the center line. Using this method ensures that we have all vertices aligned, leaving everything tidy for mirroring later.

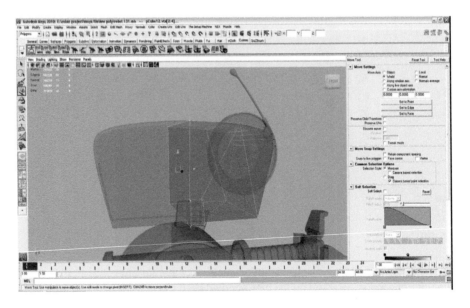

FIG 6.93

Next, we will take a look at the eye. I'm using a 16 division cylinder for this to keep the integrity of the curve. If the eye weren't such a focal point of the character, I may have been tempted to make it lower resolution.

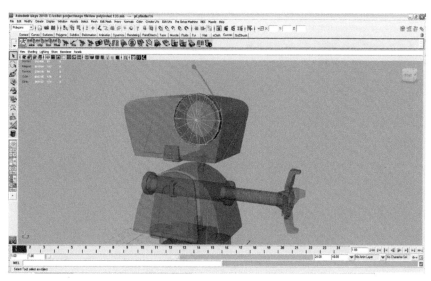

FIG 6.94

I have taken his eyebrow/antenna the presmoothed model and given them the standard reduction treatment we have been using. The antenna is also given several extra edge loops down its length to allow for greater flexibility when animated.

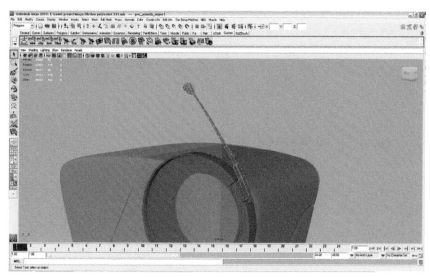

FIG 6.95

Next, we need to construct the low poly neck piece. Once again I have started with the presmoothed geometry, and using a process very much the same as the leg and arm sections just model the new version.

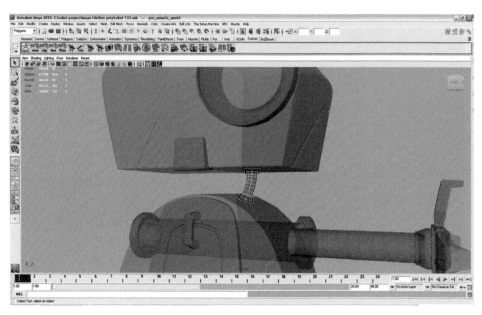

FIG 6.96

The final component is the ankle bolt, which is shaped from the presmoothed geometry.

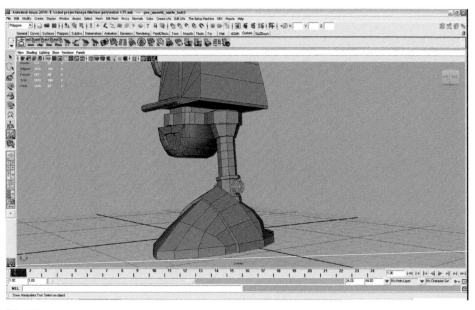

FIG 6.97

We now have our high and low poly robots with all components mirrored, etc.

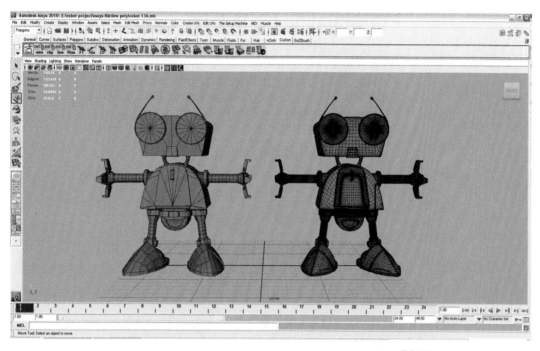

FIG 6.98

Finally, we just need to do a quick silhouette check to make sure both versions look similar even though they are different resolutions.

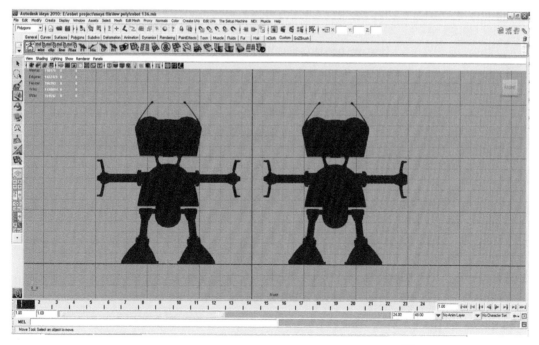

FIG 6.99

Unwrapping the Robot

To UV the robot, we'll begin at the foot. Here I have selected the foot object and assigned a checkerboard material to it. We use a checkerboard so that we can see if any texture that we apply to the model will stretch with the UVs that we apply. Sometimes it's hard to see stretching if a relatively flat colored texture map is used.

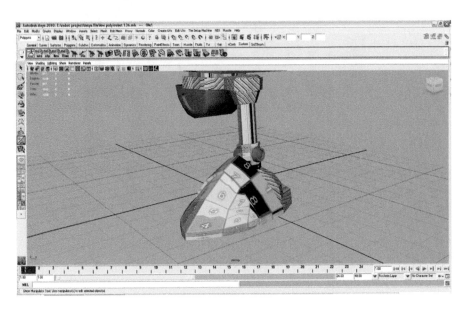

FIG 6.100

Next, we need to select the individual faces that we want to UV.

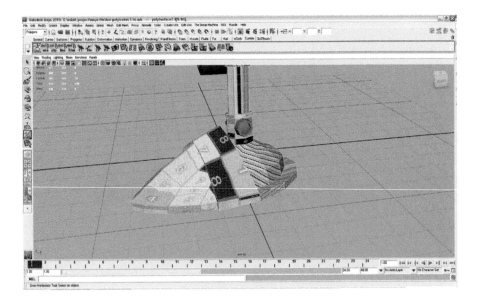

FIG 6.101

Then just select **Planar Mapping** from the Create UVs dropdown.

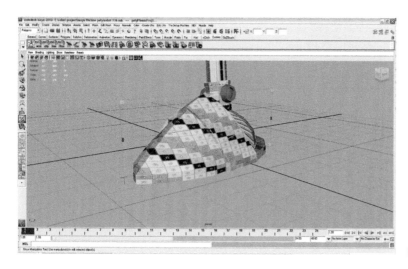

FIG 6.102

The planar projection will often be in the wrong orientation, clicking the red **T** will bring up a transform manipulator, which will allow you to reposition the plane. At this point, it is often a good idea to open your UV Texture Editor also.

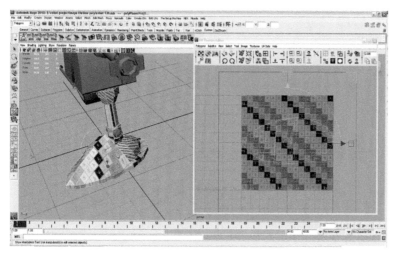

FIG 6.103

Change the selection to UVs, select one and then in the **UV Texture Editor**, CTRL + right click and select **To Shell**. This will select all the points in the UV shell that we just created for the foot – then move this to one side. We can then select all the remaining UVs for the leg object in the same CTRL + right click fashion, move those out of the way for now too. Finally we need to select **Border Edge** display and shade UVs both from the UV Texture Editor top bar.

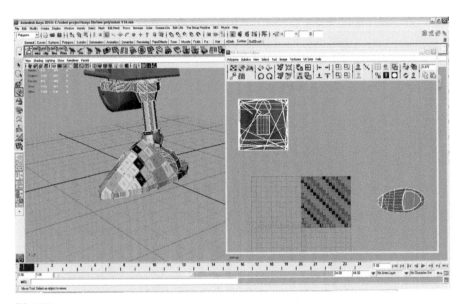

FIG 6.104

Next, **select** the loop that runs around the base of the foot.

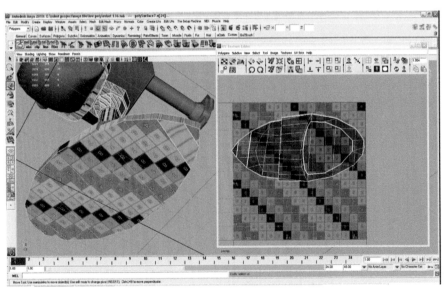

FIG 6.105

Next select the faces of the bottom of the foot and CTRL + right click to UVs. In the UV Texture Editor, right click **Select UVs**. Using the **Move** tool you should now be able to separate the sole of the foot shell from the rest of the foot shell. Notice that they are in blue (the correct way around) whereas the rest of the foot is red – the UVs will need to be flipped.

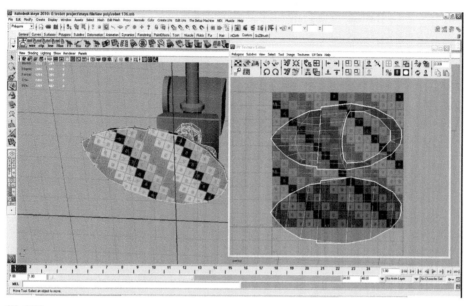

FIG 6.106

We have flipped the UVs and rotated the shell 180 degrees. Select the bottom
edge of the foot again, and in the UV Texture Editor, CTRL + right click to UVs.
Then deselect the UVs on the bottom of the foot and scale the border edges
of the main foot shell out slightly.

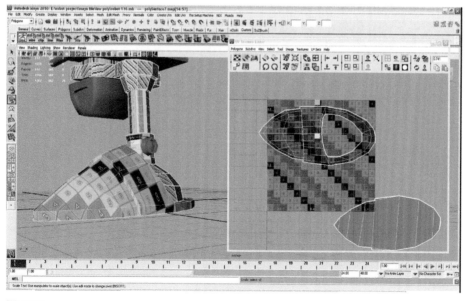

FIG 6.107

The UVs for this central edge need to be moved out slightly.

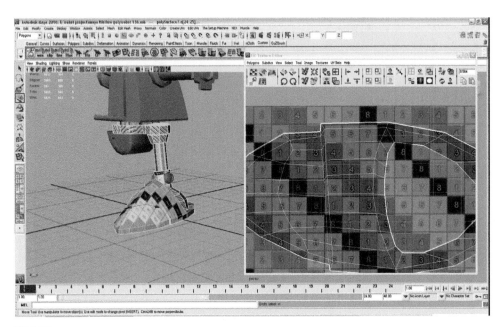

FIG 6.108

Now we need to start to move the other UVs a little, so that the checker pattern looks as even and unstretched as possible.

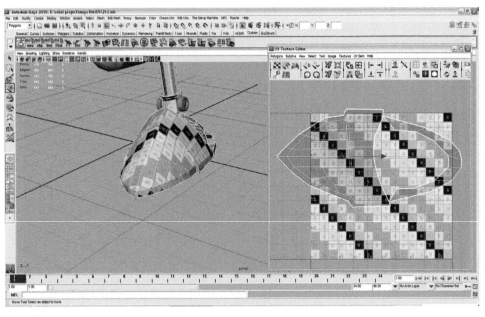

FIG 6.109

For the next step, I decide to **planar map** the faces shown, individually, using the same process as before.

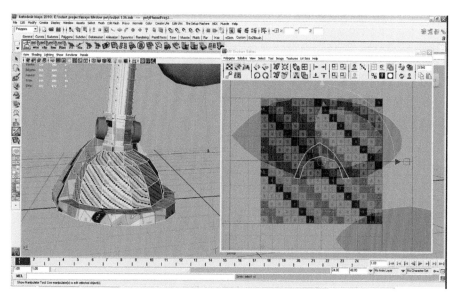

FIG 6.110

The back of the foot now needs to be **detached**, and some of the shells are scaled smaller, such as the sole of the foot. We scale the UVs smaller for areas like the sole of the foot as it will rarely be seen so it doesn't require the same texture space. We then move this off to one side.

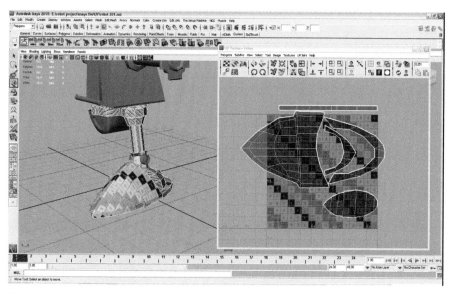

FIG 6.111

The faces for the next shell are selected. Due to the nature of the shape that we're UV'ing, I decide upon a spherical unwrap this time. Once again the red T is clicked to allow me to reposition and scale the projection. It's not perfect, but it's a good start.

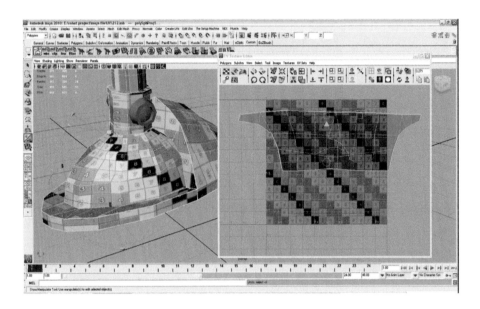

FIG 6.112

Select all the UVs and use **Unfold** (from the Polygons dropdown in the UV Texture Editor). You may need to modify one or two UVs to get it looking neat. Once complete, move the shell off to one side.

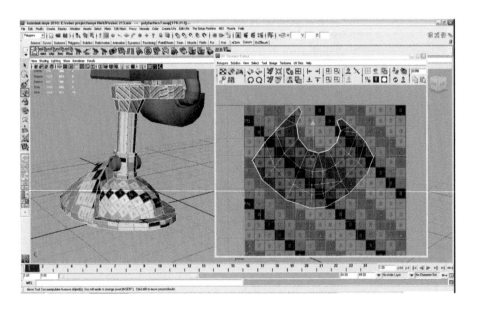

FIG 6.113

Once again using the basic shape of the model as a guide, choose the best style of mapping for the leg selection. Clearly a cylindrical map should be used for the selected faces.

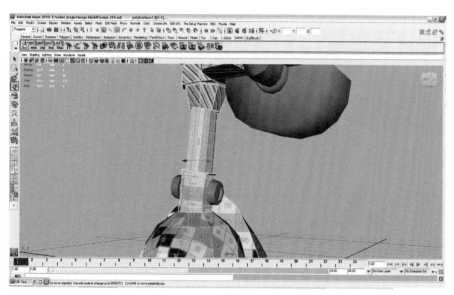

FIG 6.114

The projection is again manipulated until I am happy, then we move to modifying the UVs.

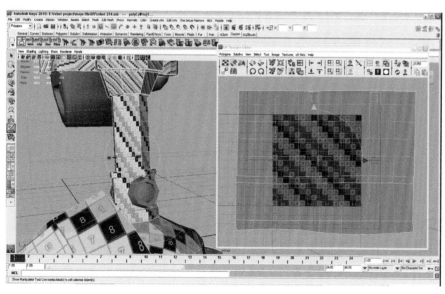

FIG 6.115

In this instance, I am aligning rows of UVs using the **Align UV** buttons at the top of the UV Texture Editor to help to neaten up the UV shell.

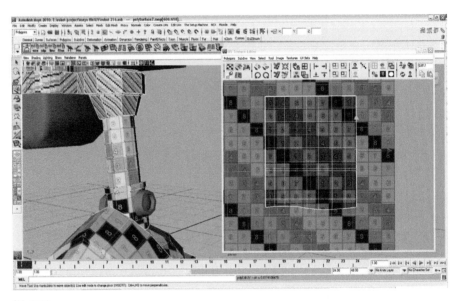

FIG 6.116

Next, let's finish up the UVs for the leg object.

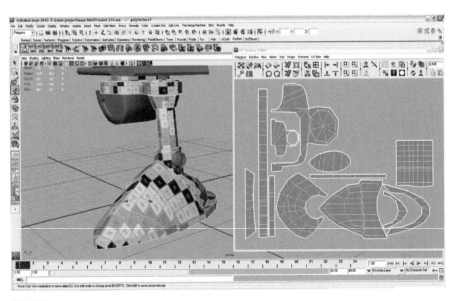

FIG 6.117

The checker material is assigned as a quick cylindrical unwrap on the ankle bolt, with a planar unwrap for the end caps.

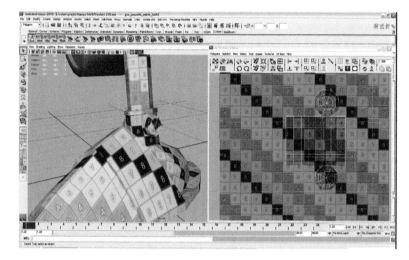

FIG 6.118

The same treatment is applied to the groin. A mix of **cylindrical unwrap** for the curved areas and **planar** for the flat areas. Notice that along with scaling down areas that will be mostly hidden or not frequently in sight, we are also beginning to think about texturing and areas such as the plate in the center of the groin should be detached from the main shell and scaled up. This will give us a better texture resolution, so that when we get into Photoshop, we will be able to add some nice details in the texture.

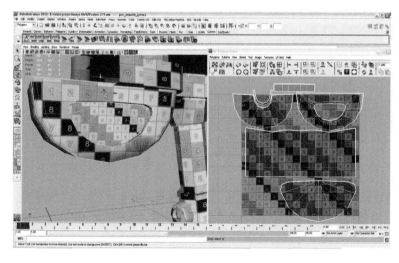

FIG 6.119

The rear pipe was simply done using a **cylindrical unwrap** on each segment and then the shells are stitched together. I would follow this method for a longer section of pipe, but it works well in this instance.

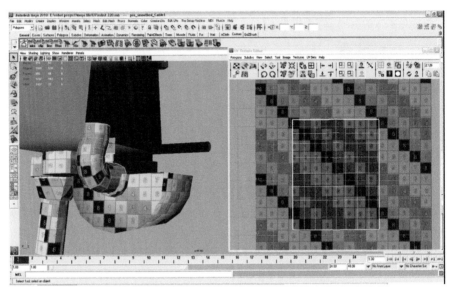

FIG 6.120

The torso is unwrapped using the same methods as the groin.

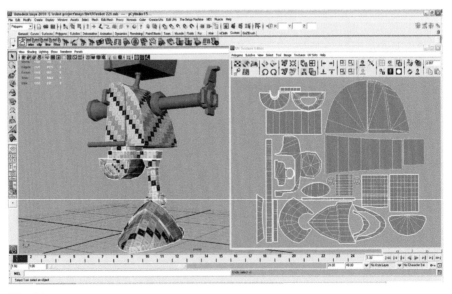

FIG 6.121

Next, we'll look at the shoulder piece and then the main cylinder of the arm.

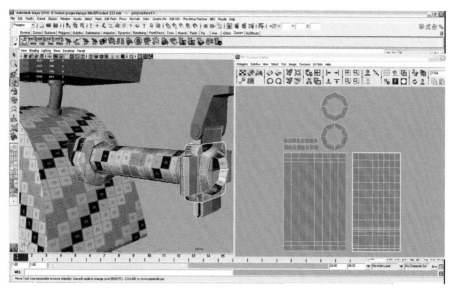

FIG 6.122

The palm is unwrapped with a combination of planar (for the two flat areas) and automatic mapping (for the edge). We then stitched these together, trying to keep the seams out of sight as much as possible.

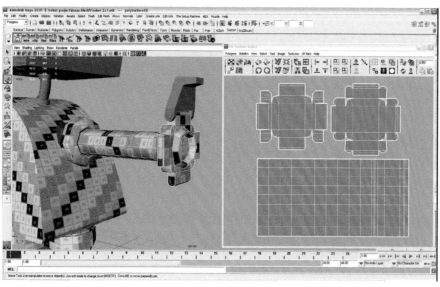

FIG 6.123

The head comes next. The mouth piece was detached and given extra resolution to ensure that we get good definition for the extra details that we are baking into that area.

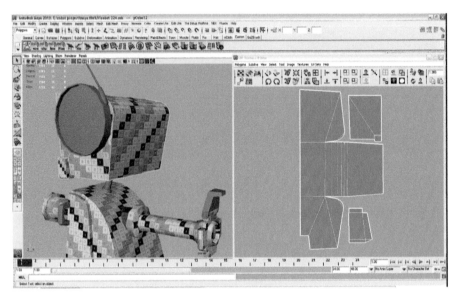

FIG 6.124

Next, we tackle the neck pipe, torso hinge, and handle using all of the same techniques as we have throughout this process.

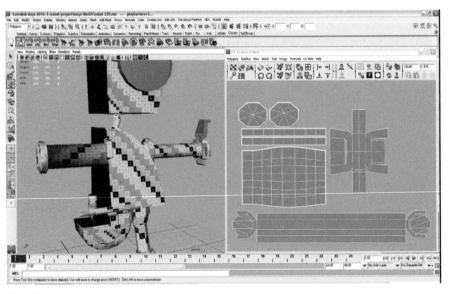

FIG 6.125

Now we can move onto the lonely finger.

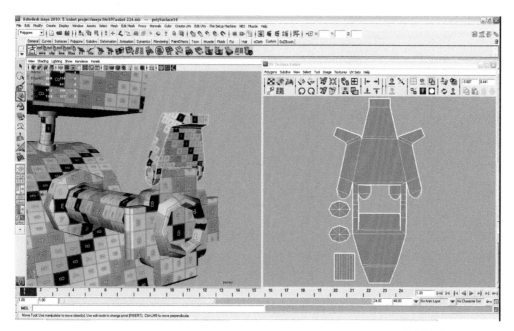

FIG 6.126

Finally, we UV the eye and antenna.

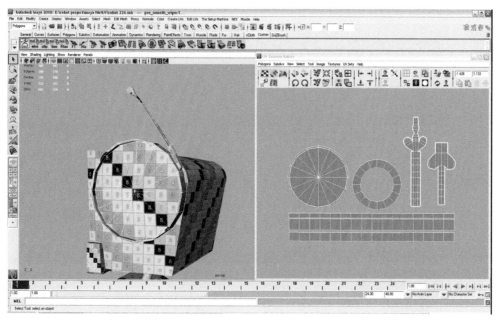

FIG 6.127

Now that we have every one of or parts UV'd, we need to arrange the UVs in the 0-1 section of the grid. Make sure that they all fit and don't overlap.

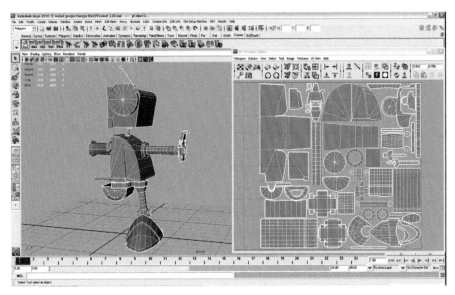

FIG 6.128

The last step in the UV process is to **mirror** any parts that are only half modeled, and place the UV shells outside of the 0-1 section. This is to help to eliminate seams in our normal map.

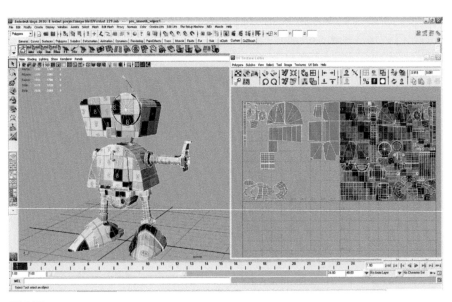

FIG 6.129

Baking the Texture Maps

For the texture bake section, first we begin by mirroring anything that requires it, so that we have a complete, high poly model of the robot. This is so that we have the correct shadows when baking the ambient occlusion maps.

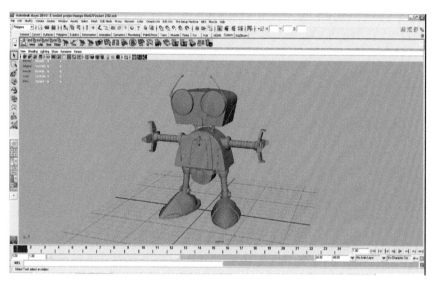

FIG 6.130

Next, we need to ensure that the normals on any floating geometry are facing outward, away from the model, otherwise these will not bake correctly.

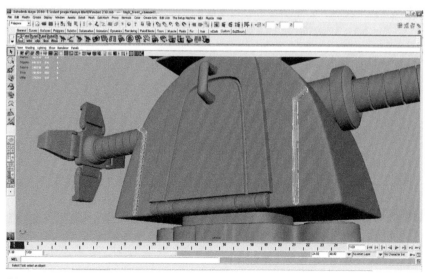

FIG 6.131

We then select an area of geometry and create UVs using the automatic mapping tool.

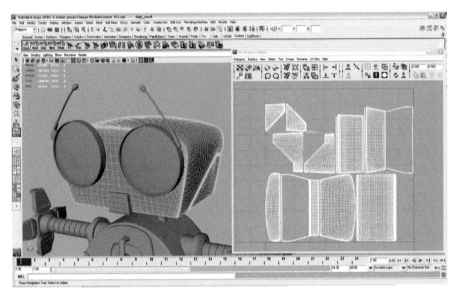

FIG 6.132

In the color menu, we select the **batch bake** (mental ray) options box and set it as shown before hitting convert.

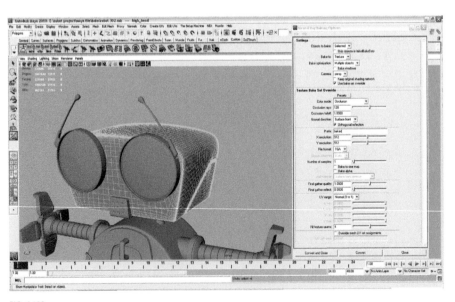

FIG 6.133

Then, we have our first AO bake. Maya will automatically assign a new material for the bake, which can cause issues in more complex high poly models with numerous parts. You can group objects together and bake them if you don't want a lot of material nodes though.

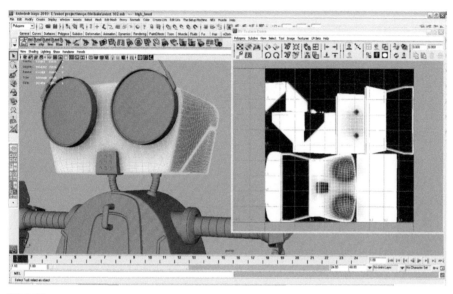

FIG 6.134

Now, in the objects material attributes open the **Incandescence Channel** .

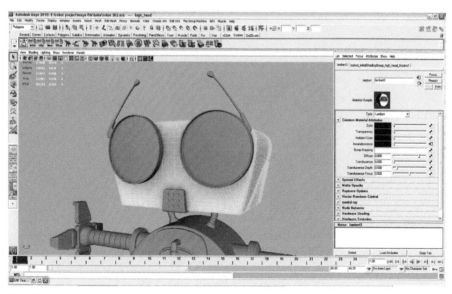

FIG 6.135a

In **File Attributes**, hit **edit** .

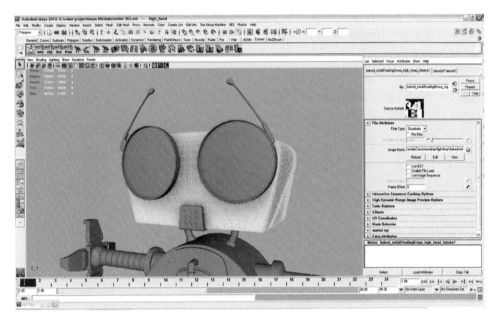

FIG 6.135b

This will then open the map in your assigned image editor – Photoshop, in my case.

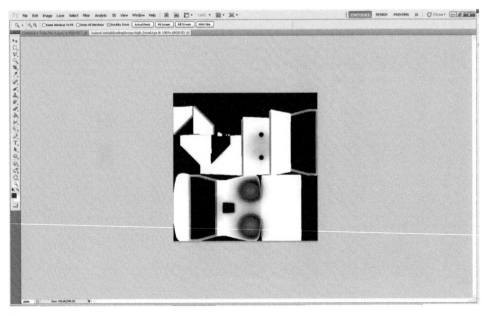

FIG 6.135c

Then just save the map somewhere you will be able to find it again. I save mine as a 24-bit .tga file.

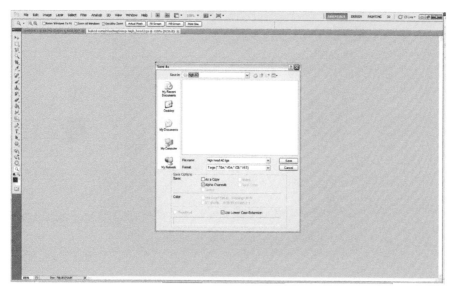

FIG 6.135d

Next, jump back into Maya, select the **Material Attributes Editor** again, Right Click **Incandescence** and **Break Connection** .

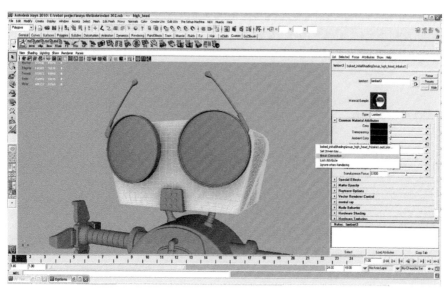

FIG 6.135e

Then, assign our newly created **Ambient Occlusion** (or AO) map to the **color channel** of our high poly object.

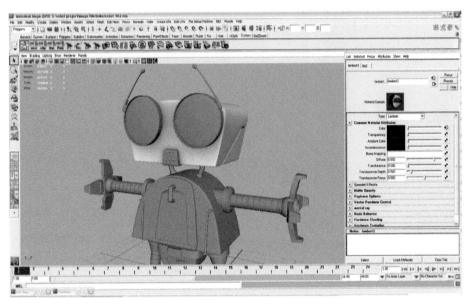

FIG 6.135f

We need to do this for each object in the high poly model that we will be baking normal information from, not necessarily every object on the model.

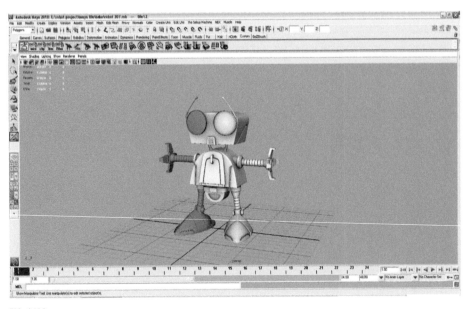

FIG 6.136

Then we need to **delete** the unnecessary parts for the normal bake, and combine chunks of the mesh in a sensible fashion. This is also a good point to organize your object names if you haven't been doing so as you have been modeling.

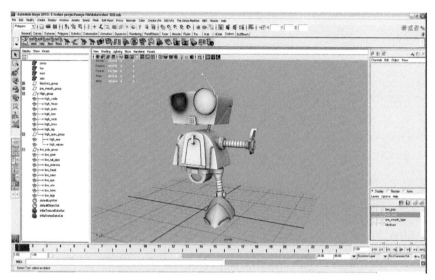

FIG 6.137

The dropdown line is changed to rendering and the low poly and high poly model layers are both turned on. Then the low poly torso is selected.

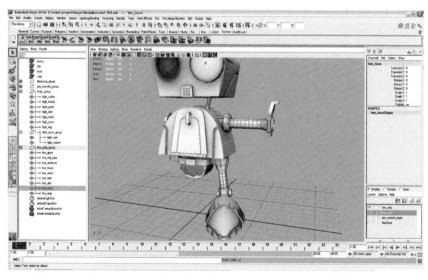

FIG 6.138

241

In the **Lighting/Shading** dropdown we select **Transfer Maps** .

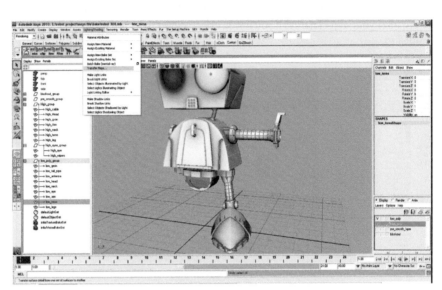

FIG 6.138a

This will bring up the **Transfer Maps option** box. First select the high
poly model and hit **Add Selected** in the source meshes, the low poly is
automatically loaded in the target mesh slot as it was the active object when
the transfer maps option box was opened. We select both normal and diffuse
output maps and set the destination folders for both, as well as changing the
file type to .tga.

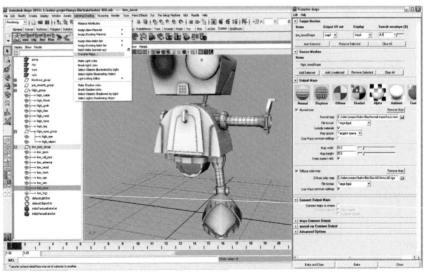

FIG 6.138b

Now we need to set the map height and width, and uncheck **Use Maya Common Settings**. Then open the **Mental Ray Common Output Settings**, change the **map size**, also increase **Fill Texture Seams** to 3.

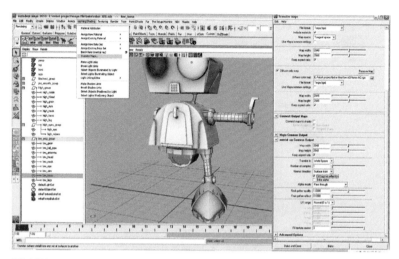

FIG 6.138c

Now we need to have a look at the envelope found in the **Target Mesh** es section, from the **Display** dropdown. We want it to cover the high poly version, but be a snug fit. The overall size can be adjusted in the search envelope slider, and individual vertices can be adjusted if necessary. Once we're happy with the envelope we re-select the mesh in the display dropdown. Next, we need to select all the edges of the low poly model and soften them before finally we hit bake.

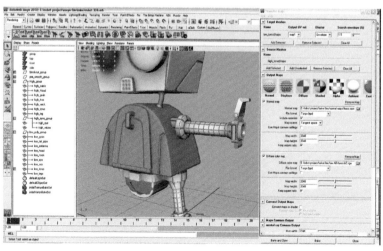

FIG 6.139

Now we assign a new material to the torso, and connect the newly created maps to the diffuse and bump channels, before previewing with the high quality rendering.

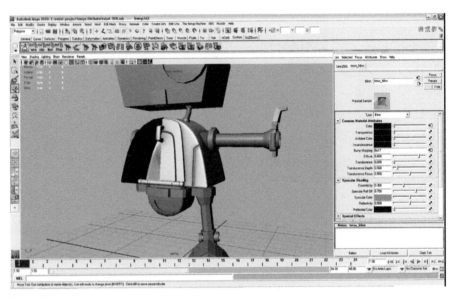

FIG 6.140

To get a true representation of the object, we need to delete the messy half of the mesh, and mirror across the good side. We need to merge the vertices to create a single object again to soften the resulting edge.

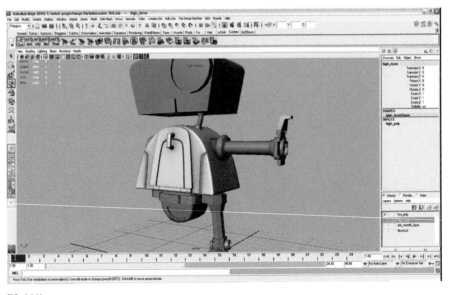

FIG 6.141

We then need to follow the same process on the rest of the parts of the model.

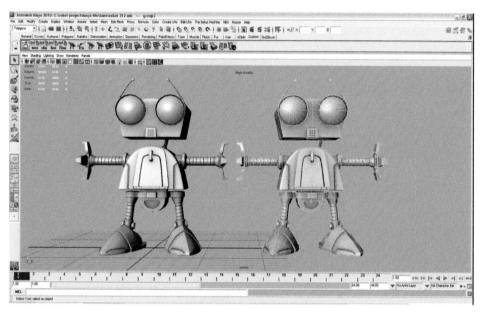

FIG 6.142

Next, open the normal maps in Photoshop, and stitch them all together to form a single image.

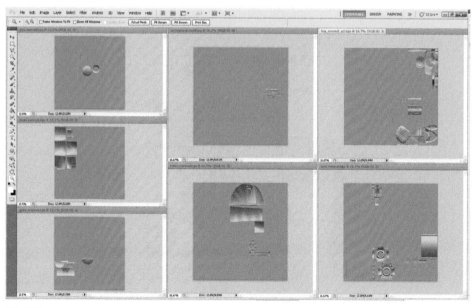

FIG 6.143

Once you've stitched them, all together, you should have something that looks similar to mine. Once you do, save it out as a .tga. We then do the same with the AO bakes that we have, but save these as a .psd.

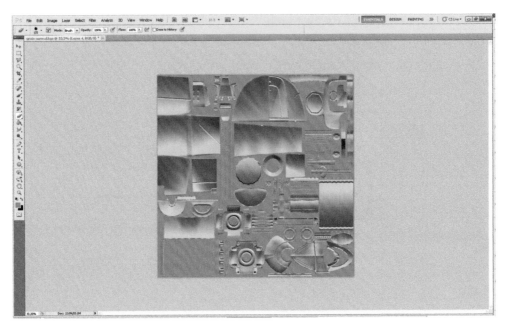

FIG 6.144

FIG 6.144a

Moving back into Maya we will need a copy of the UVs to lay over our AO .psd. We need this so that we can begin texturing. Select the low poly model and turn off the texture display in the UV Texture Editor.

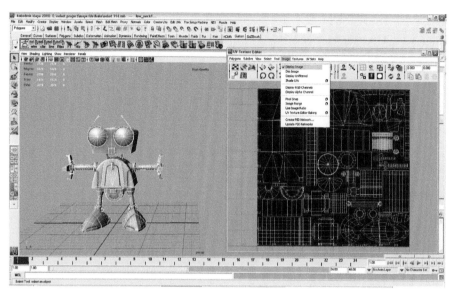

FIG 6.145

From the **Polygons** dropdown of the **UV Texture Editor**, select **UV Snapshot** . This will bring up the **UV Snapshot options box** .

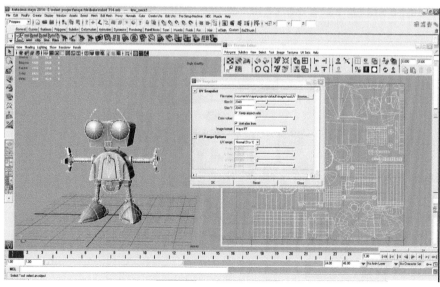

FIG 6.145a

Browse the file to the directory that you have your texture maps in and set the X and Y size to match the same as you have used for the Normal and AO maps. This time keep the file type as an .iff. This will preserve the transparency of the UVs.

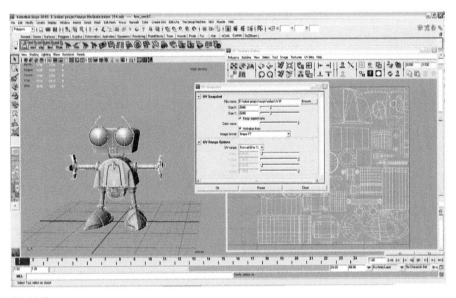

FIG 6.145b

Now we need to open the UV.iff in Photoshop and paste it over your AO layer. I tend to save this as Name of the project_diff_master. This is just a habit for me, but it makes sense.

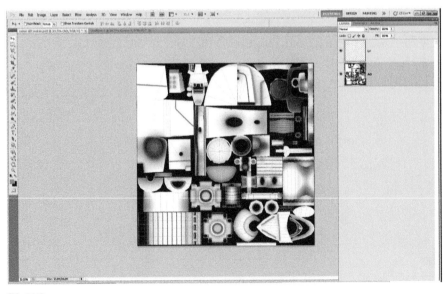

FIG 6.145c

Jump back into Maya again. We now need to select all of the parts of robot, duplicate them and combine them to form a single mesh. A new **blinn** (robot_blinn) is created and the stitched normal map imported into the **bump channel**. We then put the robot diff master .psd into the color slot. Next, **High Quality Rendering** is turned on, just so that we can see the normal map.

Our robot is now ready for texturing.

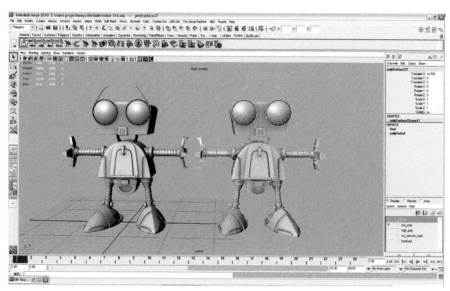

FIG 6.146

FIG 6.147

Texturing the Robot

Well done for getting this far – we're onto the final part of the build – texturing the robot.

In Photoshop, we first need to add a base metal texture underneath the UV and AO layers. As some areas of the texture will be mirrored, the metal is given a once over with the Clone Stamp tool to remove any noticeable imperfections. Once done, we then set the AO layer to multiply.

FIG 6.148

Next, we need to block in the basic colors for the different areas of the robot, on separate layers.

FIG 6.149

Create a new selection with the **Color Range tool**, using the **AO** as the **active layer**. Move the **fuzzyness** slider up until you have a clear distinction between the black and white areas.

Then **create** a new layer beneath the eye, and **bucket fill** it with an oily blue color using the selection created. Now reduce the opacity to around 30% of its full strength.

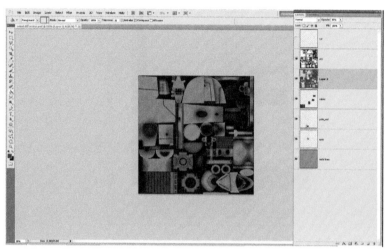

FIG 6.150

Now we begin to work back on our color layers. Set the red palm layer to overlay and create a new layer above it. Then, using a soft edged brush, paint in the center of the palm.

FIG 6.151

Next, we need to create the eye shine. We will do this using **lighting effects** from the **Filter** dropdown, under **Render**. The spotlight is placed directly over the eye in the preview, and the intensity is increased a little.

FIG 6.152

Let's tidy things up a little. Grab all the diffuse layers and place them into a folder before starting on the specular map for the robot.

FIG 6.153

Next, the base of the spec is the same metal texture, so we need to copy it, and put it in a new folder named Spec.

FIG 6.154

Now we need to use the color range tool to select the darker areas of the metal, this selection is then copied to a new layer and set to multiply.

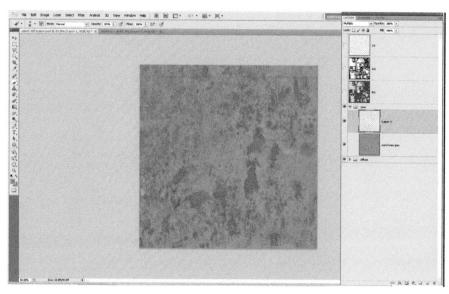

FIG 6.154a

We then use a high pass filter over the base metal to remove most of the noise and color variation.

FIG 6.154b

Next, the tint layer is copied and set to color burn at roughly 50% opacity. The Wand tool is then used to create a quick selection of the full black areas of the AO map and then that selection is filled with the Bucket tool in black just to neaten up the layers a little.

FIG 6.154c

Using their respective diffuse layers we need to create selections for the eye and palm area. We then save these as a selection.

FIG 6.154d

The selection is used to **erase** the dirt layer, and anything inside the selection in the tint layer. We then use it on its own layer to fill with a lighter color.

FIG 6.154e

255

Now we need to select all of the cable parts and with the aid of the diffuse layer, erase the dirt and fill with a darker color.

FIG 6.154f

The layer is then run through the sponge filter, just to break up the flat gray. The layer is then set to multiply.

FIG 6.154g

The resulting map is saved as a .tga file and we turn off the Spec folder. Now, turn on the diffuse folder and save that as a .tga also (using a relevant name). Then we go back into Maya and plug the maps into the correct channels of our robot mesh. Finally, turn on **high quality rendering** and we're done! Congratulations!

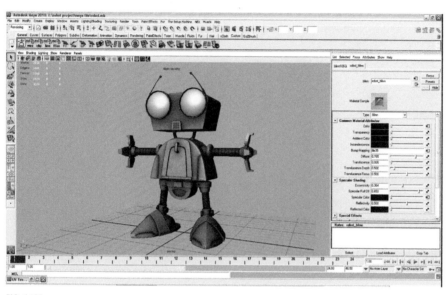

FIG 6.155

Now we have the basic model of the robot textured, let's take it a little further. We're going to use the Marmoset engine to create a better looking render. Feel free to skip this section if you like, although at some point you'll want to learn how to make your models look the very best, for your portfolio or applying for jobs.

FIG 6.155a

As you can see in the concept art, the robots eyes and palm areas both glow. To achieve this effect we'll need to go back to Photoshop. Create a new layer and a new selection from using the **Magic Wand** tool on the eyes layer and the red palm layer. Next, we need to **Bucket Fill** the background making it black.

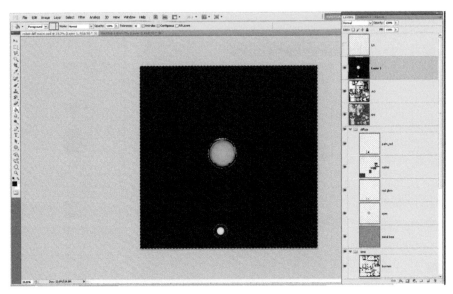

FIG 6.156

Now, switch to Quick Mask, to refine the selection.

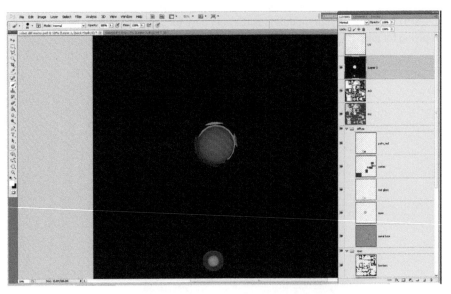

FIG 6.157

Keeping the remaining background painted black, **Save** the image as a .tga.

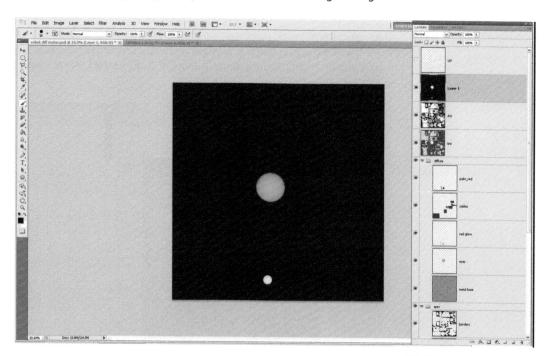

FIG 6.158

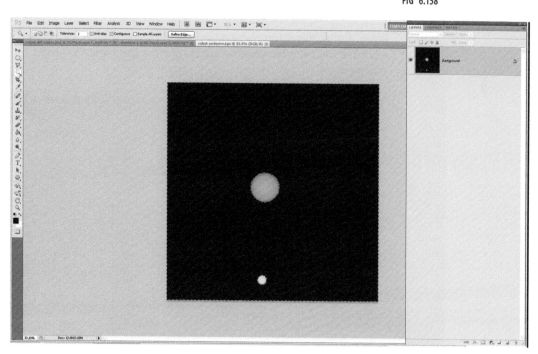

FIG 6.159

Next with the emissive .tga you've just created, use the **Magic Wand** tool to create a selection of the background.

Then select the channels palette, and create a new layer. This new layer will be alpha 1, **invert** the selection that we have and with a soft edged circular brush paint in the highlights. Reduce the brightness slightly and then save the .tga as a 32-bit image.

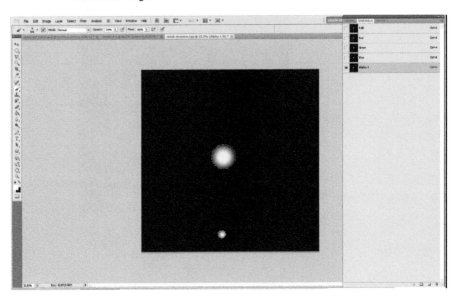

FIG 6.160

Before putting this all together in Marmoset, we need to export the mesh of robot as a .obj. Once complete we need to open up Marmoset and import your mesh.

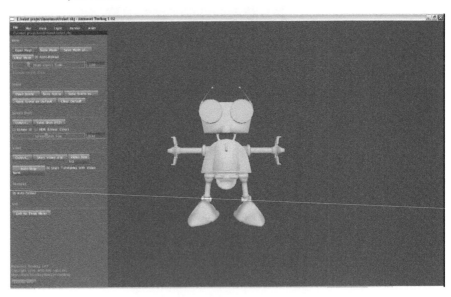

FIG 6.161

Next, we need to create a new material and load our maps into it. Then select
your mesh (robot), select the material, and hit **Apply Selected Material** .

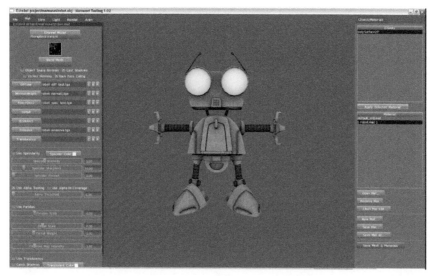

FIG 6.162

Next, we need to move to the **Light tab**. Because we want to show off the
emissive material we will select **Night** from the **pre-assigned lighting types** .

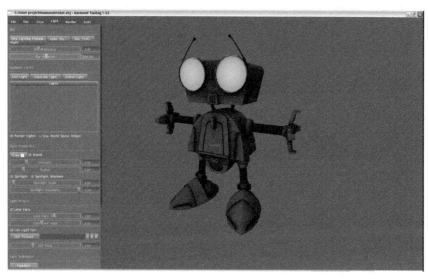

FIG 6.163

Now, go back to the **Material** tab. We need to check **Use Specularity** and adjust the **Intensity Sharpness and Fresnel** until we have something that we are happy with. We also need to change the specular color to warm the metal tones up a little.

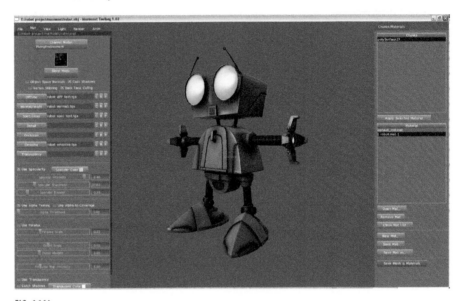

FIG 6.164

Now we need to go back to the **render** panel. Next, we need to adjust some of the post effects. First adjust the **Sharpness** until you are happy with the result. Then check the **Bloom** box and adjust the **Gamma** until you get a nice glow from your emissive material.

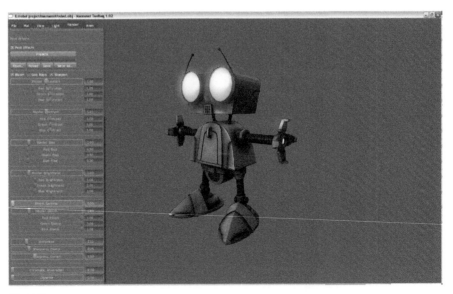

FIG 6.165

In File, set your output folder for screenshots, and if you are happy with your setup, then hit **F12** (or push the button).

Marmoset has many more features that can be used such as **Turntable Recording** and **DOF rendering** (Depth of Field Rendering), but for our robot we shall keep it simple, and just add a faint black outline in the view panel.

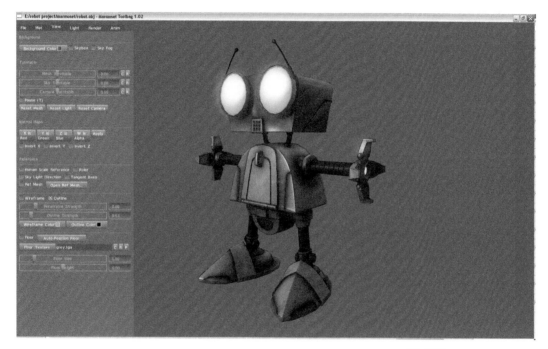

FIG 6.166

Finally, here's our finished render.

CHAPTER 7

Gallery

I'd like to show you a few images to inspire you, which have been created by a few of my friends.

FIG 7.1

FIG 7.2

Here, Johal Gow has taken some generic photographic references and produced a stunning disaster render. See more of his work at www.johalgowcg.com

3ds Max Modeling for Games
© 2012 Taylor & Francis. All rights reserved.

265

FIG 7.3

This concept was created by Andy Manns, THQ.

FIG 7.4

Mr. Bad Guy was created by John Gibson who is currently the head of the
Character and Animation department at Pitbull Studio Limited.

FIG 7.5

Ceated by John Gibson.

FIG 7.6

Nick Igoe created this World War 2 bomber for the short animation **Mila** .
Details of the film can be found at www.MilaFilm.com and there is also a
fantastic opportunity (at the time of going to print) for you to get involved in
making the film too. Just log onto www.3d-for-games.com/forum, register,
and then send a message to me **Andy Gahan**, and we'll get you started on
some of the assets.

FIG 7.7

This render of a Japanese building was created by Rob Blight for the game Sudoku Logic created by The Pixel Bullies (www.ThePixelBullies.com). Again, there are opportunities for you to get involved in making their games on the forum too.

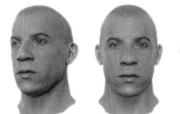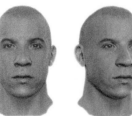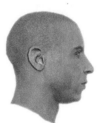

FIG 7.8

Created by John Gibson.

FIG 7.9

Wheelman character line-up created by John Gibson.

FIG 7.10

Created by Johal Gow.

FIG 7.11

Created by Johal Gow.

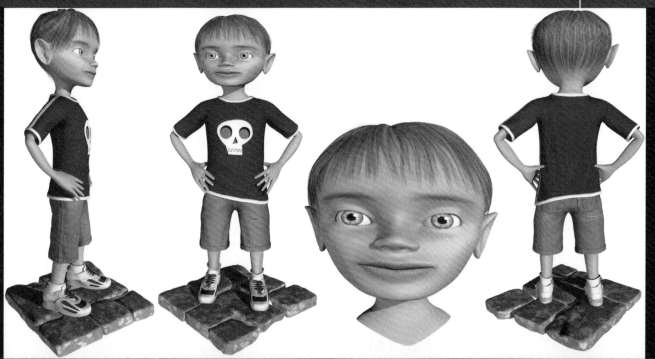

CHAPTER 8

Modeling the Character Robert Using Zbrush

Welcome to the character modeling tutorial. Here, I will show you my creative processes from the base modeling of our Robert character in Maya, through to the detailing of him in Zbrush. Hopefully, this will give you a good insight into how to go about building a character from a concept sketch.

FIG 8.1

3ds Max Modeling for Games
© 2012 Taylor & Francis. All rights reserved.

First, let's talk about my character pipeline. This usually depends on the structure of the character itself. In most cases, I start with a base mesh created in Maya that has good clean topology and UVs. I only really rely on Zbrush for the high resolution sculpting stages, especially for this project.

Some character artists prefer to block out their characters in Zbrush using **Zspheres** and then they rework the topology later. I prefer to do most of my mesh building within Maya first as I can quickly model a character and get it into the game engine to get a rough example of what it could look like in-game and quickly decide whether it will work or not, saving valuable time if it looks like it won't.

Whichever approach you choose, there is always a considerable back and forth between Maya and Zbrush throughout the modeling process, so settle on whatever works for you.

This tutorial will assume that you are familiar with the basics of navigation in Zbrush and a modeling package.

Maya Modeling

For this character, I'll be creating the base meshes using simple polygon modeling techniques. These are very similar in most 3D software, so feel free to use whatever is most comfortable for you if Maya isn't your main modeling software.

This will be an animation mesh. By that I mean that the topology will be laid out to support animating the character. With this in mind, I'll be making sure there are enough polygons around the joint zones to allow proper skinning later on. For this tutorial, I won't be covering skinning or in-game setup and will be only concentrating on the low and high meshes for the boy character. Skinning and in-game setup is a more specialized skill which most of you probably won't be interested in, certainly to begin with.

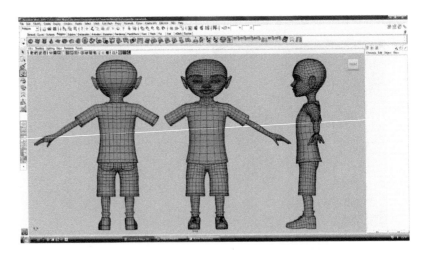

FIG 8.2

Starting with the legs I have created a **primitive cylinder** with four subdivisions along the Y axis. After resizing it to the correct length and diameter I further subdivided again. Selecting the first edge and converting the selection to Edge Loop (**Select > Convert selection > Edge Loop**).

I then rescaled each edge loop until I achieve the desired leg shape. For the sock I simply extruded the bottom edge a few times to create the basic shape. This can be refined later on within Zbrush.

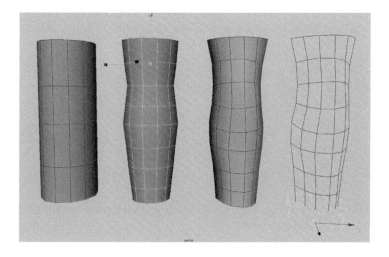

FIG 8.3

Exactly the same modeling process was used for the arms. It's worth mentioning at this point that as this is an animation mesh, the topology around the knee and elbow joints will need more subdivisions. This is to allow for better skinning and will prevent the model from distorting around these joints when animated.

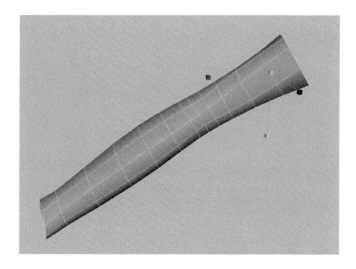

FIG 8.4

The hand was built using a cube as the base volume. It was subdivided to form the palm of the hand, then subdivided again with each finger face extruded and subdivided to create the fingers themselves. Once happy with the overall shape of the hand I next rounded off the fingers by repositioning vertices and edges until I achieve the desired smooth topology.

Even though Robert is a cartoon character, it still needs the hand (and other body parts) to be slightly realistic, so I always use an anatomy reference. I found it very useful to cast my own hand in plaster and then I always have the perfect reference which I can view from all angles. The cast being detailed enough to show all the creases, wrinkles, and veins, which is useful for more realistic sculpts.

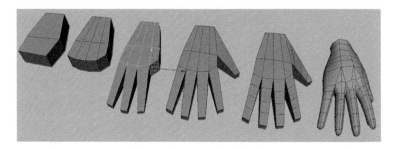

FIG 8.5

The t-shirt and shorts were also constructed using basic primitives and simple polygon modeling techniques.

For the t-shirt I created a primitive cube, created a second edge and added the sleeves by extruding each of the top sides. I then repositioned the vertices until I had a basic t-shirt volume. By subdividing, repositioning more vertices and subdividing once again I got a basic shape that I was happy with. The shorts followed exactly the same procedure, except this time I added the pocket, belt, and trouser turn-ups by using simple extrusions. These meshes could also have been built in Zbrush using primitives.

Time permitting I sometimes like to use both modeling methods, practice makes perfect after all.

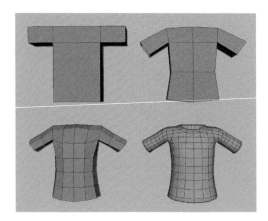

FIG 8.6

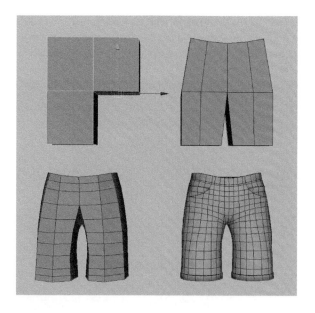

FIG 8.7

The head started off as a primitive sphere, which had a neck tube attached to it. I subdivided this and roughed out the basic volume by adding edges and repositioning the vertices until the basic head and face shape was achieved.

I then took the mesh into Zbrush and adjusted the shape a little, then re-importing it back into Maya. This was quicker than doing all the shaping in Maya alone. Simple spheres were created for the eyes and positioned within the eye sockets.

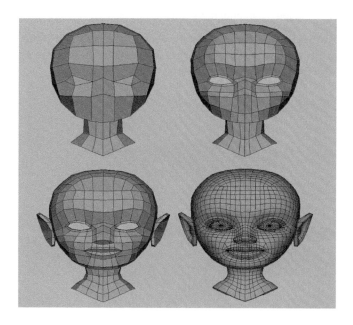

FIG 8.8

The next task for the head is to export it back into Zbrush and make some more refinements to the shape and to adjust the proportions of the model. This is to get the resulting mesh more like the concept images.

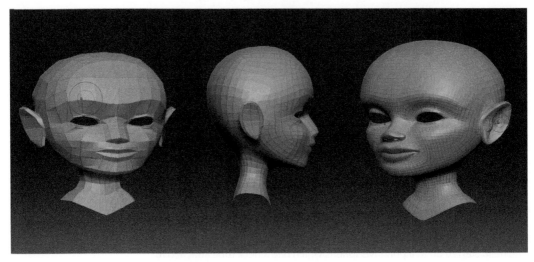

FIG 8.9

Using the **Move** brush I tweaked the shape of the head mesh making the forehead wider and making the ears stick out a little more. I also added a slight tilt to the eyes and moved them down slightly.

I then added a little more definition to the lips and nose before subdividing the head mesh. Subdividing the head two more times gave me enough polygons to shape the interior of the ears and the lips.

The nose took more time to complete, widening the nostrils and giving them more depth. The head was imported back into Maya for the final tweaks, such as filling in the backs of the eye sockets.

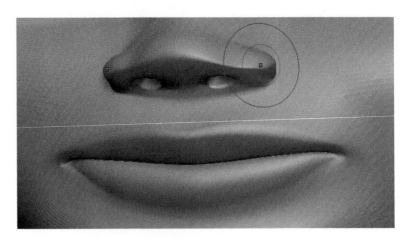

FIG 8.10

Myfinal Maya modeling task was to create the training shoes. For these, I created a rough shoe shape from a cube by adding extra edges and repositioned the vertexes.

Further subdividing and modifying the vertices gave me the rough shape I was looking for. After creating the UVs, I exported the mesh into Zbrush.

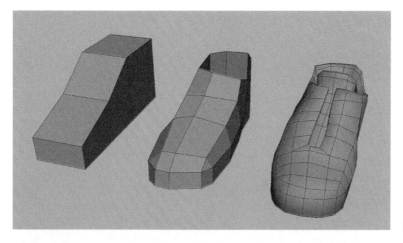

FIG 8.11

By using reference photographs of various types of training shoes, I hand painted a mask for the sole and inverted it. Next I opened the Deformation menu and Inflated by a value of 3. Using a combination of hand painted masks, I was able to quickly create all the panels and lace holes.

Since this is a nonrealistic character, I chose not to include any wrinkle or stitching detail on the training shoe. The tongue for the shoe was created in Maya and imported as a separate subtool into Zbrush.

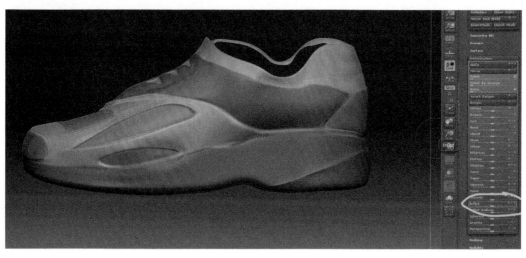

FIG 8.12

Once the sculpting phase was completed, I used a plugin called **SubToolMaster** , which can be downloaded from the Zbrush website. This is a handy plugin as it allows more control over your subtools. Once installed into the Zplugins folder it can be accessed via the Zplugin menu. By selecting the Training Shoe subtool, I used it to copy and mirror it in the X axis.

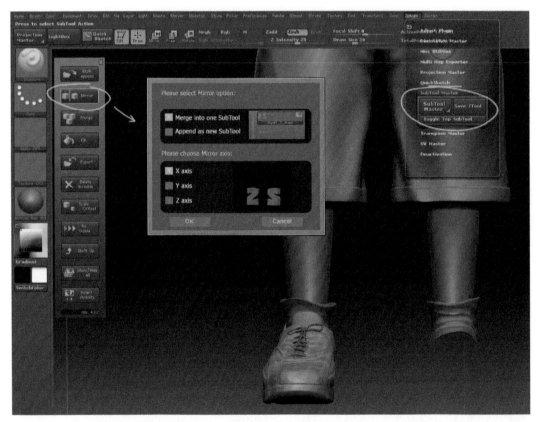

FIG 8.13

UV Maps and Texturing

Once all the component meshes have been completed, I then create all my UV maps in a program called Unfoldmagic3d.

I use this software because it is specifically designed for mapping UV texture coordinates quickly and easily. I find the tools in Maya and Zbrush not necessarily ideal for creating UV coordinates for my models.

Unfold 3D allows me to select and cut the edges where I want to unfold the mesh and further tweak the results until I am happy with the end result.

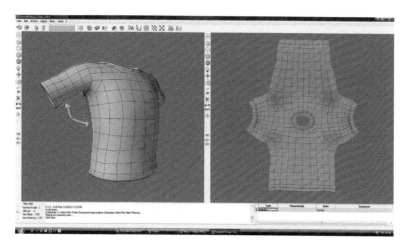

FIG 8.14

Once all of the meshes have been unwrapped and re-imported back into Maya, I can now position all the UV shells and merge them into one texture page. Here I try to keep the pixel density equal and utilize as much space on the texture page as possible. For the head, I will make the UVs larger to allow more detail to be painted on that area of the texture. The face is one of the first things the viewer sees on a character, so we want to have more texture detail in this area.

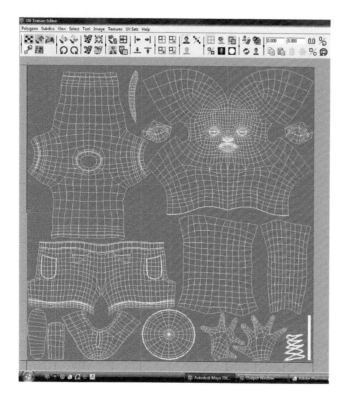

FIG 8.15

I like to create my textures double the size of the final in-game texture as it allows me to paint more detail without losing much when scaled down. Also you never know if a high version is needed for the client or your portfolio. With this in mind, I have made the base texture 2048 × 2048.

I exported the UV map from Maya and opened this in Photoshop to use as a template to paint from. Here I painted the base colors of each body part.

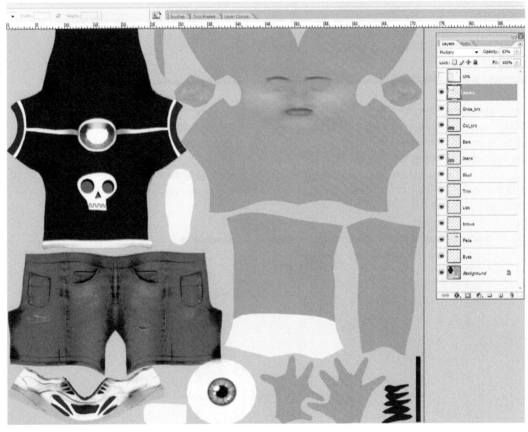

FIG 8.16

The texture for the shorts was taken from a photograph of some jeans. I then made it fit the UV shell and I added some seam and damage details painted on top.

The face and eyes were painted by hand.

The training shoe had an ambient occlusion map created within Zbrush once I'd sculpted the panel details. I overlaid this on the base color to produce the panel edges and shadows. I repeated this for the t-shirt and shorts too.

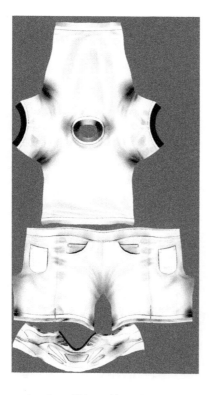

FIG 8.17

Now that all of the meshes have UVs and have been positioned nicely, my final task was to re-export all the meshes as **.obj's**. I make sure to name everything correctly (head, arms, etc.) to avoid confusion later on.

Zbrush Detailing

I'm now ready to continue with the project by taking the base meshes and start to sculpt them in Zbrush.

So the next task was to import all the individual character meshes into Zbrush and check them for any errors.

Now that all the component meshes are saved as individual subtools, I'm ready to start adding details such as the folds in the fabric for the t-shirt and shorts and some minor wrinkles on the face, arms, and legs.

I want to keep the detailing on any areas of skin as subtle as possible, but just because I'm creating a cartoon character I shouldn't ignore the rules of anatomical construction – maybe just bend them a little.

The first task for the t-shirt was to subdivide it a few times so that I could paint a crisp mask (hold CTRL and paint) for the sleeve edges, waist edge, and the upper arm panels running from the end of the arms to the collar. Remember that the polygon count increases by a multiple of four for each subdivision. For this I will turn on symmetry in the X axis, so I only have to paint on one side of the mesh.

Once I was happy with my mask, I inverted it (**Tool > Deformation panel**)and next inflated by a value of 1. Then using the smooth brush on a very low setting I tidied the edges as they had some noise from the extrusion process.

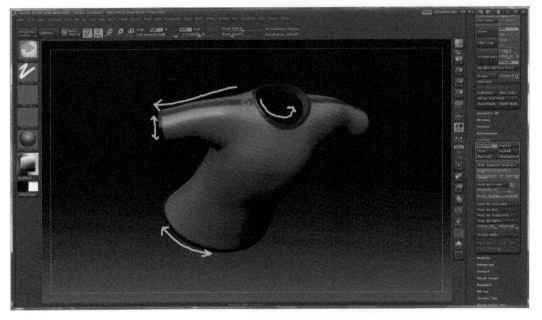

FIG 8.18

FIG 8.19

You could always do this in your preferred 3D software on the t-shirt mesh before importing it into Zbrush. Some artists like to create a medium polygon mesh from their in-game version and add these extra details before importing the meshes into Zbrush.

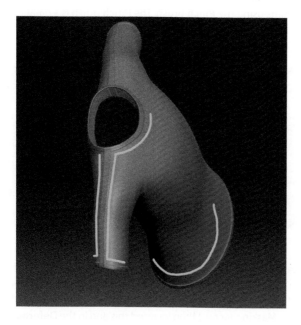

FIG 8.20

Now that I have my panel edges defined, I can start sculpting the folds. Folds can make or break a character model and I always make sure I have proper reference pictures to help my sculpting.

Over the years I've built up an extensive library of reference photographs, either taken from the Internet or photographs of friends or family posing in various articles of clothing.

Switching back to subdivision level 1, I can begin to rough out the folds using the Standard brush.

Zbrush has a large set of powerful brushes, one for almost any job. These are controlled by the **Z Intensity slider** – A value of 0 has no effect and 100 has the most effect. Using **Zadd** and **Zsub** settings, I push and pull the areas of geometry to achieve a folded cloth look. I am always referring back to my reference pictures, while keeping my brush strokes fluid and natural.

It's quite easy to make folds look overworked, which is why sculpting at a low subdivision level allows me to quickly block in the overall shapes. I'll only increase the subdivision levels once I start to refine the individual parts.

If you're not sure what each brush does, hover the cursor over one, press CTRL and a dialogue box will open, explaining what it does. Take some time to explore all the brushes to see what they do.

I always create a new layer so that any work I do can be either turned off or reduced in intensity. Working in layers allows me to quickly erase errors or make subtle changes when needed, without altering the base subtool.

Using the Standard brush I add definition to the folds and finish some of the fold highpoints using the **Pinch** brush. The **Pinch** brush is a great for adding nice sharp edges.

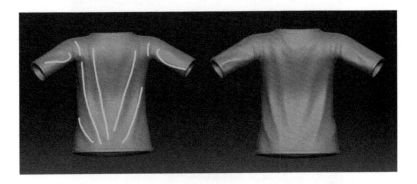

FIG 8.21

The final task on the t-shirt is to add the skull logo on the front. For this I created an alpha map taken from the main t-shirt texture. I then imported this into Zbrush, inverted it and applied this as a mask using **Create Mask From Alpha** in the Masking menu. I then inverted this and in the **Deformation** menu and Inflated this by a value of 2 – making sure I'd created a new layer first!

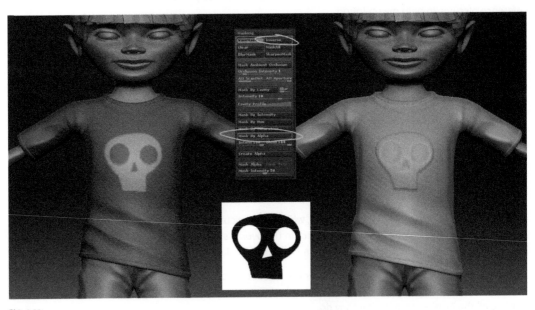

FIG 8.22

Now I can turn my attention to the shorts. These where handled in the same way as the t-shirt. A mask was made to create the pockets, zipper, and side leg seems then the folds added using the Standard brush, finished with the **Pinch** brush. I also decided to add some stitching using the Stitch1 brush.

You can make your own stitch patterns, but for this project the standard pattern is fine for my requirements.

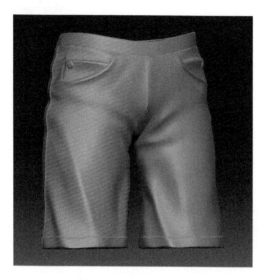

FIG 8.23

Moving onto the legs, I added folds to the socks using the basic brush and added sharp edges to some of those folds using the Pinch brush. I also used the move brush to modify the edges of the socks to make them asymmetrical. I added a few flesh creases in for the knee cap and behind the knees, although these are covered up by the shorts in the final model.

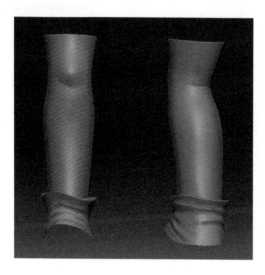

FIG 8.24

Hair

Now I want to take a look at the hair, which for this character I will create in Maya.

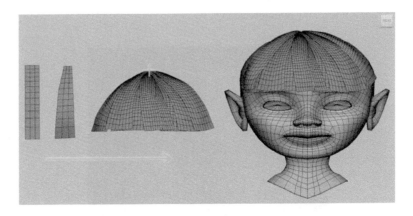

FIG 8.25

My base hair model was created from a primitive polygon plane. I created it 3 polygons wide and 12 high. By moving the vertices, I alter the plane and make it banana shaped. I taper it toward the top, making sure it has some UVs and that the pivot point is at the top.

By copying it and rotating around the pivot point I am quickly able to create the fringe section of hair. I changed the scale of every section to make the fringe look uneven – I also subdivided it.

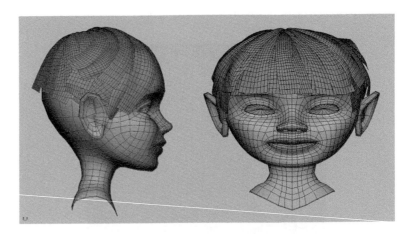

FIG 8.26

I repeated this procedure to make a side section and also a rear section. I copied and flipped the side panel in the Y axis, to create the opposite side.

Once again I scaled some of the hair strips and changed the amount of bend on several of the strips to give the hair a more natural and flowing look.

This part of the project was quite time consuming as I was constantly changing the scale and shape of various hair strips, until I was happy with the final result (or until insanity gripped me).

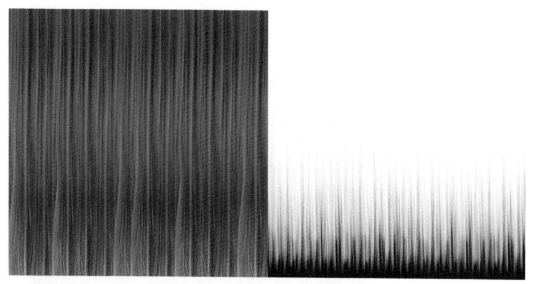

FIG 8.27

For the hair texture, I used a stock hair texture I had (why recreate the wheel after all). This had an alpha channel applied to it. I also randomized the UV placement of a number of hair planes to prevent patterns appearing.

When I'm nearing the end of sculpting work on a character, I find it useful to look at the surface in simple terms of shape and shadow. Traditional artists have always used the trick of squinting at their sculpture to reduce the visual information and concentrate on form and shape. Zbrush, being the all singing and dancing software, has an inbuilt feature which emulates this "squinting." To use this function either squint or select Preferences > Draw and press VBlur. Adjust the Radius as you see fit.

Final Stage

Now that most of the sculpting work has been completed, I will go back over all the forms and sharpen them up whilst checking for any errors.

Once the sculpting has been finally "adjusted" it's time to pose the model, for this I'll will use the **Transpose Master plugin**, downloaded from the Pixolgic website (www.Pixologic.com).

Transpose Master is a handy plugin which steps each subtool in the model down to their lowest subdivision level, so the entire model (including subtools) can be posed together, this is accessed through the Zplugin menu.

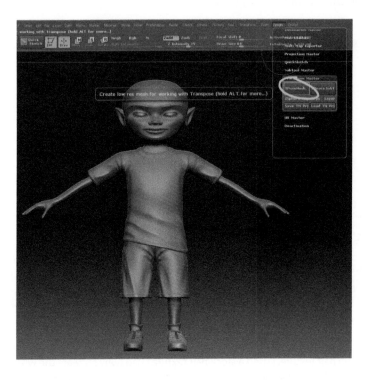

FIG 8.28

All of the subtools have now been grouped together into one mesh at the lowest subdivision level. By using simple topological masking to mask off different sections of the model in combination with **Scale, Move**, and **Rotate** functions, I can easily pose and orientate the mesh as if I were bending a wire armature.

For this character, I only need to widen the leg stance and place the hands on each hip with some slight head and face adjustments. I first create a new layer so that all my posing work will be separate from the base t-pose which I want to preserve.

There are several ways to create masks in Zbrush, and once again I'll use the easiest method. Holding down the CTRL button and using the Standard brush to paint the area I want to mask. Using the leg as an example, I hold CTRL and click and draw on the canvas to quickly create a masking box around the main part of the leg. Since I have symmetry turned on this will also affect the other side of the leg too. I finish painting the top of the legs by hand, then inverse the mask and add some blur also, this helps produce a softer bend.

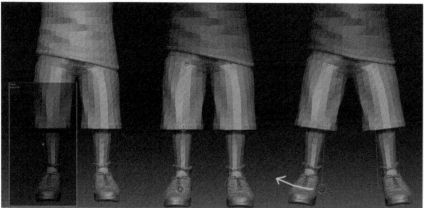

FIG 8.29

By selecting either **Move, Scale**, or **Rotate** and clicking and holding the left mouse button, I can now draw a transpose line from the hip down to the foot. The transpose line looks like an orange line with three circles along its length. I like to think of it as a skeleton. This tool can be challenging for new Zbrush users, but after some practice it will become second nature.

I can now select the red circle at the end of the transpose line on the foot and move it to the side. The leg bends at the hip joint. You can redraw the skeleton again in a new position if the need arises or close the skeleton by clicking the **Draw** button.

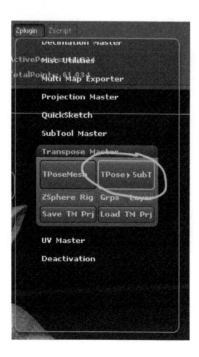

FIG 8.30

I repeated this procedure for the feet, arms, and head. The final task is to go back into the **Transpose Master menu** and click on **Tpose-subT button** .This will return the mesh back to its original subtools and also transfer the new pose to them, this may take a few minutes depending on the complexity of your model and how many subtools it has.

Posing the model has produced some deformed areas, under the arms and elbows so using the Move tool and Basic brush I repair these areas so they didn't look pinched and out of shape.

After several cycles of refinement, I'm happy with the final pose and can now apply my textures to the sculpt.

Importing and Applying the Textures

I saved my Photoshop texture out as a .jpg and imported this into Zbrush via the Texture menu. Textures always have to be flipped (Flip V button) after importing them as Zbrush always inverts them in the Y axis. I select each Subtool in turn, click on the Texture Map menu and click inside the empty gray square top left in the menu. This opens another menu box allowing the texture to be selected.

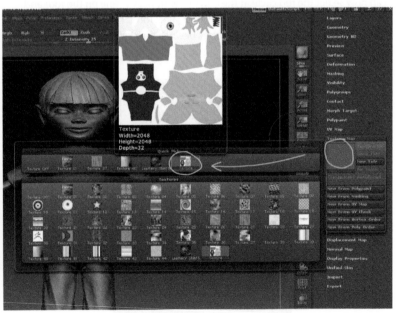

FIG 8.31

Once the texture had been applied to all of the subtools, I selected the material menu and applied the basic Skinshade 4 material. Now I can see the texture correctly.

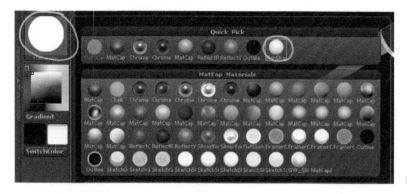

FIG 8.32

The same procedure was used when applying the hair texture, although Zbrush doesn't show alpha transparencies. There is however, a button within the **Tool: Texture Map menu** which is named **Transparent**. Clicking this will apply transparency to everything that is black within the texture. The results are poor at best so I'll leave the hair without any transparency mapping.

FIG 8.33

Rendering

Now that the model has been posed, my final task is to produce a render. For this I'll use both Zbrush and Maya with some adjustments applied in Photoshop. I won't go into much detail about rendering as this could fill an entire book by itself.

FIG 8.34

So, sticking to basics, the above image was rendered within Maya, two directional lights where used, one pointing down with shadows turned on and the other light pointing up to give some under lighting. The image was rendered using mental ray at 3000 pixels square, from several different views.

FIG 8.35

The second image was rendered using Zbrush, using the standard settings for best quality rendering and the standard SkinShade4 material.

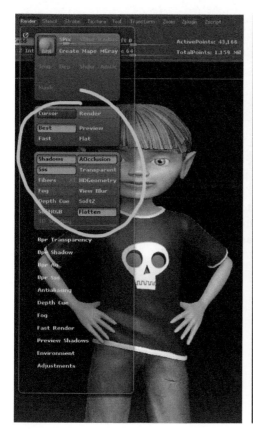

FIG 8.36

FIG 8.37

I tuned on **Shadows, AOcclusion**, and **Sss**, making sure the Best button was active. Then clicked the Render button and waited for the render to complete. The settings of these can be adjusted further for greater quality and effect, but I just stuck to the basic settings.

In the Document menu, I exported the rendered image to my desktop and opened it in Photoshop to tweak the cropping and refine the image using **Color Correction ,Brightness** ,etc.

Final

This concludes this tutorial. I hope it was useful seeing the creative process that I used to create the character from the concept art.

FIG 8.38

There are many approaches to building characters and every artist has his or her own pipeline and methods. Now that you've seen my workflow, why not experiment for yourself and also compare the methods of other artists.

CHAPTER 9

Modeling the House

For this chapter, we will be modeling the house for our scene. As you can see, we have some nicely detailed concept art, which shows us exactly what we need to produce.

Looking at the concept images we can see that the main materials for the construction of the model are wooden planks, glass, windows, doors, and tiles/corrugated sheeting for the roof areas.

Start by gathering reference for all these materials. High resolution images are best as you really need to see the detail. Also, images that are as front facing (or top down) will be better for texture reference as you won't have to work as hard to correct them.

The elements in the concept, like the windows, should not be illuminated as we will be creating the asset in a neutral setting. Light glows and effects can be added at a later stage.

After you have a good amount of reference, create a modifier set (see Chapter 3 for full details) to use for this chapter and call it "Chapter 8." The tool set should include: Edit Mesh, Edit Poly, UVW Map, Unwrap UVW, as well as some standard modifiers such as Bend, Taper, and FFD 2 × 2 × 2.

FIG 9.1 The house concept art.

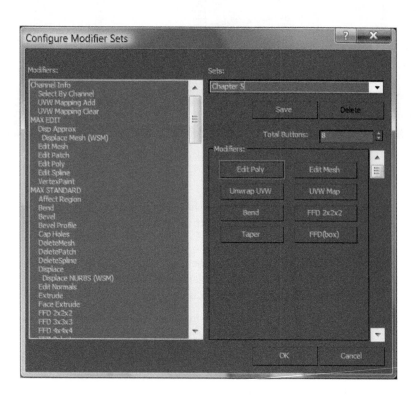

FIG 9.2

The latter sets are not essential but will come in handy should you wish to loosen up the form when the asset is constructed. Either way, try to keep the buttons down to a manageable number that you will actually use when modeling an asset of this type.

Next, create block-out objects as rough estimates of scale and color for the house model, then group them together. The bounding dimensions should be approximately: length 700, width 900, and height 700. Exact dimensions are

FIG 9.3

not essential as the model can be scaled later on, just focus on attaining the correct aspect.

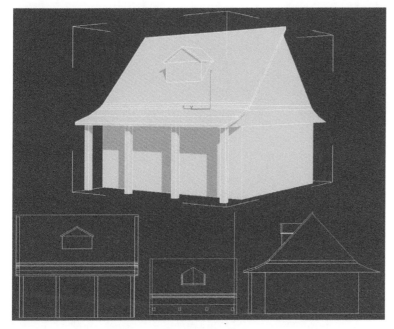

FIG 9.4

Blocking out an object can help you to work out the best method of creation. In this instance, we have windows and doors as separate objects. This means that the bulk of the house, the walls and roof, can be one object, and as such will use the same UVs and texture map.

297

We will create the main structure first. Study the concept again and you should notice the front and rear of the house are the same. This means we can make half the structure and rotate a clone of it to complete the shell of the house.

Start by creating the front of the house, including the roof and the right side wall.

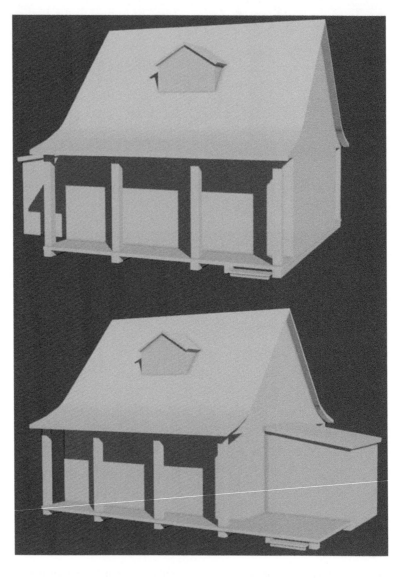

FIG 9.5

As mentioned earlier, the model can now be cloned and rotated 180 degrees. Attach the two halves, weld the vertices and add the outhouse section and the additional pillars as shown in Fig. 9.5.

The image shows the front and rear views of the model.

Before moving on, refer to the concept art and adjust the scale and angle of any surfaces you are not happy with.

Save the file and tidy up the UVs so they fit in the same texture page. Surface types can be grouped together so the outhouse roof and main building roof can occupy the same texture space.

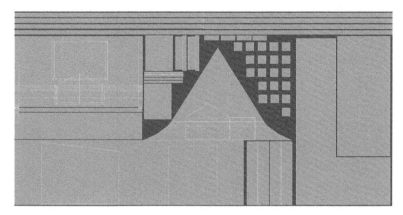

FIG 9.6a

As there is a lot of texture information to cram into one page here, we can move from the standard square texture page to a rectangular one. Texture pipelines in game engines work along the principle of the power of two, so that being the case, make the texture width double its height. The example shown here is 2048 × 1024. This is pretty big but it can be halved later if needed.

Remember to keep high res versions of all your textures in case you need to add or change any detail. Smaller versions may be needed for various reasons ranging from engine requirements to machine strength (to speed up rendering).

FIG 9.6b

Now the bulk of the building (and its texture work) is complete. Smaller scale detailing such as the windows and doors can now be constructed. The rough

FIG 9.7a

scale can be appropriated from the block out model and refined using the texture work of the building as a reference point.

Be sure to leave some additional space for the final parts of the concept – the satellite dishes, the solar panels, etc.

An example layout can be found in Fig. 9.7b.

FIG 9.7b

For the next step, we need to place the windows in place as instructed by the concept images.

Once the front is complete, clone and rotate the windows and doors to the other side. Next, rearrange the layout as suggested in the concept. If you have not already done so, put both materials in a Multi-Sub object (house in slot 1, windows in slot 2) and attach everything together into a single mesh.

FIG 9.8

This completes our simple house. Next we'll look at polishing your scene and a few modeling projects you can take on for yourself to fill it out.

CHAPTER 10

Polishing Your Scene and Modeling Projects to Complete

n this chapter, we will bring together the various elements we've created to make a scene.

The first thing we need to do is look at grounding, as this will provide a literal common ground for the objects to share. In the scene concept image, we can see the house and the surrounding area. We have the house, the foliage, and flora, but what we are missing is the ground and the fencing to give us a population plane and to separate foreground from background.

Looking at the concept we can see three types of fence – all similar but varying in scale. We won't need the large fence, so we can focus on the fence directly connected to the house, and the fence running parallel to the house. These are easy to make (create from a cube and add length segments, pulling up every other vertex to create the saw tooth effect). These can be mapped using the house texture for continuity purposes. We will need two objects that will be used to make the fence lines and as many variants as you feel are needed (texture variants to break up tiling, damaged panels, etc.).

3ds Max Modeling for Games
© 2012 Taylor & Francis. All rights reserved.

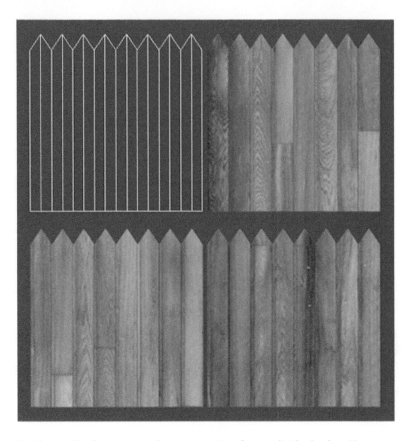

FIG 10.1a

For the smaller fence, create the section piece from individual cubes. These can then be slightly offset and rotated/scaled to provide an aesthetic in keeping with the house style. As with the larger fence, create enough variants to mask any obvious tiling.

The scale between the two types should resemble Fig. 10.1b.

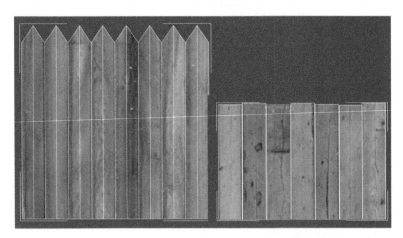

FIG 10.1b

304

The scene can now be assembled. Begin by merging in the house object and placing a plane underneath it. This plane will be replaced later.

Now, create a targeted camera, close to the floor with the house just a little off to the center (see Fig. 10.2a).

FIG 10.2a

Right click on the camera name tag, and from the drop-down menu select **Show Safe Frame**. This will create a yellow square around the camera clipped to show only what will be rendered.

Adjust your zoom and placement to compensate for this change in view.

The view as it stands lacks a little drama, so experiment with the camera controls to create something more dynamic. Try to stick with the following commands; **Roll Camera (rotate), Truck Camera (pan), Perspective**, and **Orbit Camera (rotate within view)**. The dolly distance should not be changed as we will need to place other object in front and behind the house.

An example of this can be found in Fig. 10.2b.

The camera is now set and population of the scene can begin.

It's important to set the camera first before we populate, so we can add only what we need to the scene and nothing more. This saves time with the population and rendering, but more importantly, the scene is only as complex as it needs to be.

Using the fence panels we created earlier, populate as seen in Fig. 10.3a, paying attention to the concept art.

FIG 10.2b

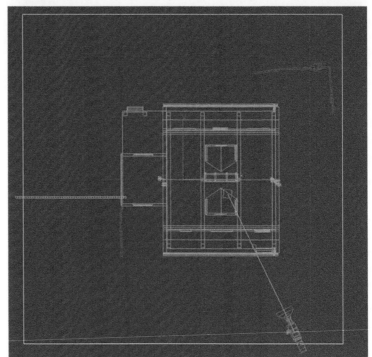

FIG 10.3a

In camera, the geometry looks like Fig. 10.3b.

So, while the camera gives away no gaps or spaces, the view from above shows that the layout is actually quite bare. Both views are required, so from this point on, work with a split view of at least two viewports in 3ds Max.

FIG 10.3b

When you are happy with the position of the objects, the placement can be fine tuned for better effect. This can be done in the camera view (this is my desired technique).

Next, bring in the palm tree and the invention to color it. The machine should be closest to the camera as it is the smallest asset. It will be the focus of the render, so it needs to have compositional prominence.

FIG 10.4

Adjust the layout and camera slightly to reflect this.

FIG 10.5

The palm should go in-between the machine and the house to help establish a foreground and background.

The floor is now noticeably absent. **Create** a **plane**, approximately 200 m² and map it with a grass material. When you're happy with it, create the paving stones. These can be made from cubes and chamfered/smoothed to give a better lighting profile. Map the path with a stone texture.

FIG 10.6

308

All the major elements are now in place and we can set the ambience. Go to **Rendering > Environment >** and under **Global Lighting** set the ambient to a low, cool color such as RGB 4, 8, and 10. Next create a **Skylight (Create > Lights > Standard > Skylight)**. Move this above the scene and set the RGB to a cool color higher than the ambient level, maybe something like 12, 17, and 28.

FIG 10.7

Render the scene and the result should be something like Fig. 10.7 if your settings were similar to mine.

To achieve the gradient effect seen in the image, create a gradient material and change the **Mapping** slot to **Screen**. Now go to **Rendering > Environment: Background**, and check **Use Map**. Then in the open slot choose the gradient material you have just made.

The ambience is now set. This is as dark as the scene will get. We don't need to return to rendering the scene until we set up the lights and atmospherics.

Low-level population is next. Bring in the grass and small bush objects and populate them on the grass plane. Do this in the camera view, so that you only place them where they are needed. Focus the density in the open areas around the palm and the invention.

With the objects set, work can begin on the more advanced aspects of the objects materials. Starting with the palm, we can add the rainbow effect caused by the invention by using a composite material and a gradient.

Go into the Palm leaf diffuse slot and change **Bitmap** to **Composite Material**.

Keep the current material as a submaterial when prompted.

FIG 10.8

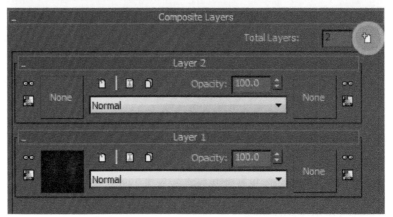

FIG 10.9a

When the composite slot is created, change the **Total layers** number to 2 as shown in Fig. 10.9a. In the new layer, in the empty slot on the left hand side, click to create a **Gradient Ramp** material. The right hand side slot is for a layer mask should one be required.

Now add a **Gradient** material in the **Self-Illumination** slot. Darken the color #2 tone to a near black and change its position from 0.5 to 0.25.

Now, go back to the gradient ramp in the diffuse slot.

Change the mapping channel for this material to 2. Then change the gradient type to radial and adjust, and then add colors to create a spectrum as shown in Fig. 10.9c. This image also shows the palm leaves from above, when mapped with the gradient ramp.

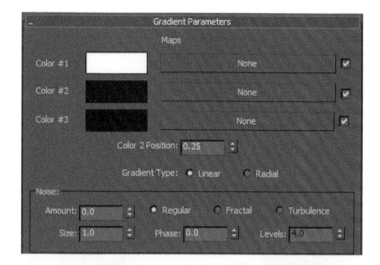

FIG 10.9b

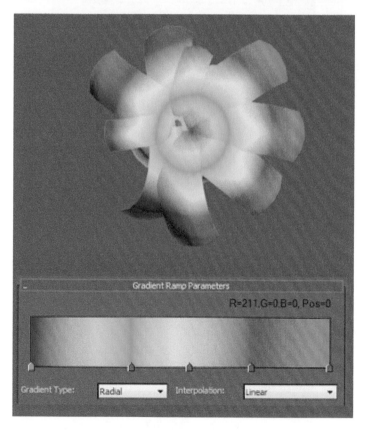

FIG 10.9c

To achieve this, go to the top view and UV map the leaves using planar mapping. Change the mapping channel to 2 and fit the gizmo to the extents using the fit command.

Now add a colorized gradient onto the palm bark (not a gradient ramp). In the empty mask slot, create a gradient similar to the palm leaf illumination gradient and black out color 2.

When complete, add a gradient to the selfillumination channel, with the same values as the palm leaf's illumination gradient.

In the maps rollout, reduce the illumination number down to 60 to prevent it from flattening out the detail of the texture.

The rendered result should look similar to Fig. 10.9d.

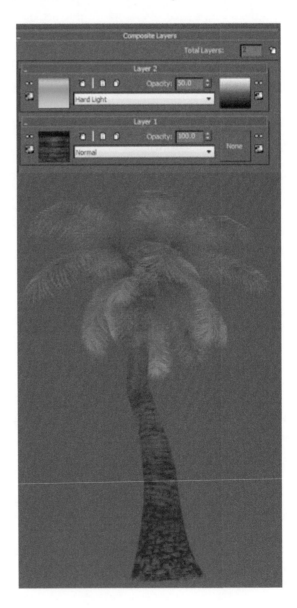

FIG 10.9d

With the population roughly complete, we can look at details such as the cable connecting the invention to the palm tree.

First, hide everything except the invention, the palm tree, and the path.

Now, create a spline running from the underside of the invention to the base of the palm. Create this from the **Top** orthographic view, then change to the **perspective** view to add any additional vertices required. Finally, move the points in all axis so that they organically flow from the beginning to the end, naturally crossing the path.

Once complete, with the spline selected, go to **Compound Objects** and create a loft using this spline as the path. Use an N-Gon as the loft target, keeping the number of sides low.

With the loft created, make a connection piece for either end. A socket at the invention end and a plate at the palm tree end will suffice. Then, texture map the two new pieces using the machine material.

The progression of this technique can be seen in Fig. 10.10.

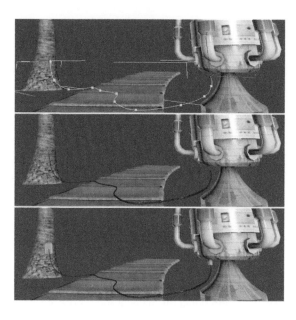

FIG 10.10

Before we can move onto the lighting, we need to prepare the major materials with normal mapping.

This can be done with a dedicated package like **Crazy Bump** or the **NVIDIA** plug in for Photoshop (which is free).

The **NVIDIA Normal Map Filter** creates normal maps from gray scale height maps. The filter's user interface provides a list of options, the most noticeable being the scale option that defaults at 0.2.

Change this to a higher number, such as 0.4 for more dramatic results. All other settings can be left as default. In Fig. 10.11, we can see how the house texture is prepared for the normal map filter by creating a stripped down gray scale height texture. Using this method, create normal maps for the remaining textures (windows, doors, the invention, and the palm tree).

FIG 10.11

To add the newly created normal maps to the relevant material, load up the **normal map** in the **Bump** slot of the material and choose the material type **Normal Bump**.

Once loaded, in the **Normal** slot, load your **normal map** texture.

The default is 30, increase this until you are happy that the effect is pronounced enough.

We now have enough to set up the lighting for the scene.

To get a clearer view of the background, hide the palm and the machine objects.

Next, using three-point lighting method, we start with the key light. This light is the main source of illumination. We are aiming for an early morning look so the light is quite low. Use a **Free Direct Light** to match the results in Fig. 10.12a.

FIG 10.12a

The ambient lighting we set earlier depended on cool tones. To enhance the depth further, we will use color contrast: warm versus cool. The effect should be used on the background gradient too to help provide a consistent and natural color spectrum for our objects to sit in.

The key light, even though it is coming from the reverse angle needs to be a very warm hue. Set the color to a warm yellow.

To get the right level of luminance, you may have to increase the multiplier so "over brightness" (specular exposure beyond the provided texture limits) can be achieved.

To achieve the "sun" effect, go to **Rendering > Environment > Effects** and add **Lens Effects** from the list.

Choose**Glow** and for the source click on **Pick Light** and select the key light in the scene.

Now, when the scene is rendered, a glow will appear as a posteffect where the light is. **Size, Color**, and **Intensity** can all be changed in the **Effects Dialogue Box**. Experiment with the settings and color values until you're happy with the results.

The next two steps are subtle, but I've included them to help to show that lighting can add depth through color contrast.

The fill light should be created next (Fig. 10.12b). This should be an **Omni Light**, placed toward the left side of the view in front of the house. The color should be cool in tone, but warmer than the ambient spectrum. In the example, a pale peach color has been used.

FIG 10.12b

Ray Traced Shadows should be turned on, and the attenuation fields should not extend beyond the house object. Using the Exclude function, exclude all objects except the house.

When placement is set, go to **shadow parameters** for the light and change the **shadow color** to a deep blue. Render in-between adjustments to check the results and enhance the contrast by tweaking the light color and illumination level.

No glow effect should be added for this light.

Finally, the bounce light should be created. This light is traditionally opposing the key light and can act as a rim light, but as we are using the key light to create a rim effect already we will use the bounce as a complimentary light source.

Using the key light as a guide, create another **Free Direct Light**.

This light should not have **Overshoot** turned on as we need it to attenuate from right to left.

Place the light above the key light, but rotate it so that it has a more horizontal path from right to left. Rotating it to be completely horizontal should be avoided as this will create a stronger effect and be harder to fade convincingly.

FIG 10.12c

Again, this light should not have any **glow. Shadows** are not needed either.

The color for this light should be warm, more toward the red part of the spectrum.

In Fig. 10.12c, you can see how this light and the key combine, creating a stronger shared key effect and a falloff that changes color. This is the benefit of using a complimentary system.

In the higher end of the illumination scale, we are complimenting colors, and in the darker end, we are contrasting colors. This is because the ambient tones take up a greater area of the image and need clearer definition.

In Fig. 10.12d, we can see what the light set up now looks like (I have the newly created bounce light selected). Working with numerous lights can be overwhelming, so to help navigate the scene, name the lights accordingly. This is especially important for light that only affect one or two objects.

To finish off the look of the main light rig, add an additional **glow** to the key light.

Turn off **Glow Behind** and change the occlusion to around 60.

Saturate the color and choose either a deep orange or a red to create a warm light haze effect. Adjust the intensity until you feel the effect is subtle enough.

The main light rig is now complete. Additional lights from this point forward will be object specific.

Next, **Hide All Objects** and **Unhide** the machine.

FIG 10.12d

FIG 10.12e

To justify the machine against the background, create a **Free Direct Light** behind it, with a cool color. This is coming from the mid ground so should feel neutral in nature. This being the case, cyan or a desaturated green should work. Exclude all other objects except the machine (Fig. 10.13).

To bring the machine to life, we need to work up the material with some additional effects.

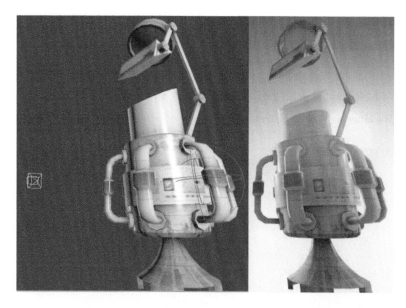

FIG 10.13

In Fig. 10.14a, you will see the necessary textures in order: **Diffuse, Specular, Glossiness, Illumination, Normal**, and **Reflection Mask**. For the reflection slot, use a mask material with the texture shown as a mask and a reflect material as the target.

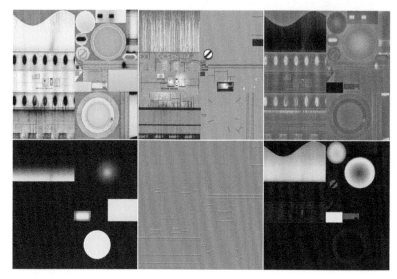

FIG 10.14a

Render to check the results and adjust the sliders for the material shading appropriately.

Next, create three new lights (which effect only the machine). One **Free Direct** with very close attenuation and two small **Omni lights**.

All these new lights need glow effects.

The one outside the casing should be green suggesting that the liquid inside is creating a ball of illumination. The smaller one, red showing the power light, and the direct light should call a **volume light** effect (found under **Atmospheres** under the light rollouts).

The latter is creating the light glow from the prism, powering the machine.

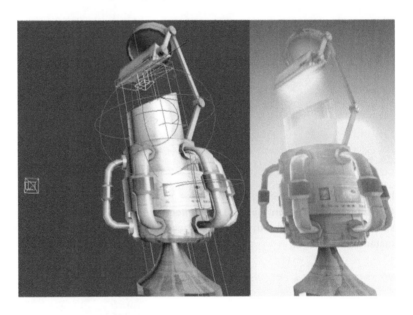

FIG 10.14b

In Fig. 10.14b, we can see the placement, attenuation and finally the rendered effect of the lights that we have just set up.

The machine and its lights can now be hidden until we need them again.

Unhide the palm tree and create the additional textures needed (**Specular, Gloss**, and **Normal**) if you haven't already created them. Reflectivity would

FIG 10.15

320

also be useful for the palm leaves. The glossiness for the leaves will have to take into account the alpha areas.

The rendered result should match Fig. 10.15. Hide the palm once the material is complete.

Unhide the house and surrounding terrain. Copy the **Free Direct Light** from the machine with the volume light effect added, over to the top window of the house to create a light glow. Once complete, replace the gradient background with a subtle sky image to help frame the objects (Fig. 10.16).

FIG 10.16

Finally, unhide all objects and lights and render to check how they sit together. Add a small **Omni Light** to the far right of the image to illuminate the large fence slightly (excluding all other objects). The palm will also need some backlighting to help lift it from the background. This should only be a subtle edging effect though as a powerful rim effect will bring it too far forward.

With all elements now balanced, the resulting rendered image should match Fig. 10.17 .

To add some variety to your scene or to differentiate your work from others doing this tutorial, add a few more assets to your scene or play around with the camera and composition, lighting, color, contrast, etc. – go wild, it's your work.

FIG 10.17

FIG 10.17a

FIG 10.17b

FIG 10.17c

After you're comfortable with setting up a scene, composing and populating and balancing the lighting set up, try creating a new scene…

FIG 10.18

Setting a scene in the back yard allows for some reuse and will be a useful exercise for stylistic continuity.

FIG 10.19

FIG 10.20

The concepts show new elements; a work shed and a tree house area. One of these would work as a focal point for a new scene. Remember, layout can be adjusted to suit camera composition and staging so the concept layout should work as a logical starting point and ongoing reference guide.

When sourcing lighting, as with most references, try and source as varied a cross section as possible. Skies are usually the best place to start as they reflect an entire color spectrum from key light source to multiple light reflections. New elements to try out could be scene fog (for distance cueing) and depth of field to enhance perspective.

To give you a few ideas, have a look at the following concepts, or create some ideas of your own.

FIG 10.21

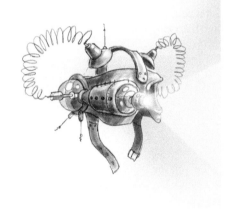

FIG 10.22

FIG 10.23

FIG 10.24

FIG 10.25

FIG 10.26

FIG 10.27

FIG 10.28

FIG 10.29

FIG 10.30

I'd love to see some of your finished compositions posted on the 3D For Games forum on www.3D-For-Games.com/forum in the Work In Progress or the Showcase threads.

CHAPTER 11

Portfolio and Interview

Portfolio

If you've been through the whole book, you've created some images and learnt how to render them, you've got yourself a portfolio, right? Wrong! The first rule about putting a portfolio together is that ***the work must be your own***. I've put this in emphasized type, because it is the single most important rule when sending off your portfolio and applying for a job.

It's okay to show your friends and family all the great renders that you've created by working through this book, but if you're going to send work off to a professional reviewer, you'll have to throw it all out and start again, from scratch – sorry! The main reasons for this are as follows:

- Although you have technically completed the projects in each chapter, don't include them in your portfolio, as it's not all your own work. You'll need to create similar pieces of work based on the skills you've learnt. That way, the projects won't be recognized by anyone as a tutorial and will truly be your own creation.

- If the reviewer recognizes one piece of work in your portfolio from a tutorial that they know or a book they own, they will most likely throw the whole portfolio out and you'll never get another chance with them, or possibly even that company, ever again.
- It's important to be original. Lots and lots of portfolios are sent to recruiters every day. Although you need to demonstrate that you can do the basics (as covered in this book), you'll need an edge to impress them. Also, if you've bought this book and created a portfolio from it, you probably won't be the only one. So take what you've learnt; apply it to a few different models, themes, and subject matter; create a stunning portfolio of your own work, which you can be truly proud of.

If you feel that you've gone through this book and completed some or even all of the tutorials but you're not quite ready to apply for a job (or don't even want to), then there are a few things that you can do next:

- You can go back to the tutorials that you enjoyed and redo them, this time creating something similar using your own reference or concept material.
- You can browse the texture and reference photo folders included on the DVD and build something from those.
- You can take some of your own reference photos and build something completely new, from scratch.
- You can even create something completely new that you can't take reference photos of, for example, something futuristic, some inner workings of a machine or animal or even something fictional.

Your portfolio is your advertisement of your work. It highlights your skill and talent as well as your problem-solving abilities, so have some fun with it. Just remember to include enough of the basics to satisfy the employer. If you're not sure what to include, here's some advice.

What to Include in Your Portfolio

I'm assuming that you want a job in the games industry (or a related industry), because of the title of the book, so I'll base my advice on that assumption. To find out what people look for while looking at portfolios, I asked a number of industry professionals what they look for. Here are a few things that came up a number of times:

- General artistic ability and command of traditional art principles (drawing and sketching, especially)
- Creative ability
- Strong original ideas
- Controlled and manageable topology and good UV layout
- Attention to detail and good observational skills (including technical detail: naming conventions, pivot points, file formats, and so on)
- Good variety of work

The bottom line is to include only your best work. If you have only five good pieces of work, then that's all that should be in your portfolio. Padding your portfolio out with everything you have ever done not only reduces the overall quality of your portfolio, but also advertises every single mistake you've ever made – not what you want to be doing. So, be strict about including only work that you believe to be flawless. Ask yourself, "Is this the best I can do, or are there any small improvements that I can make?" If there are, do them; it's really important not to rush getting this together. A rushed portfolio can hold you back for many years. If you've included only your best work so far, you may have only a few renders. As you flick through them, the small number of pieces may be the catalyst you need to buckle down and produce some more work. If not, it should be. If your portfolio is brimming with everything you've ever done, you won't feel the same sense of urgency, so try to be aware of what you really have, and what you need to do about improving it.

How do you decide what to include? Well, it all depends on the job you want. If all you want to do is model cars and other vehicles, then your portfolio should include a lot of good examples of that—one or two just isn't enough. However, if you're happy to do anything, then you'll need to have a good variety of work. If you're not sure what position you'd like to apply for, here are a few of the more common roles:

- 3D artist (does a bit of everything). This tends to be a more junior role.
- Vehicle artist (depending on the company, this can cover aircraft, military, cars, trains, and sci-fi).
- Character artist (these range from photorealistic, real-world, cartoon alien). This role can include weighting and rigging, as well as modeling and texturing.
- Environmental or level artist (real-world, alien, cartoon, fictional).
- UI (user interface artist: the selection screens you navigate between game levels).

If you're still not sure whether you want to specialize in any of the specific roles, keep everything generic at this point and do a bit of everything. Remember that originality is king here. You should create brand new conceptual forms if it allows you to flex your artistic muscles. I would much rather see a beautifully dirty and damaged vehicle for an imaginary sci-fi scene than yet another shiny Ferrari.

Ask for help if you're not sure what your best work is. Luckily, there are lots of forums and galleries to post your work for your fellow artists to critique for you. Two of the most popular are www.deviantart.com and www.cgsociety.org

Some of the best artists in the industry post work on these websites, so brace yourself: this is whom you're competing with for work. Also, some of the best artists will routinely comment on your work or works in progress and offer valuable advice, which you'd struggle to get anywhere else—and the best thing is that it's free advice.

Let's move on to the more difficult question: what you shouldn't include.

What Not to Include

First and foremost, don't include any sloppy work (unmapped polygons, stretched UVs, holes in geometry), because the mistakes will stand out from a mile away and if you haven't spotted such errors in your portfolio, then the reviewer will wonder what your mistakes will be like from day to day and you'll probably be rejected.

Don't include old work. For some reason, a lot of artists feel the need to sign and date their work, especially life drawing. If I see a date on a portfolio piece that's more than a few years old, it makes me wonder, "What have they been doing recently?" If all the work is old, it puts me off. If you must include old work, make sure you remove any dates, or better still, don't add them in the first place. Again, if all your work is too old, you will most probably be rejected.

Unfinished work should not be included, unless it's your latest piece and it's looking really good. I love it when an artist comes for an interview and shows me a piece of work that he has been working on specifically for Evolution Studios or one of the projects we're developing. It's great when a piece of work has been created just for the interview.

Artists do this a lot if there are gaps in their portfolio, when the work they have been doing is a different style or subject matter than the company or role they are applying for, to prove that they can do the job, or even to show how much they want the job. If you do try something like this, casually drop it in at the end, saying something like, "And there's this, which I was working on last night/week while preparing for today; it's not finished, but…" (and then point out what you need to do to round it off). Obviously, do this only with work that is close to completion; otherwise, it will have a negative effect.

I spoke to some of my lead artist contacts in other companies about what they really don't want to see in interviews. Here are some of their responses:

- Clichés(spaceships, Amazonian beauties, churches)
- Sloppy work (unmapped polygons, stretched UVs, poor quality)
- Unfinished work
- Scenes or exercises from books or (worse) from the 3ds Max tutorials

Overall, get as many people to look at your work as you can and listen to what they say to you. If you really like a piece but no one else does, drop it from your portfolio. By all means, keep it in a personal portfolio, but don't send it off to companies or take it to the interview.

One very important point to note is that you should not under any circumstances send original pieces of work that is, only the hard copy of something you've drawn. These will not be returned to you and you'll lose them forever.

Now that you have an idea of what you want to do, you have to produce the work, or, if you already have it, you get to organize it.

Producing the Work

If you feel that you might not have enough good work in your portfolio, you'll need to plan what you need to do. It's really important that you make a plan and stick to it. Some people create lists and work through them from top to bottom, but I prefer to use S.M.A.R.T goals. S.M.A.R.T stands for Specific, Measurable, Achievable, Realistic, and Timed. For example, if I'm applying for a new role, I might identify four new pieces that I need to produce for my portfolio, aimed at this new role. Here's how I work out what my goals should be:

- **Specific.** I want to create four new pieces of work similar to (for example) my first portfolio page.
- **Measurable.** I identify the target quality from an existing portfolio piece. I then need to list everything I need to model, texture, compose, light, and render in the scene to hit this level of quality.
- **Achievable.** I take each set of time estimates for the four pieces of work that I intend to build and add rough estimates for each task, in hours. I then add all the estimates for each piece of work and see roughly how long it will take me to make all of them. Once I have this total, I can compare it with the total amount of time that I think I can spend on this work (maybe 5 hours a day, for example). Comparing these estimates shows me how much work I have to do and how long I have to do it in.
- **Realistic.** If the total of amount of work is less than the time I have to do it in, it's a realistic goal. If it is slightly more, I may decide that if it all goes well, I can probably still do it, so it's still fairly realistic. If the amount of work to do is far more than the amount of time you have, it's an unrealistic goal and you should probably reconsider the amount of work.
- **Timed.** The closing date for applicants for the new role is (in this example) 6 weeks away, so to be sure I make it on time, I'll plan out 4 weeks of work.

For this example, if I think each piece will take me approximately 2 weeks of work, then it's obvious that I don't have time to do the four pieces I wanted to. In this case, I'll opt for doing two of the pieces or re-plan the whole lot using a simpler piece of work as the quality bar.

This technique is extremely important when planning any work. Breaking down the tasks into smaller actions makes it easier to estimate accurately, which is very important for hitting deadlines, and also really useful for pricing freelance work as a contractor. To find out more about S.M.A.R.T. goals and other planning techniques, try an Internet search—there are plenty of resources that go into planning in a lot more detail.

Now that you have your work, let's organize it.

Organizing the Content

If you're sending your work in to studios via email or disc, or if you're compiling a printed portfolio, you must put your best work first. In a lot of cases, a reviewer might look only at the first couple of pieces, so you have to blow them away with the very first piece. If you don't, you'll be in the trash – it's as simple as that. You can organize your work as simply as a set of images, or a movie, but keep it simple. Finding and downloading strange codecs to view someone's work really puts me off. A lot of people present their website portfolio, but clearly labeled folders of JPEGs work just as well.

This is how it works in some companies. A well-known developing company that makes great games and is advertising for staff might get ten or more show reels or portfolios a day from independent applicants (the number can be even higher, if recruitment agencies are involved). If the art manager or recruiter looks at these once a week, they'll have more than fifty show reels to look through; if they're really busy, as most are, and do this only once a month... Well, you can do the math.

Whenever I'm faced with such a task, I know that I can spend only a small amount of time on each. If the first few images are well below the standard that we require, I'll make a note "thanks, but no thanks" and move onto the next one. However, if the first few images are good, I'll look a lot further through the portfolio, even if I see a few poor pieces of work, just to make sure that I'm not making a mistake or missing out on finding a good candidate. Often slightly junior members of the team are tasked to filter the applicants first. This may improve your chances if your first few pieces aren't the best, but don't risk it.

In addition to putting a few of your best pieces at the start of the portfolio or show reel, you'll need to put some of your best at the end. This will leave the recruiter with a good feeling about your work, improving your chances. I prefer to use fully rendered scenes containing lots of models for the start and end of my portfolio and then focus on individual assets in the middle. I often include wireframes and texture pages as half of the portfolio, so that it is clear how efficiently the models are built and rendered. This is just my preference – have a look at some online portfolios and try to work out why the artist has organized them the way they have.

Final Presentation of Your Portfolio

Once you've produced and organized the work, you need to present it as well as you can. If you are sending in a show reel on disc, it must be in a box, with a cover, and the disc should be either printed or clearly labeled. Both the cover and disc should have your name, your contact details (email and phone number), and also your website address. If you are taking in a paper portfolio to show, it should be in a clean binder of a suitable size for your work. I always used to use two matching leather portfolios for interviews.

One was 420 × 594 mm (A2) with all my illustration, life drawing, pastel, charcoal, and painting and the other was 297 × 420 mm (A3) and had all my 3D modeling shown as full-color renders. The smaller portfolio sometimes had magazine scans of articles and high review scores of the games I'd worked on, depending on the role I was applying for.

If you're sending a demo reel, always remember to name your files properly, for example, AndrewGahan001.jpg, so that your work can be easily identified if it gets mixed up with someone else's.

If you are scanning or copying work to include in your portfolio, remember to do everything in color. Even pencil drawings should be scanned or photocopied in color, as all the gray tones will be lost if you just use the black and white settings.

Now that you have your portfolio sorted out, go ahead, and apply for that job.

Don't take my word for it!

As this is so important, I've asked a few of my colleagues and friends to tell me what they looked for in portfolios too, along with their pet likes and dislikes.

Gavin Moore – Art Director – Sony Computer Entertainment, Japan, www.scei.co.jp

First things first. Tailor your portfolio for the job that is on offer. I have seen so many portfolios applying for jobs where they do not have the required skills for the job and the portfolio does not contain work that reflects the position that we are trying to fill. If you are a BG Artist, please do not apply for a job as a Concept Artist, especially if your portfolio does not contain any 2D work. It doesn't matter how good you are as a BG Artist, it's an automatic fail.

Quality versus quantity. I would rather see a small portfolio of high quality than a portfolio stuffed to the brim with mediocre works. Or even worse, a portfolio that varies in quality. Be very critical of your own work and if you don't think a piece is of sufficient quality, don't put it in. Your future employer is going to be far more critical than you are.

Mixing quality in a portfolio just to make it seem that you have done a lot just shows a lack of self-censorship. It tells me that you cannot judge the quality of your own work.

That means that you cannot be relied upon to self-manage the quality of your work if you get the job.

If it varies in quality, it's an automatic fail. Sometimes that is a terrible shame.

Your portfolio reflects you. Take your time when creating your portfolio. Make sure that it is laid out simply and effectively to show off your work. I do not care for lacey and frilly edges, or a portfolio that is covered in your mad scribbles. It does not sway me in your favor.

It's not good if your portfolio is online and I have to wait for it to load for more than a minute or so. It may have a lot of fancy flash animation but I'm not looking for a flash artist. I just want to see your work. A simple website is best, just showcase your work quickly. Once you get the interview, you can let your personality run riot.

If there are two portfolios of the same high-quality of work, I will always choose the one that is more effective at showing the work to the best potential. It shows that the person cares about what they make. That shows me that they will care about what they make if they get the job.

Variety is king. I like to see variety in portfolios. Working for a large corporation like Sony, you may be called upon to work on various projects throughout your career. These projects can vary from the ultrarealistic to cartoony—even projects that are not games but are service-based products that require strong graphic skills. Show your future employee that you are flexible.

Remember the quality-versus-quantity rule though. This overrides all other rules. Don't throw something into your portfolio just for variety's sake.

First timers. For all the Junior Artists or you guys trying to get into the industry for the first time.

Stick to your strengths. Don't try and reach further than you can. A good employer will see that you have potential. Just stick to the rules seen earlier and you will be ok.

If you manage to get the interview, be humble! The guys sitting across that desk have seen it all before. Let your work speak for itself and show that you can communicate and are a team player.

My personal dislikes. Make sure I can find your contact information. Don't copy other peoples' work.

If it's a group project, tell me what you did on that project.

Stop sending me portfolios that contain Final Fantasy character look-a-likes.

Anne L. Michaels – President – Morpheus Digital, USA, www.MorpheusDigital.com

I could care less what qualifications students have learnt in school and/or while in training. I would prefer to see the name of the actual projects they have worked on if they are allowed to disclose and what they did on each project. It's important for me to know what software the work was created in and the turnaround time from the beginning to the final product of each piece.

Resumes aren't terribly important. I prefer to use the artist's website to tell me how the artist wants his work to be displayed and revealed to everyone. It shows what they take pride in.

Sameer Yamdagni – Lead Character Artist – Page 44 Studios, USA, www.SameerYamdagni.com

When I see a modeling demo reel, there are a few things that I look for before deciding whether or not to conduct an interview.

Work should be original and credit should be clearly given to anyone that helped. If someone else has painted the texture map or UV'd the model, that should be clearly stated.

Untidy topology is important to me, since I work closely with the rigging and animation teams. Since these teams are mostly off-site, poor topology can really slow down the pipeline with multiple revision passes on the assets being needed. It is important that modelers know the difference between creating organic models, and creating organic models with animation and deformation in mind.

Wireframe-on-shaded model turntables are important for me to see. Good use of UV space. In video games, because texture space is often limited by platform restrictions, it is vital that UV space use be maximized and UV shells be efficiently positioned. Smart use of mirrored UVs where necessary and fully laid-out UVs is also important to me.

Texture maps should be shown on the reel to see how you make use of UV space.

Work should be recent and not years old. Older work should be at the end of the reel if at all.

Models should be textured only if the modeler is a good texture artist as well. It is better to have a grayscale model than to have a model that is half-painted or poorly painted. A poorly textured model is much worse to see than a plain grayscale model, since a bad texture job will detract from the good modeling work.

There should be at least one realistic human model on the reel to show an understanding of human anatomy. It's fine to have dozens of bizarre monsters and aliens, especially if the company you're applying to specializes in games of that genre, but I do like to see one realistic human so that I know that the artist has training in understanding the human form.

Overly complex UI (user interface) elements in a reel can be distracting and annoying. Special effects and visual "bling" should be minimized so that the 3D work can speak for itself.

I often watch reels on mute if the music/sound effects are too annoying. If there is a background track to the reel, it should be soft and rhythmic, and flow with the pace of the model turntables. Bad music can leave a bad impression, and as they say "You don't get a second chance to make a first impression." Avoid any music with cussing in it and lyrics. Stick to ambient and instrumental.

335

Avoid lewd content on the reel. I have never worked for a company where seeing x-rated content has been favorably viewed. Try to think of the genre of work that the company to which you are applying produces and build models along those lines. If you want to create a reel that is more general, choose work that reflects various styles and content such as realistic models, cartoony models, and hard surface vehicles.

People often have two reels; one for organic modeling and one for hard surface modeling. Something you might want to consider if you are aiming for a specific niche role.

When creating a website, be sure that it is optimized so that loading times are negligible. Nobody likes to wait, and if a company is looking over dozens of resumes, portfolios, and websites, if something doesn't work quickly, they are quick to move on to the next person. Time is money, after all!

Try to have a one-page résumé on your website as well as on paper. It is easy to consolidate the important information. Nobody wants to read an essay or a breakdown of your previous nonindustry related work. Stick to the qualifications that you feel make you an ideal candidate for the job you are applying for.

Mike Engstrom – Owner – Honey Badger Studios, UK, www.HoneyBadgerStudios.com

Do you have any particular content that you like to see or dislike seeing?

This depends on what the job is for. I look for artists who can match certain roles. For example, are they hard-surface artists modeling vehicles and buildings? Or are they organic modelers building characters and environments? Are they technical and knowledgeable or are they super talented. I like it when an artist knows what he wants to do; it helps me to work out where to fit them into the team. I also like to see a few polished finished pieces rather than lots of unfinished messy attempts. It shows commitment to the work.

Have you seen something recently that made or killed the chance of an interview?

I recruited an artist who had a weak 3D portfolio a few years ago, because his 2D skills were outstanding and I knew I could train him up to be one of the best artists. I was right.

Do you have any advice for junior artists when applying to companies?

Be relentless; it took me 2 years to get into the industry, so don't give up and apply for every role you are suitable for – even if you think it's too basic a role. If you are good, you will soon be doing the cool stuff.

Stuart Cripps – Creative Lead – Evolution Studios, Sony, UK, www.uk.playstation.com

Here are the main points that I consider when hiring for the concept team at Evolution Studios.

Well-presented work – be professional – employers are looking for professionals.

Focus on work relevant to the role you are after. (Other stuff could serve as a distraction?)

High standards – if you aren't sure then don't put it in (one or two bad pieces can sour the deal).

Do not plagiarize, not even a little bit (we have seen this in the past and an artist's rep went from "great!" to "steer well clear").

Play to your strengths, if there are areas or skill sets you are still working on/honing, then do not show anything unless specifically asked about/required.

Diversity, in both types of project and when possible any skill sets or software knowledge.

Be awesome! It really helps ☺

Barry Meade – Director – Fireproof Studios, UK www.fireproofstudios.com

Presentation. Simplicity, tidiness, and clarity. From the layout to the typeface, everything you show says something about your skill, taste, and artistic eye. You don't have to rule out any of these presentation elements, but you really don't want to be terrible at any of them. If you are, get your graphic design mate to help you.

3D work. Tidy polygons and textures, used economically – I'm not overly impressed with high poly stuff. A demonstrated ability to "build for purpose." It should be clear what you were trying to build and what you ended up with. I like to see wireframes of each finished mesh along with good lighting.

Overall. The number one thing I want to see is an artistic eye and thought (which can be interpreted as "having taste" I suppose). Why have a great model displayed under poor lighting that ruins it? Why craft a wonderful scene in 3D and then plaster it onto a web page layout that makes me think you were born without eyeballs?

The reason is that it lends the impression that you cannot be trusted on your own and that you would need a lot of direction to come good.

Nobody talks about it in games but taste and beauty really matter in 3D art and you need to earn or learn some of both.

Rules for applicants. Do not show unfinished meshes, and that includes models with no textures applied.

Again, nobody is impressed by any z-brush model unless it's a sculpture of amazingly intricate detail. Try and keep everything to a consistent quality – if that means losing some pieces from your portfolio, so be it. Also, don't put anything in it that you can't proudly talk about.

Real tip. Those who improve, win.

If you have one or two newer pieces that are obviously better quality than some others, go back to those old pieces and improve them using what you've learnt. This constant renewal and improvement is EXACTLY what you have to do on the job – if you can demonstrate that kind of determination and lack of preciousness, you will go straight to the front of the queue. We hired a graduate who spent the 12 months after graduation throwing out every piece of coursework he'd done in 3 years and replacing it with pieces of his own that he was proud of. He is the star of our studio.

Tony Prosser – Managing Director – RealtimeUK, www.realtimeuk.com

I certainly agree with the advice you've already mentioned but would just add that in this world of email, if your work stands up well to being printed (say matte painters, concept artists, character artists etc.) then actually printing your work on a quality ink jet printer and sending it in a hard-backed envelope can potentially help you stand out from the "email crowd." It can also ensure that your work is presented as you intended (avoiding browser or monitor issues that could show work in a lesser light).

I'd also enforce your point about presenting and labeling work as professionally as possible and to leave out any "border line" work that doesn't demonstrate a consistent ability to hit a high-quality benchmark –it's so tempting to put more work in but believe me, less is more!

Tom Painter – Owner – Bigman3D, www.bigman3d.com

I was wondering if you would mind telling me what you look for in a portfolio, or what you really don't like to see?

This depends on the job role really. One thing that I really like to see these days is a blog.

These show passion, and give me a lot more feeling about the applicant's personality that you can normally get from a CV.

The more recently updated the blog, the better as it shows they are active in advancing their craft.

It's nice to see the development of the job, to see the wireframes, and a bit of concept art can show me a lot about someone's working practices.

Do you have any particular content that you like to see or dislike seeing?
I think I'm truly bored of cars, fantasy characters, spaceships, and robots. These don't normally help applicants stand out amongst the crowd unless they are really putting a twist on the old clichés.
If I'm looking for an ideas person I like to see imaginative images that I haven't seen before, but for many production jobs, I like to see good photo-realistic work.
I like to see life drawings too as these prove knowledge of proportion and anatomy.

Have you seen something recently that made or killed the chance of an interview?
Spelling mistakes in a covering letter are always going to look bad, especially in these days of spell-checking programs. Also CC'ing more than 1 company in an email application is a big "no no" to me! I like to see that the person has done their research and made an effort to explain how they might be relevant to our company.

Do you have any advice for junior artists when applying to companies?
As a junior artist, don't try and spread yourself too thinly; try to specialize in a role that currently has a feasible number of vacancies at your level. To be a strong generalist takes years of work and it's my opinion that it's not the easiest route into the industry.
Always write a nice personalized covering letter. Try to get feedback from any interviews you attend, especially if you are unsuccessful. Constructive criticism is what feeds excellence in the industry, so don't be afraid to seek out what industry people (or you can even ask your friends and family) don't like in your work.
Also, if you want that job then never give up until you get it, keep iterating on your work and constantly try to improve upon your weaknesses. Don't be scared to write back to companies that might have previously not had the right role – jobs can pop up overnight at busy studios.

Applying for a Job

I recommend that you look for your first (or next) job in these two main ways. The first, and the one I recommend the most, is to apply directly to companies that are hiring. To do this, look at the relevant magazines of your country (or the country you want to work in) and browse the advertisements from the companies looking for staff. In the United Kingdom, one of the best for this is *Edge* magazine, which is readily available in newsagents. You can also try looking on the websites for companies that you'd like to work for – often there are positions advertised that have not been in the press yet, which might get you a slight head start on the position. There are also a lot of advertisements on various websites such as http://www.gamasutra.com and http://www.gamesindustry.biz; just search for "games industry jobs" in any major search engine, and you'll find lots of positions advertised.

Which leads me to the second method of finding out who's hiring and the approach to take if your direct applications don't get you the results that you want. Again, look through the relevant trade magazines or Internet search engines, but this time, concentrate on all the recruitment agencies. You will probably find these a lot easier to find than the actual companies. Browse through their listings. If there is something specific that you like the look of, drop them a line or apply direct through the website. If there isn't, send an email with the sort of position you're looking for.

You'll find that the second method might get you more responses, but possibly not for the exact job you want. The recruitment agencies will often fire off your CV and show reel to every company on their books and get you lots of interviews. On the other hand, you might end up in a pile of other artists while the agency does all the hard work to place the more senior jobs. Remember that interviews cost money to attend, so take care how many you agree to attend and if you are invited to one, ask if they'll pay your expenses. In a lot of cases, they will.

The recruitment agencies work on commission and they will charge from 10 percent up to 30 percent of your starting salary to the company hiring you. For this reason alone, a lot of companies will not use them, so do your research and find out which companies do.

The most important thing you need to do with recruitment agencies is to keep calling them every week and ask for an update. If you don't, you might get lost in paperwork.

Finally, if you're going to start applying, you're going to need a résumé or curriculum vitae.

Résumé or Curriculum Vitae and Cover Letter

Every good job application should come with a cover letter, a résumé, or curriculum vitae (CV) and a show reel or demo disc. Let's look at them in a little more detail.

A Cover Letter

The cover letter is your way of introducing yourself to the company and should explain why you want this particular job. It should give the employer some insight into your desire and your personality. It should be no more than one-page long and should describe how you are qualified for the position. This is a good opportunity to make an impression and maybe stand out from the crowd. This is also a good opportunity to make a bad impression, so be careful what you write. A letter that lacks specifics about the position or company that you're applying to will look like a mass mailing and will show lack of effort and thought. Always use a spellchecker on all your text; spelling mistakes show that you have poor attention to detail – this really does matter. Also ask someone you trust to proofread your letter, as they may see grammatical errors that you missed, which must be corrected.

Résumé/CV

A résumé or curriculum vitae (CV) is a list of your skills, experience, interests, and successes; nothing more. It should not contain page after page of details about your hobbies or spare time and it should not be used as an opportunity to hype every single thing you've ever done. A good résumé will be easy to read and no more than two pages (maybe three if you have had a lot of relevant experience). It should have lots of open space and be presented in a clear, easy-to-read font such as 12-point Arial. You should print it on good-quality paper and put it in a matching envelope. Recruitment agencies routinely take personal information off CVs when they send them out; this often messes up the formatting, making them difficult to read. Obviously, if you apply for positions personally, you get full control over how you are presented. Also, it's important not to go mad with jazzy paper and gimmicks – we've seen them all before and are not usually impressed by anything that is supposed to shock or amaze us.

You can use the following checklist to produce a good CV directly:

- Contact information (phone numbers, email address, and mailing address)
- Objective (the exact position to which you are applying)
- Experience (employment dates, job titles, and brief descriptions of responsibilities)
- Skills (Maya, 3ds Max, Photoshop, Illustrator, and so on, including version numbers)
- Education(degrees, certifications, and additional training)
- Other relevant skills (related skills, personal successes)

There is also a mountain of free advice on the Internet for creating good CVs and résumés. Just search for "CV or résumé" and you'll find a lot more detailed advice.

One important point about your contact information is that if you are currently using an email address that you set up in college that is something like "biggy69@hotmail" or "sexyboy1980@yahoo," then you'll need to change it to something more professional. You should definitely have your own website when looking for a job, even if it's just a one-page résumé that you're putting online. It is so cheap to create and maintain a website these days that it's pretty much a no-brainer. In addition to letting you circulate your name and qualifications worldwide, it's also a permanent email address for life, which is important: you're permanently reachable through you@you.com instead of having to rely on a hotmail address. It comes off as very professional and shows good thought and consideration.

The best thing to do is to register a web domain that is your name or similar and generate a new email address using the new domain. You should also get a website hosted on this domain showcasing your best work (your portfolio) and any new work that you complete. There are loads of cheap web hosting organizations (I use http://www.streamline.net) and if you're not a web developer or don't know anyone who is, you can get cheap websites done for you by using http://www.elance.com or by getting your local web developer to put together a single-page site. If you do put your own website together, always remember to use images to show your email address or contact number – this will cut down on the amount of spam you get from bots searching your site for contact information.

At the Interview

There is a wealth of advice available about interviews, techniques, and what you should and shouldn't do, but here are a few key points directed to the creative industry in general, and more specifically, the games industry:

- **Preparation.** Preparation is extremely important and will give you some confidence in the interview. Know the company you are applying to. Find out what games they've made, who the key staff are, and especially, what they are working on now. If you can't find out what they are currently working on, the project must be unannounced, which gives you a great question in the interview.
- **Arrive on time.** You're going to meet some very busy people and they will not be amused if you're late. If you have to be late, make sure that you telephone in as soon as you know and give them a realistic time when you're going to arrive. This will give them time to reschedule. If you're late and you don't call, you may miss your slot completely and it will be a wasted journey. Also, don't arrive too early. I've had applicants turn up one and a half hours early, which really put me on the spot. Do I leave them sitting in reception for 90 mins for a receptionist to look after or do I reschedule half my day? Either way it is a hassle that you don't want to cause anyone.
- **First impressions are lasting impressions.** You will never get a second chance to make a first impression, so try to get it right. First, smile when you are introduced; it will get you off to a good start. A firm handshake is next – not a vice-like grip or a clammy wet lettuce – just short and firm. If you're really nervous and your hands are sweating, ask the receptionist where the restrooms are and freshen up before you meet anyone. Dress is also important. You'll need to look professional. Wear a nice long-sleeved shirt, some smart/casual trousers, and some clean shoes. As it's the creative industry, most people will be very casual, but don't assume that the people interviewing you will be. They are likely to be fairly senior staff

and may well be very tailored. You can dress down once you have the job. Finally, use eye contact, but don't glare. Keeping eye contact will make you look more confident than you may feel. If two people are interviewing you, it's easier, as you can switch between them. If you talk to people while looking away, they might think that you lack confidence or even interest.

- **Listen.** I realize that this sounds obvious, but it's really important to listen to the questions you are being asked before you answer them. Wait until the interviewer has finished speaking and then answer that question only, without waffling. Your answers should probably be only a couple of minutes long. Remember not to talk too much, too.
- **Stay positive.** Sometimes an interview feels like it's not going well, but as you can't be sure, you need to stay positive and enthusiastic. It's okay if you're asked a particularly difficult question and you don't answer it very well; just move on and focus on your successes and all the great work in your portfolio.
- **Ask questions.** If you can get a couple of good questions in early, without coming across as pushy, you will be able to tailor some of your responses to suit what the interviewer is looking for. Here are two good examples of questions you could ask:
  - What would be my responsibilities if I get the position?
  - What qualities are you looking for in the ideal candidate?
  - Try to keep a good dialogue going, as well as answering the questions, and try to ask some of your own – don't just leave them to the end.
- **Be honest.** It's very important to be honest in interviews, as well as on CVs. A lot of companies check references and career histories to make sure that candidates have actually done what they say they have. A friend of mine told me that he did a background check on someone he had just interviewed and discovered that he'd lied about a role on his CV. Although the candidate was very talented and would have got the job without the lie, my friend could not trust him and didn't make him any offers. It's a common myth that most people lie on their CVs; they don't and you shouldn't either. If you lack experience, then your work must stand out on its own. If it doesn't, keep working hard, posting on forums and learning as much as you can. What we do isn't rocket science and if you persevere, you'll get your break into the industry.

There are also a number of things that you shouldn't do, but (skipping the obvious) here are a few essentials:

- **Don't disrespect previous employers, tutors, or colleagues.** One of the best ways of talking yourself out of a job is saying negative things about previous employers, professors, or colleagues. It won't help you in any way if you do it – so don't.
- **Salary and holidays.** This question comes up more than any other when I ask junior artists if they have any questions for me. Obviously salary and holidays are important, but don't bring it up unless they do. Besides,

you can always call the HR representative of the company or whoever booked the interview once you know that they like you or in the second interview.

- **Have some questions prepared.** It is not a good sign when I ask a candidate if he or she has any other questions, and the candidate says, "No." If you've prepared for the interview, which you definitely should have, you should be able to ask the interviewer a series of good questions about the company, the direction it's going in, expansion, new projects, or whatever. If you have nothing to ask, it shows that you haven't done your homework, you're not interested enough in the job and that you're wasting everyone's time.

- **Don't forget to follow up.** Even if you think that you made a complete disaster of the interview, don't forget to follow up with a written note thanking everyone for the interview and reiterating your interest in the position and the company.

If after doing all of this, you are still rejected, don't take it too personally and don't see it as failure. It's just a result; not the result you were looking for, but a result that you can learn from. I have had artists applying to me more than once, and in some cases, I have hired them the second time around. There are a number of reasons why you weren't picked for the role, but if you keep improving and working as hard as you can, you'll get there.

CHAPTER 12

Creating the Initial Cover Image

s a bit of a bonus I thought I'd explain how the cover image was created for those of you interested in rendering.

Layout

To start off with, we need a rough sketch or layout of our composition. This can be done loosely on a paper and scanned in, or it can be created in Photoshop, as I have done here.

This should be as basic as possible defining the main three or four elements. In this image, we are showing three main elements – two characters and one background. Each separate element must be justified against the others.

FIG 12.1 Our layout created in Photoshop.

Composition and the Rule of Thirds

The rule of thirds is probably the most common rule of composition. Feel free to Google it to see how different people and industries explain it. It is commonly used in 3D, fine art, design, and photography, and it is really well documented and taught – justifiably so, as it is the main guideline responsible for well-composed images and renders.

The rule of thirds (or sometimes known as "the golden section") was documented as early as 1757 in a book as a rule for proportioning scenic paintings, but was used much earlier as well.

The basic principle behind the rule is that your page, view, or image should be divided into nine equal sections with four imaginary lines, two each running vertically and horizontally, as shown in Fig. 12.2.

FIG 12.2

Place important elements of your composition where these lines intersect, as shown in Fig. 12.3 .

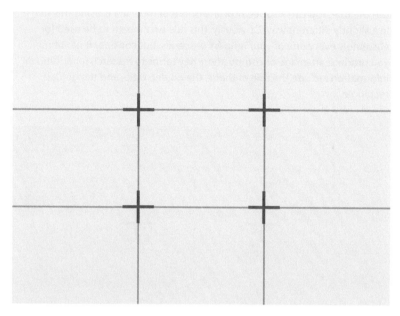

FIG 12.3

You can also arrange key areas of your image into bands that occupy one-third of your page. A great use for this would be a horizon, but other less-obvious ones could be the eyes of a subject in a photo, or a combination of a horizon and a tree, using two intersections.

FIG 12.4

In this photograph of a seascape (Fig. 12.5), the land mass is roughly taking up the bottom third and the remaining two-thirds are sky. Browse through some classic landscape paintings online and see just how many use the rule. You can also see how the photo of the child is using this rule in a slightly different way. Obviously, this rule isn't meant to be used for absolutely every one of your renders or scenes, but consider it next time you produce an image or composition. Key terms to research for additional information include the rule of thirds, the golden ratio, and the golden rectangle.

FIG 12.5

Using the "Rule of thirds," the golden section of the image is calculated and the character positions can be tweaked. We now have a rough guide and move onto the assets. The more simplistic the image, the easier it will be to remember. Anchor points such as the golden section and the vanishing point are needed to help element alignment, perspective, and focus.

As we can see in Fig. 12.1, the juxtaposition of the robot character against the boy – robot – in the foreground makes him the "hero" character so we'll look at him first.

Robot

In Fig. 12.6, we can see the base robot model. To get the most of the character design, I've decided to make some adjustments for this image. The main reasoning is to add personality, lighting range, and bridge the stylistic gap

FIG 12.6

FIG 12.7

between the two character styles such that they fit nicely as they appear side by side.

In Fig. 12.7, we see the process of enhancing the model well under way. We can see that the detail has increased dramatically and the pose has been adjusted in preparation for the rendered shot. An important point to note at this stage is that some smaller details suggested via texture have been remodeled in 3D to strengthen the form. We can see evidence of this in the arms but the legs have yet to be completed.

The increase in detail has caused some UV tears on the chest area and around the "mouth" area, which will need to be fixed before the render can be made.

Robot Render layer

After the model is finished, the pose is altered to best suit the composition (note the head tilt). The asset is now lit with a four-point light rig and is ready for the production render shot.

A camera is set up for this render shot to use. The other character will render with the same camera to ensure that perspective and depth are the same.

349

FIG 12.8

FIG 12.9

Three- and Four-Point Lighting

The three-point lighting technique is another well-documented technique widely used in games, television, film, and digital media. It is a very simple but effective method of lighting a scene, which often forms the basis of most lighting.

The reason that it is so widely used is that the artist, photographer, or game designer can illuminate the subject (in our case, the robot) while controlling or almost completely illuminating any shadows produced by direct lighting – giving us full control over how our character looks.

The technique is called "three-point" lighting (as you may have guessed), because it uses three main lights. These three lights are the key light, the fill light, and the back light. I'll explain how each one works and what it is used for.

The "key" light is the main light in the scene, as its name suggests. This light is usually the strongest in the scene and shines directly on the subject, serving as its key illuminator. The intensity, color, and angle of this light set the lighting in the scene.

Next is the "fill" light. This light is the secondary one, which is usually placed on the opposite side from the key light, illuminating the shaded areas on the front of the subject created by the key light (such as the shadow cast by a subject's nose). This light is less intense than the key light and softer (often half as much), and it is used more as a flood. Not using a fill light often creates very sharp contrasting shadows from the key light.

Finally, we have the "back" light. This is also known as the "rim" or "hair" light. This is normally placed at the rear of the subject, and rather than providing direct lighting (as the key and fill lights do), it is used to create subtle highlights and definition around the subjects' outlines. These are normally used to lift the characters away from the background they are standing against and to provide a stronger 3D look.

Here's how the lights look from above, looking at our robot:

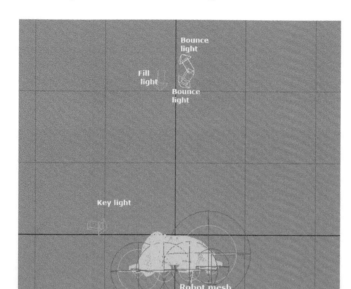

FIG 12.10

Do a little Internet research for other lighting combinations, also do your research and see how different people use different techniques from different industries.

Robert

FIG 12.11

FIG 12.12

In Fig. 12.11, we see the preliminary character as created in Zbrush. To get this to tie in with the style that the robot is rendered in, we need to make few adjustments.

We can't see too much change here but a more natural look will help the render. The head is scaled in and the hair is scruffed up a little to give it a more organic look. The smile is slightly rounded and the neck is made a little shorter. Essentially, we're just making a few proportional changes.

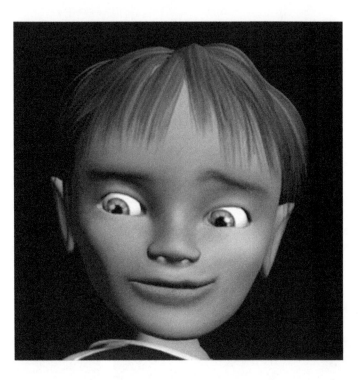

FIG 12.13

Next, using soft selection in a similar way as we did with the robot, a touch of the character is added to help provide personality. The changes are only small but already we can see a more interesting lighting profile. The more you get right in the early stages, the less you have to correct in the latter stages.

Robert Render Layer

As with the robot, a 4-point lighting rig is created (following the robot's rig closely), material settings are adjusted until the desired shading is achieved and the production render is created as shown in Fig. 12.14.

You should notice that both the characters are rendered against a base gradient.

This is so that they both antialias against the same color tones. The gradient itself has a vanishing point that can be used to establish a false floor for the

FIG 12.14

background. This was indicated in the initial layout image. The gradient will also use on its own to slightly ghost over the Robert layer later on.

FIG 12.15

Background

Starting with the gradient and using a variety of layers, a background scene is created that will match the projected lighting and be ambiguous enough to not draw away from the characters.

Once the character layers are added (and masked off using layer masks derived from the rendered alpha channels), the gradient is added between them on a very low opacity setting so that it is almost invisible (10% or thereabouts). This will help differentiate the contrast between the two characters and help justify the robot into the foreground.

FIG 12.16

Robert 2D Fixes and Final Polish

FIG 12.17

FIG 12.18

Here, we can see the character render and the subtle changes that are applied to achieve final quality. Lighting inaccuracies (such as around the upper lip and beneath the nose) are corrected in Photoshop and highlights are added to suggest a higher level of detail and organic use of form.

Robot 2D Fixes and Final Polish

FIG 12.19

Here, we can see the composited robot render and the subtle changes that are applied in Photoshop to achieve final quality. Additional form isn't really needed in this case (with the exception of the mouth/grating area). This being the case, additional texture and material properties are enhanced – a more detailed, worn metallic effect, glossier glass lenses, and an additional specular pass in the form of rim lighting.

FIG 12.20

Foreground FX

The final additions to the robot character added in Photoshop are the particle "energy" FX, along with some color glows and washes to help increase the blue range and prevent it from flattening the image.

Final Composition

After all these elements are in place, colors are tweaked and balanced in Photoshop, additional scene elements such as reflections and shadows are added, contrast is aligned, and the image is complete.

FIG 12.21

Index

Page numbers followed by *f* indicates a figure and *t* indicates a table.

Printed and bound by CPI Group (UK) Ltd, Croydon, CR0 4YY

21/10/2024

01777057-0012